access to history

The Cold War 1941–95

DAVID G. WILLIAMSON

THIRD EDITION

HODDER
EDUCATION
AN HACHETTE UK COMPANY

To Saul, Luca and Marco

The Publishers would like to thank Nicholas Fellows and David Ferriby for their contribution to the Study Guide.

The Publishers would like to thank the following for permission to reproduce copyright material:

Photo credits: p13 Library of Congress, 3a33351; **p27** Library of Congress, LC-USZ62-7449; **p38** Kem image courtesy of Richard and Alexander Marengo; **p65** dpa/dpa/Corbis; **pp77, 88** Presse und Informationsamt der Bundesregierung ; **p103** Jack Esten/Picture Post/ Getty Images; **p110** Bettmann/Corbis; **p112** Library of Congress, 3c17124; **p113** Presse und Informationsamt der Bundesregierung; **p118** Bettmann/Corbis; **p129** https://commons. wikimedia.org/wiki/File:Mao_Zedong,_1935.jpg; **p132** Ullstein Bild/TopFoto; **pp135, 141** TopFoto; **p149** AFP/AFP/Getty Images; **p157** TopFoto; **p162** Bettmann/Corbis; **p166** This image is a work of an employee of the Executive Office of the President of the United States, taken or made as part of that person's official duties. As a work of the U.S. federal government, the image is in the public domain; **p188** The Official CTBTO Photostream (this file is licenced under the Creative Commons Attribution 2.0 Generic licence); **p200** Ullstein Bild/TopFoto.

Acknowledgements: are listed on page 252.

Although every effort has been made to ensure that website addresses are correct at time of going to press, Hodder Education cannot be held responsible for the content of any website mentioned in this book. It is sometimes possible to find a relocated web page by typing in the address of the home page for a website in the URL window of your browser.

Hachette UK's policy is to use papers that are natural, renewable and recyclable products and made from wood grown in sustainable forests. The logging and manufacturing processes are expected to conform to the environmental regulations of the country of origin.

Orders: please contact Bookpoint Ltd, 130 Milton Park, Abingdon, Oxon OX14 4SB. Telephone: +44 (0)1235 827720. Fax: +44 (0)1235 400454. Lines are open 9.00a.m.–5.00p.m., Monday to Saturday, with a 24-hour message answering service. Visit our website at www.hoddereducation.co.uk

© 2015 David G. Williamson
Third edition © David G. Williamson 2015

First published in 2001 by
Hodder Education
An Hachette UK Company
Carmelite House, 50 Victoria Embankment
London EC4Y 0DZ

Impression number	10	9	8	7	6	5	4	3
Year		2019	2018	2017	2016			

Cover photo © Corbis
Produced, illustrated and typeset in Palatino LT Std by Gray Publishing, Tunbridge Wells
Printed and bound by CPI Group (UK) Ltd, Croydon CR0 4YY

A catalogue record for this title is available from the British Library

ISBN 978 1471838668

Contents

Dedication

Keith Randell (1943–2002)

The *Access to History* series was conceived and developed by Keith, who created a series to 'cater for students as they are, not as we might wish them to be'. He leaves a living legacy of a series that for over 20 years has provided a trusted, stimulating and well-loved accompaniment to post-16 study. Our aim with these new editions is to continue to offer students the best possible support for their studies.

CHAPTER 1

The origins of the Cold War

The Cold War was a period of political hostility between capitalist and Communist countries, in particular between the USA and the USSR, which, from its onset in 1945, lasted for over 40 years. Several times, it brought the world perilously close to another global war. This chapter looks at historians' attempts to define what the Cold War was and its origins from 1917 to 1945 through the following themes:

★ What was the Cold War?

★ The opposing ideologies of the Cold War

★ The Soviet Union and the Western powers 1917–41

★ Tensions within the Grand Alliance 1941–5

★ The liberation of Eastern and Western Europe 1943–5

★ The Yalta Conference, February 1945

★ The end of the war in Europe

Key dates

1917	Oct.	Russian Revolution	1944	Aug. 23	Formation of coalition government in Romania
1918–20		Russian Civil War		Sept. 9	Communist coup in Bulgaria
1939	Sept.	Hitler and Stalin partitioned Poland		Oct. 9	Anglo-Soviet 'percentages agreement'
1941	June	German invasion of USSR		Dec.	British suppressed Communist uprising in Greece
1943	Sept. 3	Italian Armistice			
	Nov.–Dec.	Tehran Conference			
1944	June 6	Allied forces invaded France	1945	Feb. 4–11	Yalta Conference
	July	Red Army entered central Poland		May 8	Unconditional German surrender

1 What was the Cold War?

▶ *What were the main characteristics of the Cold War?*

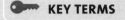
The term 'cold war' had been used before 1945 to describe periods of extreme tension between states stopping just short of war. In 1893 the German **socialist**, Eduard Bernstein, described the **arms race** between Germany and its neighbours as a kind of 'cold war' where 'there is no shooting but … bleeding'. In May 1945 when the USA and the **USSR** faced each other eyeball to eyeball in Germany this term rapidly came back into use. The British writer George Orwell, commenting on the significance of the dropping of the atomic bomb (see page 37), foresaw 'a peace that is no peace', in which the USA and USSR would be both 'unconquerable and in a permanent state of cold war' with each other. The Cold War was, however, more than just an arms race. It was also, as the historian, John Mason, has pointed out, 'a fundamental clash of **ideologies** and interests'. These are discussed in more detail in the next section.

The US historian, Anders Stephanson, has defined the essence of the Cold War as follows:

- Both sides denied each other's legitimacy as a regime and attempted to attack each other by every means short of war.
- Increasingly this conflict became **polarised** between two great powers: the USA and the USSR. There was an intense build-up of both nuclear and conventional military weapons and a prolonged arms race between the USA and the USSR.
- Each side suppressed its internal **dissidents**.

Most historians would more or less accept this definition, although there is less agreement on the timescale of the Cold War. The British historian, David Reynolds, whose chronology is for the most part followed in this book, argues that there were three cold wars:

- 1948–53
- 1958–63
- 1979–85.

These were 'punctured by periods of *détente*'. Two Russian historians, Vladislav Zubok and Constantine Pleshakov, however, provide a slightly different model: they define the Cold War as lasting from 1948 to the Cuban Crisis of 1962 and the subsequent 27 years as no more than a 'prolonged **armistice**' rather than actual peace. The problem with this interpretation is that it ignores the impact of the Vietnam War and the outbreak of the 'Third Cold War' in 1979.

While the chronology of the Cold War is open to debate, and the beginning of the 'Second Cold War' could as easily be dated from October 1956 as from

November 1958, it is important to grasp that the years 1945–89 formed a 'Cold War era', in which years of intense hostility alternated with periods of *détente*, but, even then, the arms race and ideological competition between the two sides continued. Both sides also continued to engage in **proxy-conflicts** in the developing world. The US historian John Lewis Gaddis argues that the Cold War lasted for so long because of the nuclear balance. Soviet military, particularly nuclear, strength disguised the essential economic weakness of the USSR, which eventually caused its collapse (see page 216).

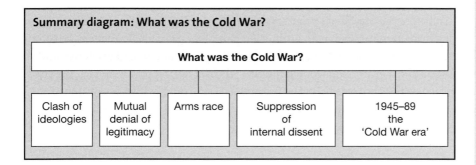

Summary diagram: What was the Cold War?

What was the Cold War?				
Clash of ideologies	Mutual denial of legitimacy	Arms race	Suppression of internal dissent	1945–89 the 'Cold War era'

2 The opposing ideologies of the Cold War

▶ *In what ways did the ideologies of the opposing sides differ?*

The main intellectual basis of communism was constructed in the nineteenth century by two Germans, **Friedrich Engels** and **Karl Marx**. Their thinking provided the foundations of **Marxism–Leninism**, which, in the twentieth century, became the governing ideology of the USSR, much of Central and Eastern Europe, the People's Republic of China, Cuba, and several other states.

Marx argued that capitalism and the **bourgeoisie** in an industrial society would inevitably be overthrown by the workers or **proletariat** in a socialist revolution. This initially would lead to a **dictatorship of the proletariat** in which the working class would break up the old order. Eventually, a true egalitarian Communist society would emerge in which money was no longer needed and each gave 'according to his ability' and received 'according to his need'. Marx idealistically believed that once this stage was achieved then crime, envy and rivalry would become things of the past since they were based on greed and economic competition.

KEY TERMS

Proxy-conflicts Wars encouraged or supported by major powers without their direct involvement.

Marxism–Leninism Doctrines of Marxism which were modified by Lenin, who adapted Karl Marx's teaching to the situation in Russia. Unlike Marx, he advocated the creation of a party dictatorship, which would have absolute powers, even over the workers.

Bourgeoisie The middle class, particularly those with business interests, who Marx believed benefited most from the existing capitalist economic system.

Proletariat Marx's term for industrial working-class labourers, primarily factory workers.

Dictatorship of the proletariat Marx's term suggesting that following the overthrow of the bourgeoisie, government would be carried out by and on behalf of the working class.

KEY FIGURES

Friedrich Engels (1820–85)

German industrialist and mill owner in Manchester, who co-operated closely with Karl Marx.

Karl Marx (1818–83)

German philosopher of Jewish extraction, whose writings formed the intellectual basis of communism.

Marxism–Leninism

In the early twentieth century **Vladimir Ilych Lenin** developed Marx's ideas and adapted them to the unique conditions in Russia. Russia's economy was primarily agricultural and lacked a large industrial proletariat, which Marx saw as the class most likely to revolt. Lenin therefore argued that the Communists in Russia needed to be strongly organised with a small compact core, consisting of reliable and experienced revolutionaries, who could achieve their aims of undermining and toppling the Tsarist regime. In 1903 Lenin and his followers founded the **Bolshevik Party**, which seized power in Russia in October 1917.

Just before the Bolsheviks seized power, Lenin outlined his plans for the creation of a revolutionary state in an unfinished pamphlet, *State and Revolution*. It would be run by 'the proletariat organised as a ruling class' and would use terror and force against any organisation or person who did not support it. In fact, the state would be the 'dictatorship of the proletariat', but would 'wither away' only once its enemies at home and abroad were utterly destroyed. Then, of course, the reality of communism would dawn where, it was believed, there would be no economic exploitation, crime, selfishness or violence.

Under the leadership of at first Lenin, and then Josef Stalin (see page 13), the USSR became an authoritarian, Communist state where the government was in charge of all aspects of the economy; there were no democratic elections and freedom of speech was limited. Thus, the state did not in fact 'wither away'.

Capitalism

Capitalism is an economic system in which the production of goods and their distribution depend on the investment of private capital with a view to making a profit. Unlike a socialist **command economy**, a capitalist economy is run by people who wish to make a profit and therefore have to produce what people want, rather than by the state. Opposition to Marxism–Leninism in the USA and the Western European states was reinforced, or – as Marxist theoreticians would argue – even determined, by the contradictions between capitalism, which was the prevailing economic system in the Western world, and the command economies of the Communist-dominated states.

Rival definitions of democracy

In the West there was a deep mistrust of communism as a political system, particularly its lack of **democracy**. The USSR dismissed parliamentary democracy as a mere camouflage for capitalism and its politicians as its puppets. For Marxist–Leninists, democracy meant economic equality where there were

KEY FIGURE

Vladimir Ilych Lenin (1870–1924)
Leader of the Bolshevik Party 1903–24 and ruler of Communist Russia 1917–24.

KEY TERMS

Bolshevik Party
The Russian Communist Party, which seized power in a revolution in October 1917.

Command economy
An economy where supply and pricing are regulated by the government rather than market forces such as demand, and in which all the larger industries and businesses are controlled centrally by the state.

Democracy A form of government in which all eligible citizens participate either directly, or more usually through elected representatives, in the government of their country.

no extremes between wealthy capitalists and poor workers and peasants. However, for the democratic states of Western Europe and the USA, democracy meant the liberty of the individual, equality before the law, freedom of speech and a parliament elected by the people to whom the government is ultimately responsible. Rather than economic equality under the dictatorship of the proletariat, liberal or parliamentary democracy challenges the right of any one party and leader to have the permanent monopoly of power. It is opposed to dictatorship in any form and ultimately the people can get rid of an unpopular government in an election.

Religion

Marxism–Leninism was opposed to religion. One of its core arguments was that it was not an all-powerful God who influenced the fate of humankind, but rather economic and material conditions. Once these were reformed under communism, humankind would prosper and not need religion. For Marxists, religion was merely, as Marx himself had said, 'the opium of the masses'. It duped the proletariat into accepting exploitation by their rulers and capitalist businessmen. During the revolution in Russia, churches, mosques and synagogues were closed down, and religion was banned.

In Europe, Christian Churches were among the leading critics and enemies of communism. After 1945, Catholic-dominated political parties in western Germany and Italy played a key role in opposing communism. In 1979 the election of Pope John Paul II of Poland as head of the Roman Catholic Church strengthened political opposition in Poland to communism (see page 184).

SOURCE A

From John W. Mason, *The Cold War, 1945–1991*, Routledge, 1996, p. 71.

Fundamentally the cold war was a confrontation between the United States and the Soviet Union, fuelled on both sides by the belief that the ideology of the other side had to be destroyed. In this sense ... co-existence was not possible ... The Soviet Union held to Lenin's belief that conflict between Communism and Capitalism was inevitable. The United States believed that peace and security in the world would only emerge when the evil of Communism had been exorcised [expelled].

What does Source A reveal about the nature of the Cold War?

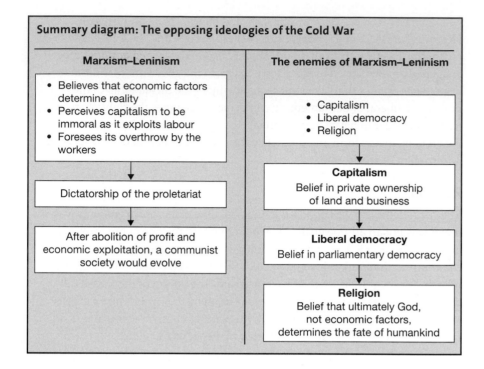

Summary diagram: The opposing ideologies of the Cold War

Marxism–Leninism

- Believes that economic factors determine reality
- Perceives capitalism to be immoral as it exploits labour
- Foresees its overthrow by the workers

↓

Dictatorship of the proletariat

↓

After abolition of profit and economic exploitation, a communist society would evolve

The enemies of Marxism–Leninism

- Capitalism
- Liberal democracy
- Religion

↓

Capitalism
Belief in private ownership of land and business

↓

Liberal democracy
Belief in parliamentary democracy

↓

Religion
Belief that ultimately God, not economic factors, determines the fate of humankind

3 The Soviet Union and the Western powers 1917–41

▶ *How did relations develop between the USSR and the main Western states in 1924–41?*

▶ *Was there already a 'Cold War' between the Western powers and the USSR in 1918–41?*

The Bolshevik Revolution in Russia succeeded against the odds, but Lenin was initially convinced that victory within Russia alone would not ensure the survival of the revolution. An isolated Bolshevik Russia was vulnerable to pressure from the capitalist world as its very existence was a challenge to it. If communism was to survive in Russia, it had also to triumph globally.

SOURCE B

From Lenin's 'Farewell Address to the Swiss Workers', April 1917, quoted in M.S. Levin, *et al.*, translators, *Lenin's Collected Works*, volume 23, Progress Publishers, 1964, p. 371.

To the Russian proletariat has fallen the great honour of beginning the series of revolutions which the imperialist war [the First World War] has made an objective inevitability. But the idea that the Russian proletariat is the chosen revolutionary proletariat is absolutely alien to us. We know perfectly well that the proletariat of Russia is less organised, less prepared and less class conscious

? How does Source B help in understanding Soviet foreign policy in the aftermath of the Bolshevik Revolution?

than the proletariat of other countries. It is not its special qualities but rather the special conjuncture of historical circumstances that for a certain, perhaps very short, time has made the proletariat of Russia the vanguard of the revolutionary proletariat of the whole world.

Russia is a peasant country, one of the most backward of European countries. Socialism cannot triumph directly and immediately ... [but] ... our revolution [may be] the prologue to world socialist revolution, a step towards it.

The USA and Russia 1917–18

The simultaneous expansion of Russia and the USA until they dominated the world had been foreseen as early as 1835 by the French historian Alexis de Tocqueville (see Source C):

SOURCE C

From Alexis de Tocqueville, *Democracy in America*, edited by J.P. Mayer, Doubleday, 1969.

There are now two great nations in the world, which, starting from different points, seem to be advancing toward the same goal: the Russians and the Anglo-Americans [English-speaking Americans, most of whose ancestors came from the British Isles]. ... [E]ach seems called by some secret design of Providence one day to hold in its hands the destinies of half the world.

What information is conveyed in Source C about the future global power of the USA and Russia?

It was, however, the First World War that brought these great states more closely into contact with each other. When the USA entered the war against Germany, it was briefly an ally of the Russians, but this changed dramatically once the Bolsheviks seized power in October 1917 and made peace with Germany. Ideologically there developed a clash between the ideas of the US president, Woodrow Wilson, and Lenin. Wilson, in his Fourteen Points of April 1918, presented an ambitious global programme for self-determination, free trade and collective security through a League of Nations, while Lenin preached world revolution and communism.

The Russian Revolution and Allied intervention 1918–22

One historian, Howard Roffmann, argued that the Cold War 'proceeded from the very moment the Bolsheviks triumphed in Russia in 1917'. There was certainly immediate hostility between Soviet Russia and the Western states. Although the Bolsheviks had seized power in the major cities in 1917, they had to fight a bitter civil war to destroy their opponents, the Whites, who were assisted by Britain, France, the USA and Japan. These countries hoped that by assisting the Whites, they would be able to strangle Bolshevism and prevent it spreading to Germany which, after defeat in the First World War in November 1918, was in turmoil and vulnerable to Communist revolution by its own workers. If Germany were to become Communist, the **Allies** feared that the whole of Europe would be engulfed in revolution. However, Allied intervention

 **KEY TERM**

Allies Britain, France, Japan, China and others were allied against Germany. The USA was 'an associated power'.

7

was ineffective and served only to strengthen Bolshevism. In 1919 French and US troops withdrew, to be followed by the British in 1920. Only Japanese troops remained until the end of the Civil War in 1922. Intervention in the USSR did inevitably fuel Soviet suspicions of the Western powers.

The Polish–Russian War 1920

At the Paris Peace Conference in 1919, the British foreign minister, Lord Curzon, proposed that **Poland**'s eastern frontier with Russia should be about 160 kilometres (100 miles) to the east of Warsaw; this demarcation became known as the Curzon Line. Poland, however, rejected this and exploited the chaos in Russia to seize as much territory as it could. In early 1920 Poland launched an invasion of Ukraine. This was initially successful, but, by August 1920, Bolshevik forces had pushed the Poles back to Warsaw. With the help of military supplies and advisors from France, Poland rallied and managed to inflict a decisive defeat on the **Red Army**, driving it out of much of the territory Poland claimed. In 1921 Poland signed the Treaty of Riga with Russia and was awarded considerable areas of Ukraine and Byelorussia, in which Poles formed only a minority of the population.

The extension of Poland so far east helped to isolate Russia geographically from Western and Central Europe. The creation of Finland, Estonia, Latvia and Lithuania helped to further this, leading to the creation of a *cordon sanitaire*, a zone of states, to prevent the spread of communism to the rest of Europe. The recovery of these territories of the former Russian Empire became a major aim of the USSR's foreign policy before 1939.

Soviet foreign policy 1922–41

Once the immediate possibility of a world revolution vanished, the consolidation of socialism within the USSR became the priority for Lenin and his successors, particularly Stalin, who after 1928 adopted the policy of **Socialism in one country**. However, this did not stop the USSR from supporting subversive activities carried out by Communist groups or sympathisers within the Western democracies and their colonies. These activities were co-ordinated by the **Comintern**, which was established in 1919 to spread Communist ideology. Although foreign Communist parties had representatives in the organisation, the Communist Party of Russia controlled it.

Hitler and Stalin 1933–8

The coming to power of Hitler and the Nazi Party in Germany in 1933 led to a radical change in Soviet foreign policy. Nazi Germany, with its hatred of communism and stated goal of annexing vast territories in the Soviet Union for colonisation, presented a threat to the USSR's very existence. To combat this, Stalin, despite the ideological differences between the USSR and Britain and France, attempted to create a defensive alliance against Nazi Germany:

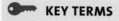

KEY TERMS

Poland In 1815 Poland was partitioned between Austria, Russia and Prussia. In 1918 the defeat of Russia, Germany, which included Prussia, and Austria enabled it to regain independence.

Red Army The Workers' and Peasants' Red Army was the Bolsheviks' armed force, which eventually became the Soviet Army.

Socialism in one country Policy aimed at strengthening socialism within the USSR even though elsewhere revolution had failed.

Comintern A Communist organisation set up in Moscow in 1919 to co-ordinate the efforts of Communists around the world to achieve a worldwide revolution.

Figure 1.1 Central and Eastern Europe in 1921. This map shows the changes made by the peace treaties of 1919–21 and how Russia (USSR) was now confined to the margins of Europe. What information about the situation in Europe is conveyed in this map?

- In 1934 the USSR joined the League of Nations, which Stalin hoped to turn into a more effective instrument of collective security.
- In 1935 Stalin signed a pact with France and Czechoslovakia in the hope that this would lead to close military co-operation against Germany. French suspicions of Soviet communism prevented this development.
- In 1936 Stalin intervened in the Spanish Civil War to assist the Republican government against the **Nationalists**, who were assisted by Nazi Germany and Fascist Italy.

🔑 **KEY TERM**

Nationalist A movement or person passionately devoted to the interests and culture of their nation, often leading to the belief that certain nationalities are superior to others.

- In September 1938, in response to Hitler's threat to invade Czechoslovakia, Stalin was apparently ready to intervene, provided France did likewise. However, Hitler's last-minute decision to agree to a compromise proposal at the Munich Conference of 29–30 September, which resulted in the **Munich Agreement**, ensured that Soviet assistance was not needed. The fact that the USSR was not invited to the Conference reinforced Stalin's fears that Britain, France and Germany would work together against the USSR.

Anglo-French negotiations with the USSR, April–August 1939

In March 1939, Germany invaded what was left of Czechoslovakia and, in April, the British and French belatedly began negotiations with Stalin for a defensive alliance against Germany. These negotiations were protracted and complicated by mutual mistrust. Stalin's demand that the Soviet Union should have the right to intervene in the affairs of the small states on its western borders if they were threatened with internal subversion by the Nazis, as Czechoslovakia had been in 1938, was rejected outright by the British. Britain feared that the USSR would exploit this as an excuse to seize the territories for itself.

Stalin was also suspicious that Britain and France were manoeuvring the Soviets into a position where they would have to do most of the fighting against Germany should war break out. The talks finally broke down on 17 August over the question of securing Poland's and Romania's consent to the passage of the Red Army through their territory in the event of war; something which was rejected by Poland.

The Nazi–Soviet Pact

Until early 1939, Hitler saw Poland as a possible ally in a future war against the USSR for the conquest of *lebensraum*. Poland's acceptance of the **Anglo-French Guarantee** forced him to reconsider his position and respond positively to those advisors advocating temporary co-operation with the Soviet Union.

Stalin, whose priorities were the defence of the USSR and the recovery of those parts of the former Russian Empire, which had been lost in 1917–20, was ready to explore German proposals for a non-aggression pact; this was signed on 24 August. Not only did it commit both powers to benevolent neutrality towards each other, but in a secret protocol it outlined the German and Soviet **spheres of interest** in Eastern Europe: the Baltic states and Bessarabia in Romania fell within the Soviet sphere, while Poland was to be divided between them.

On 1 September 1939, Germany invaded Poland, and Britain and France declared war on Germany on 3 September. The Soviet Union, as agreed secretly in the Nazi–Soviet Pact, invaded eastern Poland on 17 September, although by this time German armies had all but defeated Polish forces. By the beginning of October, Poland was completely defeated and was divided between the Soviet Union and Germany, with the Soviets receiving the larger part.

Territorial expansion, October 1939 to June 1941

Until June 1941, Stalin pursued a policy of territorial expansion in Eastern Europe aimed at defending the USSR against possible future aggression from Germany. To this end, and with the dual aim of recovering parts of the former Russian Empire, Stalin strengthened the USSR's western defences:

- He signed mutual assistance pacts with Estonia and Latvia in October 1939. The Lithuanians were pressured into agreeing to the establishment of Soviet bases in their territory.
- In March 1940, after a brief war with Finland, the USSR acquired the Hanko naval base and other territory along their mutual border.
- Stalin's reaction to the defeat of France in June 1940, which meant German domination of Europe, was to seize the Baltic states of Estonia, Latvia and Lithuania, and to annex Bessarabia and northern Bukovina from Romania.

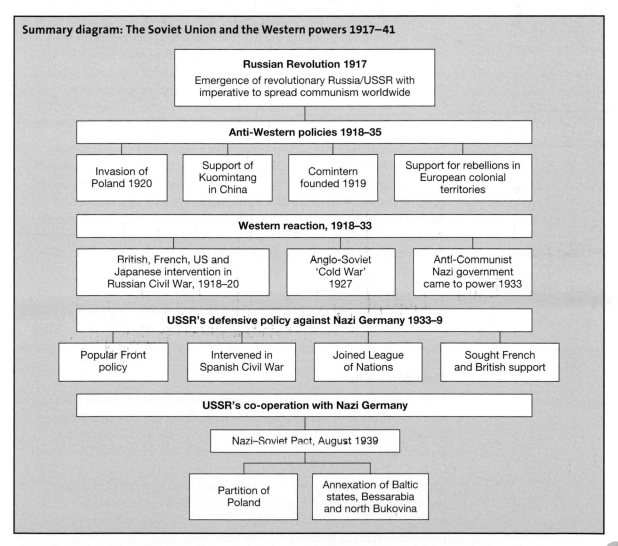

Summary diagram: The Soviet Union and the Western powers 1917–41

Russian Revolution 1917
Emergence of revolutionary Russia/USSR with imperative to spread communism worldwide

Anti-Western policies 1918–35

Invasion of Poland 1920

Support of Kuomintang in China

Comintern founded 1919

Support for rebellions in European colonial territories

Western reaction, 1918–33

British, French, US and Japanese intervention in Russian Civil War, 1918–20

Anglo-Soviet 'Cold War' 1927

Anti-Communist Nazi government came to power 1933

USSR's defensive policy against Nazi Germany 1933–9

Popular Front policy

Intervened in Spanish Civil War

Joined League of Nations

Sought French and British support

USSR's co-operation with Nazi Germany

Nazi–Soviet Pact, August 1939

Partition of Poland

Annexation of Baltic states, Bessarabia and north Bukovina

4 Tensions within the Grand Alliance 1941–5

▶ *In what ways did the war aims and ambitions of the USSR, the USA and Britain conflict?*

▶ *To what extent had the Great Powers agreed on dividing up Europe into spheres of influence by the end of 1944?*

Between June and December 1941 the global political and military situation was completely transformed. On 22 June Germany invaded the USSR. Hitler's aggression turned Britain and the USSR into allies fighting a common enemy, and on 12 July this was confirmed by the Anglo-Soviet agreement. On 7 December 1941, Japan's attack on the naval base at Pearl Harbor, Hawaii, brought the USA into the war, as it immediately declared war on Japan, an **Axis** power. In response, Germany and Italy both declared war against the USA on 11 December. Germany was now confronted with what became the Grand Alliance of Britain, the USA and the USSR, the leaders of which were known as the 'Big Three'. Although all three powers co-operated closely in the war against Germany, the USA and USSR never actually signed a formal alliance and the USSR did not enter the war against Japan until July 1945.

Both sides remained suspicious of each other's motives. Stalin feared that the Anglo-American decision not to invade France until 1944 was a plot to ensure the overthrow of communism by Nazi Germany, while Stalin himself considered a possible secret peace with Germany at least up to September 1943. **Andrei Gromyko**, a Soviet diplomat in Washington in 1942, was convinced that the Cold War began as 'the secret Cold War accompanying the "hot war" [the Second World War] as the allies … delayed the opening of the second front in Europe'.

The conflicting aims of the Big Three

As victory over the Axis powers became more certain, each of the three Allies began to develop its own often conflicting aims and agendas for post-war Europe.

The USSR's aims

In the early 1950s, most Western observers assumed that Moscow's main aim was to destroy the Western powers and create global communism, yet recent historical research, which the end of the Cold War has made possible, has shown that Stalin's policy was often more flexible and less ambitious – at least in the short term – than it appeared to be at the time. By the winter of 1944–5 his immediate priorities were clear. He wanted security for the USSR and **reparations** from Germany and its allies. The USSR had, after all, borne the brunt of German aggression and suffered immense physical damage and heavy casualties – some 25 million people by May 1945.

Josef Stalin

1879	Born Loseb Besarionis dze Jughashvili in present-day Georgia, the son of a cobbler
1917–22	Appointed Soviet commissar for the nationalities
1928	Defeated internal opposition and effectively became Soviet leader
1928–34	Introduced collectivisation of agriculture and the Five-Year Plan to industrialise the USSR
1941	Surprised by German invasion of USSR
1945	Presided over the final defeat of Nazi Germany
1947	Founded Cominform
1948–9	Berlin Blockade
1950	Secretly approved North Korean plans to invade South Korea
1953	Died

Stalin's character is important in any assessment of the causes of the Cold War. In many ways the record of his foreign policy before 1939 was cautious and pragmatic. He was ready to co-operate with Britain and France against Nazi Germany, but when he decided that they would not stand up against Hitler, he signed the Nazi–Soviet Pact with the German government. On the other hand, he was also a Marxist–Leninist, who believed in the ultimate triumph of communism, and was ruthless and brutal towards his opponents. Historians are divided as to whether he had ambitions to gain control of Germany and even of Western Europe after 1945. Some, like the US historian R.C. Raack, believed that he pursued a revolutionary and expansionary policy until 1948, when he returned to a more defensive policy towards the USA and the West. Others point out that the USSR had suffered enormously in the war and was hardly in a position to challenge the West after 1945.

To protect the USSR against any future German attack, Stalin was determined to hang on to the land annexed from Poland in 1939 and, as compensation, to give Poland the German territories that lay beyond the River Oder (see the map on page 36). He also aimed to reintegrate into the USSR the Baltic provinces of Estonia, Latvia and Lithuania, as well as the territory lost to Finland in 1941, to annex Bessarabia and to bring both Romania and Bulgaria within the Soviet orbit (see the map on page 9).

In Eastern Europe, Stalin's first priority was to ensure that regimes friendly to the USSR were set up. In some states, such as Poland and Romania, this could only be guaranteed by a Communist government, but in others, such as Hungary and Czechoslovakia, Stalin was prepared to tolerate more broadly based, but friendly, governments in which the Communists formed a minority.

By 1944 Stalin seems to have envisaged a post-war Europe which, for a period of time at least, would consist of three different areas:

- An area under direct Soviet control in Eastern Europe: Poland, Romania, Bulgaria and, for a time at least, the future Soviet zone in Germany.
- An 'intermediate zone', which was neither fully Communist nor fully capitalist, comprising **Yugoslavia**, Austria, Hungary, Czechoslovakia and Finland. The Communists would share power there with the liberal, moderate socialist and peasant parties. These areas would act as a 'bridge' between Soviet-controlled Eastern Europe and Western Europe and the USA.
- A non-Communist Western Europe, which would also include Greece.

> 🔑 **KEY TERM**
>
> **Yugoslavia** In 1918 the kingdom of Serbs, Croats and Slovenes was formed. In 1929 it officially became Yugoslavia. The Serbs were the dominating nationality within this state.

Dissolution of the Comintern

In 1943 Stalin dissolved the Comintern (see page 8) as a gesture to convince his allies that the USSR was no longer supporting global revolution. The British government saw this optimistically as evidence that Stalin wished to co-operate in the reconstruction of Europe after the end of the war.

The USA's aims

In the 1950s, Western historians, such as Herbert Feis, argued that the USA was too preoccupied with winning the struggle against Germany and Japan to give much thought to the political future of post-war Europe, since it assumed that all problems would in due course be solved in co-operation with Britain and the USSR. Yet this argument was sharply criticised by **revisionist historians** in the 1960s and 1970s, who insisted that the USA very much had its own security agenda for the post-war period.

More recently, historian Melvyn Leffler has shown that the surprise Japanese attack on Pearl Harbor in 1941, and the dramatic developments in air technology during the war, made the USA feel vulnerable to potential threats from foreign powers. Consequently, as early as 1943–4 US officials began to draw up plans for a chain of bases which would give the USA control of both the Pacific and Atlantic Oceans. This would also give US industry access to the raw materials and markets of most of Western Europe and Asia. Leffler argues that the steps the USA took to ensure its own security alarmed Stalin and so created a 'spiral of distrust', which led ultimately to the Cold War.

SOURCE D

An excerpt from an article by Melvyn Leffler, 'National Security and US Foreign Policy', in M.P. Leffler and D.S. Painter, editors, _Origins of the Cold War_, Routledge, 1994, pp. 37–8.

The dynamics of the Cold War … are easier to comprehend when one grasps the breadth of the American conception of national security that had emerged between 1945 and 1948. This conception included a strategic [military and political] sphere of influence within the western hemisphere, domination of the Atlantic and Pacific oceans, an extensive system of outlying bases to enlarge the strategic frontier and project American power, an even more extensive system of transit rights to facilitate the conversion of commercial air bases to military use, access to the resources and markets of Eurasia, denial of these resources to a prospective enemy, and the maintenance of nuclear superiority.

The USA's economic aims

Much of US President Roosevelt's policy was inspired by the ideas of his predecessor Woodrow Wilson (see page 7), who in 1919 had hoped eventually to turn the world into one large free trade area. This would be composed of democratic states, where **tariffs** and **economic nationalism** would be abolished. The US government was determined that there should be no more

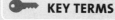

KEY TERMS

Revisionist historian
A historian who revises the traditional or orthodox interpretation of events and often contradicts it.

Tariffs Taxes placed on imported goods to protect the home economy.

Economic nationalism
A policy in which every effort is made to keep out foreign goods.

? How important is Source D in explaining the causes of the Cold War?

attempts by Germany or Italy to create **autarchic economies**, and that the British and French, too, would be forced to allow other states to trade freely with their empires. Indeed, the US commitment to establishing democratic states meant that they supported the **decolonisation** of the European colonial empires.

The United Nations

These ideas were all embodied in the **Atlantic Charter**, which British Prime Minister Churchill and US President Roosevelt drew up in August 1941, four months before the USA entered the war. This new, democratic world order was to be underpinned by a future United Nations Organisation (UN). By late 1943, Roosevelt envisaged this as being composed of an assembly where all the nations of the world would be represented, although real power and influence would be wielded by an executive committee, or Security Council. This would be dominated by the Soviet Union, Britain, China, France and the USA. For all his talk about the rights of democratic states, he realised that the future of the post-war world would be decided by these powerful states.

Britain's aims

The British government's main aims in 1944 were to ensure the survival of Britain as an independent Great Power still in possession of its empire, and to remain on friendly terms with both the USA and the USSR. The British government was, however, alarmed by the prospect of Soviet influence spreading into Central Europe and the eastern Mediterranean, where Britain had vital strategic and economic interests. The Suez Canal in Egypt was its main route to India and British industry was increasingly dependent on oil from the Middle East. As Britain had gone to war over Poland, Churchill also wanted a democratic government in Warsaw, even though he conceded that its eastern frontiers would have to be altered in favour of the USSR.

Inter-Allied negotiations 1943–4

Churchill and Roosevelt held several summit meetings to discuss military strategy and the shape of the post-war world, but it was only in 1943 that the leaders of the USSR, USA and Britain met for the first time as a group.

The foreign ministers' meeting at Moscow, October 1943

In October 1943, the foreign ministers of the USA, USSR and Britain met in Moscow, the Soviet Union's capital, in an effort to reconcile the conflicting ambitions of their states. They agreed to establish the European Advisory Commission to finalise plans for the post-war Allied occupation of Germany. They also issued the 'Declaration on General Security'. This proposed the creation of a world organisation to maintain global peace and security, the UN, which would be joined by all peaceful states. The US **secretary of state**, Cordell Hull, insisted that the Chinese President Chiang-Kai-shek, as head of a large

KEY TERMS

Autarchic economy
An economy that is self-sufficient and protected from outside competition.

Decolonisation Granting of independence to colonies.

Atlantic Charter
A statement of fundamental principles for the post-war world. The most important of these were: free trade, no more territorial annexation by Britain or the USA, and the right of people to choose their own governments.

Secretary of state The US foreign minister.

and potentially powerful allied country, should sign this declaration too. Stalin also informed Hull, in the strictest secrecy, that the USSR would enter the war against Japan after Germany's defeat in Europe.

Tehran Conference, 28 November to 1 December 1943

At the Tehran Conference, Churchill, Roosevelt and Stalin met for the first time to discuss post-war Europe, the future organisation of the UN and the fate of Germany. Stalin again made it very clear that he would claim all the territories which the USSR had annexed in Poland and the Baltic in 1939–40, and that Poland would be compensated with German territory. To this there was no opposition from either Churchill or Roosevelt.

KEY TERM

Commonwealth
Organisation of states that were formerly part of the British Empire.

The key decision was made to land British, **Commonwealth** and US troops in France (Operation Overlord) rather than, as Churchill wished, in the Balkans in 1944. This effectively ensured that the USSR would liberate both eastern and south-eastern Europe by itself, and hence be in a position to turn the whole region into a Soviet sphere of interest. It was this factor that ultimately left the Western powers with little option but to recognise the USSR's claims to eastern Poland and the Baltic states. On 29 November Roosevelt told his son Elliot, who accompanied him to Tehran, the following (Source E):

SOURCE E

An excerpt from President Roosevelt's conversation with his son, from Jonathan Fenby, *Alliance*, Simon & Schuster, 2008, pp. 246–7.

? According to Source E, what were the political implications of Operation Overlord?

Our Chiefs of Staff are convinced of one thing, the way to kill the most Germans, with the least loss of American soldiers is to mount one great big invasion and then slam 'em with everything we have got. It makes sense to me. It makes sense to Uncle Joe. It's the quickest way to win the war. That's all.

Trouble is, the PM [Churchill] is thinking too much of the post-war, and where England will be. He's scared of letting the Russians get too strong in Europe. Whether that's bad depends on a lot of factors.

The one thing I am sure of is this: if the way to save American lives, the way to win as short a war as possible, is from the west and the west alone … and our chiefs are convinced it is, then that's that! I see no reasons for putting the lives of American soldiers in jeopardy in order to protect real or fancied British interests on the European continent.

The Churchill–Stalin meeting, October 1944

A year later, in an effort to protect British interests in the eastern Mediterranean (see page 15), Churchill flew to Moscow and proposed a division of south-eastern Europe into distinct spheres of interest. This formed the basis of an agreement, the so-called 'percentages agreement', that gave the USSR 90 and

75 per cent predominance in Romania and Bulgaria, respectively, and Britain 90 per cent in Greece, while Yugoslavia and Hungary were to be divided equally into British and Soviet zones of interest.

After reflection, this agreement was quietly dropped by Churchill as he realised that it would be rejected outright by Roosevelt once it was brought to his attention. This, Churchill feared, would only lead to unwelcome tension in the Anglo-US alliance. Roosevelt had informed Stalin shortly before Churchill arrived in Moscow that there was 'in this global war … no question, either military or political, in which the United States [was] not interested'. However, it did broadly correspond to initial Soviet intentions in Eastern Europe, and Stalin did recognise Britain's interests in Greece, even denying the local Communists any Soviet support (see page 23).

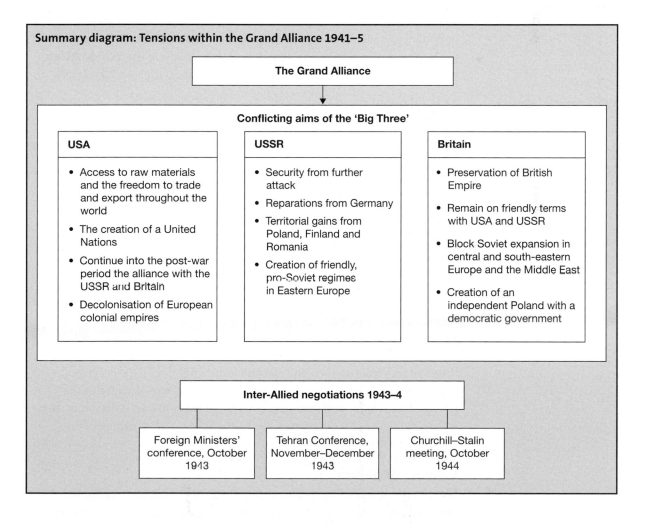

Summary diagram: Tensions within the Grand Alliance 1941–5

The Grand Alliance

Conflicting aims of the 'Big Three'

USA	USSR	Britain
• Access to raw materials and the freedom to trade and export throughout the world • The creation of a United Nations • Continue into the post-war period the alliance with the USSR and Britain • Decolonisation of European colonial empires	• Security from further attack • Reparations from Germany • Territorial gains from Poland, Finland and Romania • Creation of friendly, pro-Soviet regimes in Eastern Europe	• Preservation of British Empire • Remain on friendly terms with USA and USSR • Block Soviet expansion in central and south-eastern Europe and the Middle East • Creation of an independent Poland with a democratic government

Inter-Allied negotiations 1943–4

Foreign Ministers' conference, October 1943	Tehran Conference, November–December 1943	Churchill–Stalin meeting, October 1944

5 The liberation of Eastern and Western Europe 1943–5

▶ *How far did the liberation of Europe, 1943–5, intensify the rivalry and distrust between the 'Big Three'?*

KEY TERMS

Liberation The freeing of a country from foreign occupation.

Allied Control Commissions These were set up in each occupied territory, including Germany. They initially administered a particular territory in the name of the Allies.

Partisan groups Resistance fighters or guerrillas in German- and Italian-occupied Europe.

Allied powers Commonly referred to as the Allies during the Second World War, this group first consisted of Poland, France, Britain and others, with the USSR and the USA joining in 1941.

The **liberation** of Eastern Europe by the Soviet Army and Western Europe by predominantly Anglo-American forces in 1944–5 created the context for the Cold War in Europe. It was in Europe where the Cold War both started and ended.

Eastern Europe 1944–5

To understand the complex political situation created by the end of the war, it is important to understand the significance of the **Allied Control Commissions** (ACC), the tension between the governments-in-exile and the local **partisan groups**, and the close links between the Communist parties and the USSR.

Allied Control Commissions

Bulgaria, Finland, Italy, Hungary and Romania were Axis states. Although they were allowed their own governments after their occupation by the **Allied powers**, real power rested with the ACC. The first ACC was established in southern Italy in 1943 by Britain and the USA after the collapse of the Fascist government there. As the USSR had no troops in Italy, it was not represented on the ACC. Similarly, as it was the USSR that liberated Eastern Europe from Germany, Soviet officials dominated the ACCs in Romania, Bulgaria, Finland and Hungary. In this respect, Soviet policy was the mirror image of Anglo-American policy in Italy.

Governments-in-exile and partisan groups

Political leaders who had managed to escape from German-occupied Poland, Czechoslovakia, Greece and Yugoslavia to Britain, set up what were called governments-in-exile in London for the duration of the war. Being in London, however, they lost control of the partisan groups fighting in the occupied territories. Except for Poland, Communist partisan groups emerged as the strongest local forces and their leaders were not ready to take orders from their governments-in-exile. Sometimes this suited Stalin, and sometimes, as in Greece (see page 23), it did not.

Communist parties

In the liberated territories, Stalin advised the local Communist parties to form popular fronts or alliances with the liberal, socialist and peasant parties. Eventually these fronts became the means by which the Communists seized power in Eastern Europe.

Poland

The Polish question was one of the most complex problems facing the Allies. Britain, together with France, had gone to war in September 1939 as a result of the German invasion of Poland. The British government therefore wanted to see the emergence of a democratic Poland once Germany was driven out by the Red Army. On the other hand, Stalin was determined not only to regain the territories that fell into the Soviet sphere of interest as a result of the Nazi–Soviet Pact (see page 10), but also to ensure that there was a friendly pro-Soviet government in Poland. In effect, this meant forcibly establishing a Communist dictatorship, as the majority of Poles were strongly anti-Soviet and anti-Communist.

In principle, Britain and the USA had agreed at Tehran to the Soviet annexation of eastern Poland up to the Curzon Line (see page 8), and that Poland would eventually be compensated for this by acquiring territory on its western frontiers from Germany. Both hoped optimistically that Stalin would tolerate a democratically elected government in Warsaw.

The Soviet advance into Poland

Once the Red Army crossed Poland's eastern frontier in early January 1944, the Soviet Union annexed the territory it had claimed in September 1939. By July, Soviet troops had crossed the Curzon Line and moved into western Poland. As they advanced, they systematically destroyed the nationalist Polish resistance group known as the **Polish Home Army**. Stalin fatally undermined the authority of the Polish government-in-exile in London by establishing the Committee of National Liberation, based in Lublin in Poland, which became known as the Lublin Committee. The task of the committee was to administer Soviet-occupied Poland, and eventually to form the core of a future pro-Soviet government in Poland.

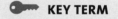 **KEY TERM**

Polish Home Army
The Polish nationalist resistance group that fought German occupation during the Second World War.

SOURCE F

From a report by Colonel T.R.B. Sanders, who was in command of an Allied mission which visited the V2 missile site at Blizna in central Poland in September 1944 after it had been captured by the Red Army. National Archives (NA HS4/146), London.

Everywhere we went (except in the forward areas) there were posters with portraits and short descriptions of the nine or ten chief members of the Lublin Committee. Other posters dealt with conscription, giving up of wireless sets, giving up of arms and payment of social insurance instalments. In addition all along the roads, there were numerous billboards with slogans in Russian and Polish such as 'Long live the Red Army!' 'Glory to our Great Leader Stalin!'

What does Colonel Sanders' report in Source F reveal about the activities of the Lublin Committee in Soviet-liberated Poland? **?**

The Warsaw Uprising

The Soviet Union's policy was revealed when the Polish Home Army rose in revolt against the Germans in Warsaw in August 1944 in a desperate attempt to seize control of parts of Poland before the Red Army could overrun the whole country. By capturing Warsaw, the Home Army calculated that it would be able to set up a non-Communist government in the capital, which would be recognised by the Western Allies as the legal government of Poland. It was hoped that this would then stop Stalin from creating a Communist Poland. Not surprisingly, Stalin viewed the uprising with intense suspicion. Although Soviet troops penetrated to within 20 kilometres of Warsaw, the Polish insurgents were left to fight the Germans alone and were defeated by 2 October.

The German defeat of the Warsaw Uprising effectively destroyed the leadership of the Home Army, and inevitably this made it easier for Stalin to enforce his policy in Poland. As Soviet troops moved further west towards the Oder River in the remaining months of 1944, the **NKVD**, assisted by Polish Communists, shot or imprisoned thousands of participants in the Home Army in a determined attempt to eliminate the anti-Soviet Polish opposition.

Britain, the USA and Poland

Despite all that had happened, Roosevelt and Churchill still clung to the hope that it would be possible to reach a compromise with Stalin about the future of Poland. In the interests of post-war Allied unity, they were both determined to avoid a premature break with the USSR over Poland. In January 1945 the USSR formally recognised the Communist-dominated Committee for National Liberation as the **provisional government** of Poland. Britain and the USA, although they still supported Poland's government-in-exile in London, played down the significance of this in the interests of the unity of the Grand Alliance.

Romania and Bulgaria

On 20 August 1944, the Soviets launched a major offensive to drive German troops out of the Balkans. The immediate consequence of this brought about the collapse of the pro-German regimes in both Romania and Bulgaria. Like Poland, both states were vital to the military security of the USSR, since, if they were under friendly pro-Soviet governments, they would protect the USSR's south-western frontiers from any future attack. Soviet control of Romania would also allow access to Yugoslavia and south-eastern Europe, and enable it to strengthen its strategic position in the Black Sea. Control of Bulgaria would give the USSR a naval base from which to dominate the approaches to the Turkish Straits and the Greek frontier (see the map on page 9).

Romania

The Soviet Union was also determined to re-annex the Romanian territories of Bessarabia and northern Bukovina, which it had occupied in 1940, and launched

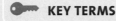

KEY TERMS

NKVD Soviet security organisation responsible for enforcing obedience to the government and eliminating opposition.

Provisional government A temporary government in office until an election can take place.

an offensive against Romania on 20 August 1944. In a desperate attempt to take control of Romania before the Red Army occupied the whole country, the Romanian king deposed the pro-German government on 23 August. The king hoped that, like Italy (see page 25), Romania would be allowed to negotiate a ceasefire with the Western allies and then form a new government in which Communists would only be a minority. This idea was an illusion based on the false assumption that Britain and the USA would begin a second front in the Balkans which would give these two allies more say in Romania's affairs. The king had no alternative but to negotiate an armistice on 12 September, with the Soviets who now occupied the country.

The National Democratic Front

Britain and the USA tacitly accepted that Romania was in the Soviet sphere of influence, and gave no help to the Romanian government, which was anxious to obtain a guarantee that Soviet troops would be withdrawn as soon as the war with Germany was over. An ACC was created and dominated by Soviet officials. A coalition government composed of Communists, socialists, National Liberals and the **left-wing** National Peasants' Party, the so-called Ploughmen's Front, was formed. This was paralysed by disagreements between the National Liberals and the three other parties. Supported by Soviet officials on the ACC, Communists and their allies formed the National Democratic Front and incited the peasants to seize farms from landowners and the workers to set up Communist-dominated production committees in the factories.

In March 1945, Stalin followed the precedent of Britain, which had intervened in December 1944 in Greece (see below) to establish a new government friendly to itself. Consequently, in March 1945 with the help of the Red Army, Romanian Communists orchestrated a coup which led to the creation of the pro-Soviet Communist-dominated National Democratic Front government.

Bulgaria

Although Stalin did not want a break with Britain and the USA, Western observers noted the anti-Western bias of Soviet policy in Romania and how Soviet officials actively supported the workers and peasant parties. The occupation of Romania allowed the Soviets to invade Bulgaria in early September 1944 and establish an ACC on 28 October.

Local Communists, including several thousand partisan troops, had already established the Patriotic Front, an alliance of anti-German left-wing forces. The Front seized power from the pro-German government of Konstantin Muraviev and established a government in Sofia shortly before the Red Army arrived. Inevitably, this success strengthened local Communists, who attempted a Communist revolution in the country. The country's former ruling class was eliminated, with over 10,000 people executed. The trade unions and police were dominated by Communists and large farms were taken over by peasants.

🔑 **KEY TERM**

Left wing Liberal, socialist or Communist.

Soviet response

This enthusiasm for revolution did not, however, fit in with Stalin's overall strategy. Essentially, he was determined to safeguard Soviet control over Bulgaria, yet not antagonise his Western allies any more than necessary while the war with Germany was still being fought, and at a time when Poland was becoming an increasingly divisive issue. Since the USSR's position was guaranteed through the key role of the Soviet chairman of the ACC, and the strong position of the local Communist Party, Stalin could afford to be conciliatory. Consequently, he attempted in the autumn of 1944 to persuade the Bulgarian Communists to pursue a more moderate policy. He wanted them to tolerate a certain degree of political opposition and to work within the Patriotic Front coalition. This was difficult to achieve as local Communists, sometimes backed by Soviet officials on the ACC, were determined to gain complete power regardless of Stalin's instructions or the diplomatic consequences.

Yugoslavia and Greece

Josip Broz (Tito) was one of the most successful partisan leaders in German-occupied Europe. As a Communist, he looked to the USSR as a model for the state he wished to create in Yugoslavia, but his very independence and self-confidence were to cause Stalin considerable problems.

Yugoslavia

After the occupation of Bulgaria, Soviet troops joined with partisan forces in Yugoslavia, launching an attack on Belgrade on 14 October 1944. By this time, Tito had created an effective partisan army which not only fought the Germans but also waged civil war against non-Communist Serbs and Croat nationalists. Tito's position had been strengthened when Britain decided in May 1944 to assist him rather than the nationalists, as his partisans were more effective opponents of the Germans. With British weapons and equipment, they effectively dominated the struggle against the Germans and nationalists, laying the foundations for a Communist takeover in 1945 in both Yugoslavia and neighbouring Albania. Whenever Tito's partisans occupied an area, they formed Communist-dominated committees which took their orders from him rather than from the Yugoslav government-in-exile in London.

To the Soviets, the key to controlling south-eastern Europe was to create a military and political alliance between Yugoslavia, Bulgaria and the USSR. Tito was not, however, an easy ally and tried to carry out his own policies independently of the USSR. Despite Stalin's reluctance to provoke a crisis with Britain and the USA on the eve of the Yalta Conference (see page 26), Tito established Communist governments in both Yugoslavia and Albania, which his forces controlled by November 1944.

Stalin was able to exercise a firmer control over Tito's foreign policy. In January 1945, he vetoed Tito's scheme for a federation with Bulgaria which would have turned it into a mere province of Yugoslavia. He made it very clear that Yugoslavia would have to subordinate its local territorial ambitions to the overall foreign policy considerations determined by the Soviet Union, although this naturally displeased Tito.

Greece

Tito and Stalin also clashed over the attempts by the Communist-controlled People's Liberation Army (ELAS) in Greece to set up a national liberation government on the Yugoslav model. During the war, ELAS emerged as the most effective resistance force in Greece and, like Tito's partisans, fought the Germans and non-Communist **guerrilla groups**. By 1944, ELAS was able to launch a Communist takeover of Greece. Yet, as Greece was an area regarded by the USSR as being well within the British sphere of influence, Stalin urged ELAS to join a moderate coalition government with non-Communist parties. When a revolt encouraged by Tito broke out in Athens on 3 December 1944, Stalin, true to his agreement with Churchill (see page 16), stopped him from helping Greek Communists and raised no objection to their defeat by British troops.

Hungary and Czechoslovakia

In neither Czechoslovakia nor Hungary did Stalin have any immediate plans for a Communist seizure of power. He wanted to keep alive the possibility of co-operation with non-Communist parties in order to protect Soviet interests. Local Communist parties were consequently ordered to enter into democratic coalition governments and to work within these to consolidate their position.

Hungary

The decision taken at the Tehran Conference not to start a second front in the Balkans ensured that the Red Army would also decide Hungary's fate. When Soviet troops crossed the Hungarian frontier in September 1944, the head of state, Admiral Miklós Horthy, appealed to the Soviets for a ceasefire, but Germany took Horthy's son prisoner and encouraged the Hungarian ultra-nationalists, the **Arrow Cross Party**, to seize power in western Hungary. It was not until early December 1944 that Red Army units reached the outskirts of Budapest, Hungary's capital.

In the Soviet-occupied section of the country, the Hungarian Communist Party was initially too weak to play a dominant role in politics, and it therefore had little option but to co-operate with the Socialist Party, the Smallholders Party (a peasants' party) and several other middle-class parties. In December 1945, when elections took place for the National Assembly, the Communist Party, despite the presence of the Red Army, gained only seventeen per cent of votes cast, but they were given three key posts in the provisional national

KEY TERMS

Guerrilla groups Fighters who oppose an occupying force using tactics such as sabotage and assassination.

Arrow Cross Party A Hungarian ultra-nationalist political party that supported Germany in the Second World War.

government. Throughout 1945, Stalin's immediate aim was to remove anything from Hungary that could be claimed as war reparations by the USSR, since Hungary had been a German ally. In the longer term he was not sure whether Hungary should be integrated into the emerging **Soviet bloc**, where it would be dominated militarily, politically and economically by the USSR.

Czechoslovakia

Of all the Eastern European states, Czechoslovakia had the closest relations with the USSR. The Czechoslovaks felt betrayed by Britain and France over the Munich Agreement of 1938 (see page 10) and looked to the USSR as the power that would restore their country's pre-1938 borders. In 1943, the Czechoslovak government-in-exile in London under Edvard Beneš, the former president, negotiated an alliance with the USSR, although this still did not stop Stalin from annexing Ruthenia, in eastern Czechoslovakia, in the autumn of 1944 (see the map on page 9).

As the Soviet army occupied more and more of Czechoslovakia in the winter of 1944–5, the balance of power tilted steadily away from the democratic parties represented by the government-in-exile in London to the Czechoslovak Communist Party led by Klement Gottwald, who was a refugee in Moscow. Stalin nevertheless forced Gottwald to accept Beneš as president and work within a coalition government. In turn, Beneš followed a conciliatory policy and was ready to co-operate with the Communist Party, enabling Stalin to achieve a harmony that had been impossible to reach in Poland. When the Provisional Government was formed in 1945, the Communist Party was able to demand eight seats in the cabinet including the influential Ministries of the Interior and Information, although Gottwald skilfully camouflaged the Communist Party's powerful position by not demanding the position of prime minister.

Finland

In the summer of 1944, when Soviet troops invaded, Finland was granted an armistice on unexpectedly generous terms. The Finns had to:

- declare war on the Germans
- cede part of the strategically important Petsamo region on the Arctic coast
- pay reparations.

However, politically, they were allowed a considerable degree of freedom. Marshal C.E.G. Mannerheim, who had co-operated closely with Germany during the war, remained president until 1946 and there was only one Communist in the first post-war cabinet. Finland was in a position to give the USSR vitally needed reparations, such as barges, railroad equipment and manufactured goods. A repressive occupation policy would have disrupted these deliveries. In addition, the Finnish Communist Party was weak and unpopular, and the USSR had little option but to rely on the non-Communist parties.

The liberation of Italy and France

Italy and France were liberated by the Western Allies. Italy was a leading Axis state, while France, until its defeat in 1940, had played the main part in the war against Germany. In both states, resistance to German occupation and its **puppet governments** helped to legitimise each Communist Party and enhance its popularity.

Italy

After the Allied landings in Sicily in July 1943, Mussolini, the Italian Fascist dictator, was overthrown and imprisoned, and in September an armistice was signed. This did not prevent German troops from seizing Italy's capital, Rome, and occupying most of the Italian peninsula. The Allies were then forced to fight their way up the peninsula, and it was only in April 1945 that northern Italy was finally conquered. Italy was the first Axis state to sign an armistice, and the way it was administered by the Allies set important precedents for the future. All Soviet requests to be involved were firmly rejected by Britain and the USA, which later gave Stalin an excuse to exclude them from Eastern Europe. An Italian government was established and it was gradually given responsibility for governing the liberated areas. This government was closely supervised by the Anglo-American ACC.

Palmiro Togliatti

Stalin had little option but to accept these arrangements, although he was determined that Italian Communists should not be excluded from participating in the new government. Palmiro Togliatti, the leader of the Italian Communist Party, was ordered to form a coalition with the Socialist Party. He was to avoid any aggressive actions, such as an uprising or a civil war, which would cause tension between the USSR and the West and so make it more difficult for Stalin to consolidate the Soviet position in Eastern Europe. Togliatti was also to draft a popular programme for reforming the Italian economy which, by promising measures that would help the workers and peasants, would prepare the way for later Communist Party electoral successes.

Togliatti carried out these instructions as well as he could, joining the new government that was formed when Rome was occupied by the Allies in June 1944. In the north, in the winter of 1944–5, Communists played a key role in the resistance against the Germans. Togliatti, only too aware of how the British had crushed the Greek revolt, managed to keep his more radical partisans in check. By the time the war ended, this resistance had won the Communists considerable support throughout Italy and made them an essential partner in coalition government. This was seen when Togliatti himself became minister of justice in the Italian government, which was formed in April 1945. At this stage, then, Stalin's policy in Italy was to push the Italian Communist Party into joining a governing multi-party coalition.

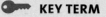

KEY TERM

Puppet government
One that operates at the will of and for the benefit of another government.

France

When Paris was liberated in August 1944, General Charles de Gaulle, the leader of the **Free French**, immediately established an independent government. His aim was to rebuild French power and to create a powerful French-led Western European bloc. To counter the predominance of the Anglo-Americans, he looked to the Soviet Union, and in December 1944 signed the Franco-Soviet Treaty of Alliance and Mutual Assistance, which committed both states to co-operate in any future defensive war against Germany.

As in Italy, the French Communist Party, having played a prominent part in the resistance, became a major force in French politics. Its leader, Maurice Thorez, was instructed by Stalin to support the Soviet–French alliance and work towards creating a left-wing coalition with socialists, which, it was hoped, would eventually be able to form a government.

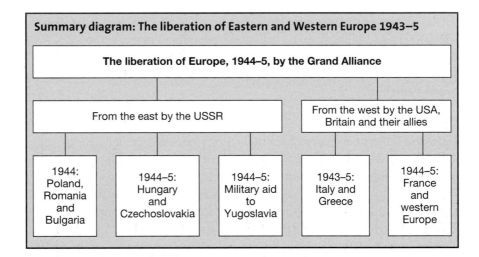

Summary diagram: The liberation of Eastern and Western Europe 1943–5

The liberation of Europe, 1944–5, by the Grand Alliance

From the east by the USSR

From the west by the USA, Britain and their allies

| 1944: Poland, Romania and Bulgaria | 1944–5: Hungary and Czechoslovakia | 1944–5: Military aid to Yugoslavia | 1943–5: Italy and Greece | 1944–5: France and western Europe |

⑥ The Yalta Conference, February 1945

▶ *What was achieved at the Yalta Conference?*

The Yalta Conference, attended by Stalin, Roosevelt and Churchill, was, to quote the journalist and historian Martin Walker, 'the last of the wartime conferences … [and] the first of the post-war summits'. Besides creating plans for finishing the war in Europe and eastern Asia, it also attempted to lay the foundations of the coming peace. Plans were finalised for the occupation of Germany by the victorious powers, among whom, on Churchill's insistence, France was to be included because he feared that the USA might withdraw its troops from Europe soon after the end of hostilities. Each power was allotted its own zone, including a section of Berlin, which was placed under **Four-Power Control** (for details of the zone divisions, see the map on page 36). The decision was also taken to establish the UN.

Poland

Poland again proved to be the most difficult subject on the agenda, and the Allies were only able to reach agreement through a series of ambiguous compromises, which could be interpreted differently by the USSR and the Western powers:

- They confirmed that Poland's eastern border would run along the Curzon Line.
- They agreed in principle, as they had at Tehran, that in compensation for the land lost to the USSR, Poland would receive a substantial increase in territory in the north and west from land to be removed from Germany. The exact details of this were not stated.

SOURCE G

The 'Big Three': Churchill, Roosevelt, who was already terminally ill, and Stalin (front row, left to right) at the Yalta Conference in 1945. No French representative was invited.

KEY TERM

Four-Power Control
Under the joint control of the four occupying powers: Britain, France, the USA and the USSR.

How valuable is Source G in assessing Allied unity in February 1945?

- The decision was also taken to reorganise the provisional government by including democratic politicians from both Poland and the London government-in-exile.
- Elections would be held as soon as possible.

Superficially this seemed to be a success for Britain and the USA, but in fact the terms were so vague that Stalin could easily manipulate them. First, the exact amount of land that Poland would receive at the cost of Germany was not fixed and secondly, words like 'democracy' and 'elections' meant very different things to the participants. For Stalin they essentially meant the domination of Poland by the Communist Party, while for Britain and the USA they meant effectively the domination of the non-Communist parties.

SOURCE H

From Norman Davies, *God's Playground: History of Poland*, volume 2, Oxford University Press, 2005, p. 364.

Given the relentless character of Soviet diplomacy over the Polish problem, it must be recognized … that Stalin's views had changed fundamentally. In 1939–41, the Soviet dictator had showed a willingness to trample on every vestige of Polish nationality or independence. From 1941 onwards he constantly reiterated his desire to restore 'a strong and independent Poland'. His understanding of 'strength' and 'independence' differed considerably from that which was held in Britain and America, or indeed in Poland, but was no less substantive for that. Anyone who has any doubts concerning the genuineness of Stalin's commitment should compare the post-war history of Poland with that of the Baltic states or the Ukraine. Stalin was the author not only of post-war Polish independence, but also of the peculiarly stunted interpretation of that concept which prevailed in the post-war era.

? What is the view conveyed by Source H on Stalin's Polish policy?

'Declaration on Liberated Europe'

To underpin the right of the liberated states to determine their own governments, Roosevelt persuaded Stalin and Churchill at Yalta to agree to the 'Declaration on Liberated Europe', which committed the three governments to carry out emergency measures to assist the liberated states and to encourage democratic governments.

With the start of the Cold War, this became, as the journalist Martin Walker observed, a key text 'upon which all future accusations of Soviet betrayal and bad faith were made'. Yet such accusations, although essentially true, completely ignored the reality of the situation in Eastern Europe. Stalin saw Poland, and indeed the other Eastern European countries, as corridors for an attack from Germany or eastern Europe on the USSR. He was therefore going to ensure that friendly governments, which in most cases were to mean Communist ones, were in place.

SOURCE 1

From 'Declaration on Liberated Europe', quoted in Martin Walker, *The Cold War and the Making of the Modern World*, Vintage, 1994, p. 14.

[The Declaration emphasised] the right of all peoples to choose the form of government under which they will live, the restoration of sovereign rights and self-government to those peoples who have been forcibly deprived of them by the aggressor nations.

To foster the conditions in which the liberated people may exercise these rights, the three governments will jointly assist the people in any liberated state or former Axis satellite state in Europe where in their judgement conditions require: (a) to establish conditions of internal peace; (b) to carry out emergency measures for the relief of distressed peoples; (c) to form interim governmental authorities broadly representative of all democratic elements in the population and pledged to the earliest possible establishment through free elections of governments responsive to the will of the people; and (d) to facilitate where necessary the holding of such elections.

How reliable is Source 1 as a guide to the immediate post-war policies of the Big Three?

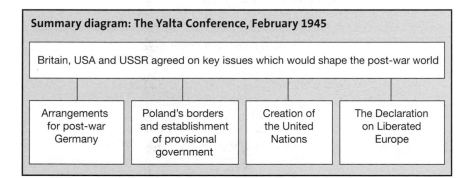

Summary diagram: The Yalta Conference, February 1945

Britain, USA and USSR agreed on key issues which would shape the post-war world

| Arrangements for post-war Germany | Poland's borders and establishment of provisional government | Creation of the United Nations | The Declaration on Liberated Europe |

⑦ The end of the war in Europe

▶ *Why did Churchill view the USSR's advance westwards with suspicion?*

Three months after the Yalta Conference, the war in Europe ended. In the final weeks of the war British and US forces raced to Trieste, Italy, in an attempt to stop Yugoslav forces seizing the port, while British troops in northern Germany crossed the River Elbe and advanced into Mecklenburg to prevent the Soviets from occupying Denmark (see map on page 36).

Churchill urged the USA to make special efforts to take Berlin and Prague to pre-empt a Soviet occupation, but the US generals were not ready to see their soldiers killed for what they regarded as political reasons, and so both capitals fell to Soviet troops.

When the war ended with the surrender of Germany on 8 May 1945, Anglo-American forces occupied nearly half the area that was to become the Soviet zone in Germany (see the map on page 36). It was not until early July that these troops were withdrawn into the US and British zones, which had been agreed on at Yalta.

The Red Army now confronted the Western allies in the middle of Germany. A few days before he killed himself in April 1945, Hitler predicted that:

SOURCE J

From F. Genoud, editor (translated by R.H. Stevens), *The Testament of Adolf Hitler: The Hitler–Bormann Documents, February–April 1945*, Icon Books, 1961, p. 107.

With the defeat of the Reich [Germany] and pending the emergence of the Asiatic, the African, and perhaps the South American nationalisms, there will remain in the world only two Great Powers capable of confronting each other – the United States and Soviet Russia. The laws of history and geography will compel these two Powers to a trial of strength either military or in the fields of economics and ideology. These same laws make it inevitable that both Powers should become enemies of Europe. And it is equally certain that both these powers will sooner or later find it desirable to seek the support of the sole surviving great nation in Europe, the German people.

> According to Source J, what will be the global consequence of the defeat of Nazi Germany?

Chapter summary

The roots of the Cold War lay in the Bolshevik Revolution in Russia and in Marxism–Leninism. This was countered by the USA's intention to open up the world to capitalism, free trade, democracy and self-determination. During the interwar years, the Soviet government focused on internal issues rather than foreign policy, but used secret agents to stir up trouble in the capitalist states of Western Europe and their empires. At first Stalin sought to co-operate with Britain and France against Hitler, but in August 1939 he signed the Nazi–Soviet Pact to regain the land lost to Poland in 1920.

The German invasion of June 1941 led to the USSR allying with the very states it so distrusted. While the Second World War lasted the USSR and its Western Allies had no option but to co-operate to defeat Germany, despite tensions in the Grand Alliance. The military campaigns that defeated Germany in 1944–5 dictated the immediate post-war situation in Europe. Eastern Europe fell under the control of the Red Army, and Western Europe was firmly within the sphere of the British and the Americans.

At the Yalta Conference of February 1945, the Big Three agreed to place Germany under Four-Power Control, and democratically elected governments were to be set up in liberated Europe.

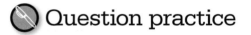 Refresher questions

Use these questions to remind yourself of the key material covered in this chapter.

1 What are the main arguments of Marxism–Leninism?

2 Why did Western liberals distrust Marxism–Leninism?

3 To what extent was Soviet foreign policy, 1920–45, aimed at consolidating the Soviet state?

4 How serious were the tensions within the Grand Alliance?

5 To what extent were the aims of the Big Three contradictory?

6 What were the key sources of political power in liberated Eastern Europe, 1944–5?

7 To what extent was Stalin's concern about post-war Poland prompted by the needs of Soviet security?

8 How did the USSR consolidate its position in Romania and Bulgaria?

9 Why were Tito's ambitions viewed with suspicion by Stalin in 1944 and early 1945?

10 What was Stalin's policy in Hungary and Czechoslovakia?

11 Why did Stalin pursue such a moderate policy in Finland?

12 How influential were the Communist Parties in Italy and France?

13 How was an agreement on Poland reached?

14 How significant was the Declaration on Liberated Europe?

15 Why did Poland cause problems for the 'Grand Alliance'?

Question practice

ESSAY QUESTIONS

1 'The wartime "Grand Alliance" between Britain, the USA and USSR was undermined by mutual suspicion.' Explain why you agree or disagree with this view.

2 How far was Soviet policy in Eastern Europe based on defensive aims?

3 How important was ideology in the origins of the Cold War, 1917–45?

4 Which of the following was the greater problem for the unity of the 'Grand Alliance' in the period 1943–5? i) The liberation of Italy. ii) The liberation of Poland. Explain your answer with reference to both i) and ii).

INTERPRETATION QUESTION

1 Read the interpretation and then answer the question that follows. 'Fundamentally the cold war was a confrontation between the United States and the Soviet Union, fuelled on both sides by the belief that the ideology of the other side had to be destroyed' (from John W. Mason, *The Cold War, 1945–1991*, Routledge, 1996, p. 71). Evaluate the strengths and limitations of this interpretation, making reference to other interpretations that you have studied.

CHAPTER 2

The breakdown of the Grand Alliance 1945–7

This chapter considers reasons for the breakdown of the Grand Alliance in 1945–7. During this period, there were tensions between the Western Allies and also between them and the Soviet Union. Much of the tension arose from the problems of dealing with Germany, which was under the control of four different states. Neither the Western powers nor the USSR could agree on joint measures for its economic and political reconstruction.

This chapter examines these issues through the following themes:

★ Transition from war to fragile peace 1945–6

★ Germany, June 1945 to April 1947

★ The Truman Doctrine, the Marshall Plan and the Soviet response

★ The 'Iron Curtain': European states 1945–7

The key debate on *page 56* of this chapter asks the question: Did the USA or the USSR start the Cold War 1945–7?

Key dates

1945	July–Aug.	Potsdam Conference	1947	Feb. 10	Peace treaties signed with Italy, Romania, Bulgaria, Finland and Hungary
1946	March 5	Churchill's Iron Curtain speech		March 12	Truman Doctrine announced
	April 21	Social Unity Party formed		March–April	Council of Foreign Ministers' Meeting, Moscow
	April–July	Paris Conference of Foreign Ministers		May	Communists excluded from government in France and Italy
	May 3	General Clay halted reparation payments from Soviet zone		June 5	Marshall Aid Plan announced
1947	Jan. 1	Anglo-American Bizone formed		Oct. 5	Cominform founded

1 Transition from war to fragile peace 1945–6

▶ *What initial impact did Truman have on US policy towards the USSR?*

▶ *In what ways did the friction between the members of the Grand Alliance increase during 1945–6?*

All three members of the victorious Grand Alliance – Britain, the USA and the USSR – wished to continue the alliance, yet for this alliance to survive there needed to be either a common danger or agreement between its members on key principles. In post-war Europe this was no longer the case. Publicly, Roosevelt had stressed the importance of the Declaration on Liberated Europe (see page 28), but privately he had recognised that Britain and the USA had little option but to accept Soviet predominance in Eastern Europe. When, only two weeks after the Yalta Agreement, the Soviets imposed a **puppet government** on Romania (see page 21), Roosevelt made no complaint to Stalin.

The impact of US President Harry Truman

Roosevelt died on 12 April 1945 and was replaced by **Harry Truman**. The new president, like his predecessor, wanted the USSR to declare war against Japan, which would potentially save the USA hundreds of thousands of casualties if it became necessary to invade Japan. Truman was both more aggressive and decisive, but less experienced, than Roosevelt. He became president at a point when the government of the USA was becoming increasingly concerned about Soviet policies in Poland, and was considering limiting **lend–lease** shipments to the USSR solely to material to be used for the war on Japan. The USA hoped that this might persuade Stalin to become more co-operative in carrying out the Yalta Agreement. In fact, the policy had the opposite effect and, unsurprisingly, merely succeeded in giving Stalin the impression that the USA was trying to extract political concessions through crude economic pressure.

SOURCE A

From Daniel Yergin, *Shattered Peace*, Houghton Mifflin, 1977, p. 72.

Truman could not believe that Russia's quest for security had a rationality. When he was finally confronted with foreign policy questions, all he had as a background was a storybook view of history and a rousing Fourth of July patriotism. He tended to see clearly defined contests between right and wrong, black and white. Neither his personality nor his experience gave him the patience for subtleties and uncertainties.

KEY FIGURE

Harry S. Truman (1884–1972)
US president 1945–53.

KEY TERM

Lend–lease This US programme (started in March 1941) gave over $50 billion ($650 billion in today's terms) of war supplies to Allied nations. This money was to be paid back at the end of the war.

What does Source A tell us about Truman's assessment of Soviet foreign policy?

Disagreements over the United Nations

In August 1944, the representatives of Britain, the USA, the USSR and China met at Dumbarton Oaks near Washington to discuss the future structure of the United Nations (UN). They agreed on the establishment of the General Assembly in which all member nations would be represented, and on the Security Council. Britain, the USA, the USSR and China would be permanent members of this, with the right to veto any decision decided on by the Assembly. In 1945 it was decided that France, too, should became a permanent member on the Security Council.

There were disagreements with the USSR over whether a permanent member of the Security Council, if it were involved in a dispute with another member of the UN, should have the right to veto a decision by the Council of which it disapproved. The Soviets also attempted to increase their influence by demanding that the sixteen member republics of the USSR should also become members of the UN. At the subsequent conference in San Francisco in April 1945, the right of each individual permanent member of the Security Council to exercise a veto was conceded but only two of the Soviet republics – the Byelorussian Soviet Socialist Republic (Belarus) and Ukraine – were given seats in the Assembly, in addition to one for the whole of the Soviet Union.

Potsdam Conference: July to August 1945

It is possible that Truman deliberately delayed the Allied summit at Potsdam until after the successful testing of the atomic bomb (see below) on 16 July 1945. He and his officials hoped that the possession of the bomb would enable the USA to force Stalin to make concessions in Eastern Europe. Stalin was impressed by the weapon and ordered the USSR's own nuclear development programme to make faster progress, but it did not make him any more flexible in Eastern Europe or Germany. In fact, it appeared to have little effect on Soviet policy.

On 17 July, Stalin, Churchill and Truman at last met at Potsdam, just outside Berlin. On 26 July, Churchill was replaced by Clement Attlee as British prime minister after a decisive Labour Party victory in the British general election. The conference continued, however, without interruption. The interlinked questions of Germany and Poland dominated the agenda.

Germany

While Britain, the USA and USSR could agree on the necessary measures for German demilitarisation, **denazification** and the punishment of war criminals, they were only able to conclude the following minimal political and economic guidelines for the future of Germany:

- the Allied Control Council (ACC)
- reparations.

KEY TERM

Denazification The process of removing all Nazi Party ideology, propaganda, symbols and adherents from every aspect of German of life.

The Allied Control Council

As there was no central German government, an ACC was established, composed of the military commanders from each of the four occupying powers. To avoid being outvoted by the three Western powers, the Soviets insisted that each commander should have complete responsibility for his own zone. This decision effectively stopped the ACC from exercising any real power in Germany as a whole. A limited number of central German departments dealing with finance, transport, trade and industry were to be formed at some point in the future.

Reparations

Agreement on reparations was difficult to achieve. The USSR had suffered immense damage in the war, and was determined to extract as much as possible in reparations from Germany. Britain and the USA, on the other hand, were convinced that the German economy must be left sufficiently strong so that it could pay for the imported food and raw materials that the Germans needed; they did not want the cost of this to be borne by the Allies. A temporary compromise was negotiated whereby both the USSR and the Western powers would take reparations from their own zones. In addition to this, Britain and the USA would grant ten per cent of these reparations to the Soviets and a further fifteen per cent in exchange for the supply of food and raw materials from the Soviet zone.

Poland

The Western allies had agreed at Yalta that Poland should be awarded 'substantial accessions of territory' from Germany to compensate for the land annexed by the USSR (see page 27). However, both Britain and the USA considered that the new boundary between Germany and Poland, lying along the Oder and Western Neisse Rivers, which the USSR had unilaterally determined, gave far too much territory to Poland. As Soviet troops occupied eastern Germany and Poland, there was little that Britain and the USA could do to change the frontier. Both powers eventually recognised the Oder–Neisse Line pending a final decision at a future peace conference. They hoped that this concession would persuade the Soviets to be more flexible about German reparations and the establishment of a democratic government in Poland.

The Council of Ministers

At Potsdam, the **Council of Ministers**, composed of the foreign ministers of Britain, the USSR, China, France and the USA, was formed to negotiate peace treaties with the former Axis powers of Italy, Romania, Bulgaria, Finland and Hungary, and to prepare a peace settlement with Germany once the Allies had set up a German government able to negotiate on behalf of Germany.

🔑 KEY TERM

Council of [Foreign] Ministers Composed of the foreign ministers of Britain, France, the USA and the USSR. Its role was to sort out the German problems and prepare the peace treaties.

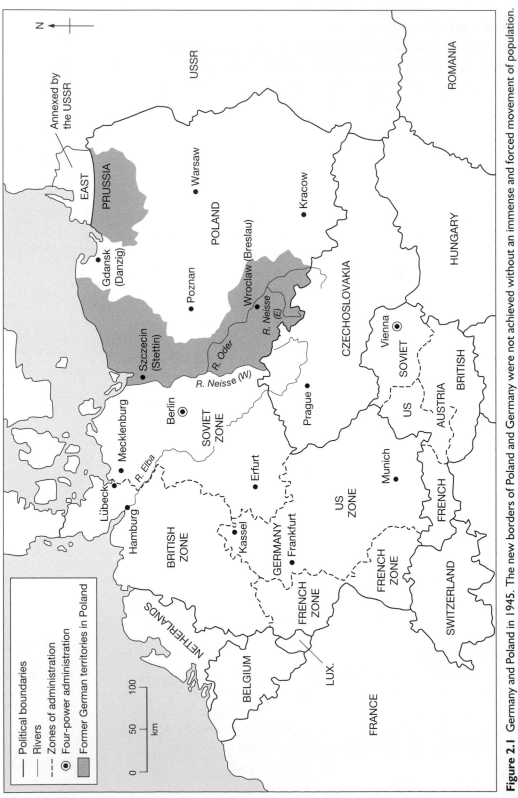

Figure 2.1 Germany and Poland in 1945. The new borders of Poland and Germany were not achieved without an immense and forced movement of population. What information about the territorial changes in Poland and Germany is conveyed in this map?

The impact of the atomic bomb

The atomic bomb was tested successfully at Alamogordo in New Mexico in the USA on 16 July 1945. Its destructive potential was much greater than expected and it was ready for immediate use against Japanese cities. On 6 August, an atomic bomb was dropped on Hiroshima, killing nearly half the population and flattening the city. Three days later, another bomb was dropped on Nagasaki, killing a further 40,000 people. The horrific destruction of these two cities with the threat of further US raids, as well as the Soviet invasion of **Manchuria**, left Japan with little option but to surrender.

Essentially, two alternatives confronted Truman's government once the atomic bomb had been shown to be effective. The first was that the USA could seek to retain its nuclear monopoly as long as possible. The second was that it could hand over the control of the bomb to the UN. Some in the US government initially believed that a monopoly on the weapon would enable the USA to dictate the terms of the diplomatic debate to the rest of the world.

SOURCE B

From John Lewis Gaddis, *The United States and the Cold War, 1941–1947*, Columbia University Press, 2000, p. 245.

But the bomb had more than purely military implications. American possession of this revolutionary new weapon drastically altered the balance of power, making it at least technically feasible for the United States to impose its will upon the rest of the world. 'God Almighty in his infinite wisdom [has] dropped the atomic bomb in our lap', Senator Edwin C. Johnson proclaimed in November 1945; now for the first time the United States 'with vision and guts and plenty of atomic bombs [could] compel mankind to adopt the policy of lasting peace … or be burned to a crisp'.

Truman's advisors were much more cautious. **Dean Acheson**, deputy secretary of state, pointed out that the US lead in nuclear science was only temporary and that the Soviets would rapidly catch up. Indeed, the temporary nature of the US lead was revealed when a Soviet espionage network was discovered in September 1945 operating in both Canada and the USA, which had already sent a considerable amount of information about the atomic bomb to the Soviet Union.

The United Nations Atomic Energy Commission

Truman, therefore, agreed in principle to the international control of atomic energy by the UN, providing that other nations also agreed to abide by its rules. In November 1945, the USA, together with the two nations that had helped it to develop the atomic bomb, Britain and Canada, called for the creation of a UN commission which would create rules for the control of nuclear weapons.

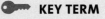

KEY TERM

Manchuria A region in the far north-east of China, occupied by the Japanese in 1931 until the end of the Second World War.

According to Source B, what is Edwin Johnson's reaction to the USA's possession of the atomic bomb?

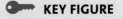

KEY FIGURE

Dean Acheson (1893–1971)

US deputy secretary of state 1945–9, secretary of state 1949–53.

These were:

- exchange of basic scientific information for peaceful ends between all nations
- establishing means for the control of atomic energy to ensure its use for peaceful purposes only
- the elimination from national armaments of atomic weapons
- establishing an effective system of inspection to prevent the clandestine manufacture of nuclear bombs.

At the Moscow Conference of Foreign Ministers in December 1945, the Soviets agreed to the establishment of the United Nations Atomic Energy Commission. They did, however, insist that it should report to the Security Council rather than the Assembly, where the Soviets could use their veto power as a permanent member if the need arose. The USA countered in early 1946 by suggesting that no country should have veto power over atomic energy matters, even in the Security Council, in an obvious effort to circumvent any Soviet interference.

Breakdown of agreement

Increasingly, however, plans for the international control of nuclear energy became a casualty of the growing mistrust between the Soviets and the Western powers. When US proposals were again discussed at the UN in June 1946, the Soviets refused to surrender their veto on the grounds that it would enable them to be outvoted on the Security Council, and instead suggested the immediate destruction of all nuclear weapons. The USA rejected this, claiming there were no safeguards to ensure that all nuclear weapons would in fact be destroyed. The Soviets retaliated in December 1946 by vetoing the US plan in the Security Council.

SOURCE C

? What information is conveyed in Source C about the importance of the atomic bomb?

'Christmas Card' by cartoonist Kem (Kimon Evan Marengo), 1945. It shows Truman (as the Statue of Liberty) with Stalin, British Prime Minster Clement Attlee, French President Charles de Gaulle and Chinese leader Chiang Kai-shek.

The Paris Peace Treaties with Italy and the minor Axis powers 1945–7

When the Council of Ministers met for the first time in September 1945 to discuss the details of the peace treaties, arguments erupted almost immediately. The Soviets pressed for a harsh peace with Italy, while Britain and the USA argued that Italy deserved more lenient treatment. The USSR also insisted that the armistice agreements, which it had already signed with Bulgaria, Finland, Hungary and Romania, should form the basis of the subsequent peace treaties. The USA, on the other hand, insisted that before the peace treaties could be signed with these states, legal governments representing their people must be formed. To save the negotiations from a complete breakdown, James Byrnes, the US secretary of state, went to Moscow in December 1945, and a compromise was reached whereby the Eastern European and the Italian peace treaties would be negotiated simultaneously. Negotiations dragged on for over a year and were frequently threatened by escalating tension between the USSR and the USA and its British and French allies. Nevertheless, in the final analysis, both sides wanted the peace treaties concluded, and were able to make compromises. In February 1947 the Paris Peace Treaties were finally concluded.

Italy

The USA argued that Italy, by making peace with the Allies in 1943, had effectively joined their side by 1945, but the USSR insisted that, as a former Axis power, Italy should accept a punitive peace. The USA was also alarmed by Soviet claims to a share of Italy's former colony, Libya, which would enable the USSR to extend its power into the Mediterranean. Only by agreeing to a severe peace with Italy, which involved the loss of territory to Yugoslavia (see page 52), the payment of $360 million reparations ($100 million of which were to go to the USSR) and controls on the size of Italy's armed forces, was the USA able to achieve agreement that Italy's former colonies would become **trust territories** under the UN. With the signature of the treaty, Italy again became an independent state.

> **🔑 KEY TERM**
>
> **Trust territories** Former colonial territories put in trust to the UN until they were ready for independence.

Eastern Europe

In Eastern Europe, the Soviets wanted the conclusion of the peace treaties with the former Axis states as soon as possible, as they wished to dissolve the ACC on which Western observers participated (see page 18) and obtain reparations. Once new governments were in place in the ex-Axis states, Britain, France and the USA were ready to accept the peace treaties. These were all signed on 10 February 1947, but disagreements about the value of former German property to be handed over to the USSR delayed the Austrian treaty until 1955 (see page 90). No treaty could be signed with Germany as disagreement between the four occupying powers prevented the restoration of an independent central German state until 1990.

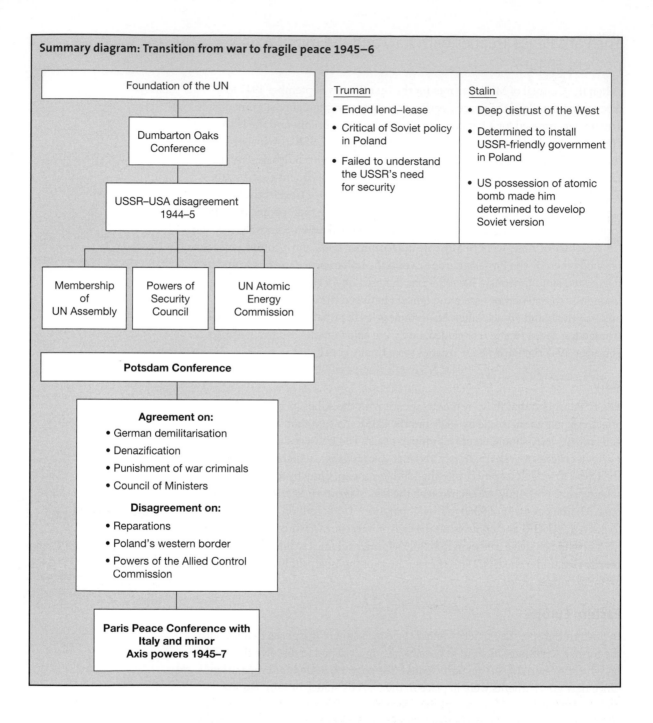

Summary diagram: Transition from war to fragile peace 1945–6

Foundation of the UN

Dumbarton Oaks Conference

USSR–USA disagreement 1944–5

Membership of UN Assembly

Powers of Security Council

UN Atomic Energy Commission

Potsdam Conference

Agreement on:
- German demilitarisation
- Denazification
- Punishment of war criminals
- Council of Ministers

Disagreement on:
- Reparations
- Poland's western border
- Powers of the Allied Control Commission

Paris Peace Conference with Italy and minor Axis powers 1945–7

Truman
- Ended lend–lease
- Critical of Soviet policy in Poland
- Failed to understand the USSR's need for security

Stalin
- Deep distrust of the West
- Determined to install USSR-friendly government in Poland
- US possession of atomic bomb made him determined to develop Soviet version

② Germany, June 1945 to April 1947

▶ *Why did the four occupying powers fail to work out a joint programme for Germany's future?*

▶ *To what extent did the USSR aim to control the whole of Germany?*

Germany's position in the middle of Europe and its potential wealth and military and economic strength ensured that neither the USSR nor the Western allies could allow the other to dominate it. Indeed, as tension rose, both sides began to wonder whether Germany itself could not perhaps be enlisted as a future ally in a possible East–West conflict. The German question became one of the central issues of the Cold War. Stalin was to appreciate this well before the Western allies did.

Soviet aims in Germany

In June 1945, Stalin explained his plans for eventually bringing a reunified Germany into Moscow's sphere of influence to the leaders of the German Communist Party (KPD). The Red Army would directly control the Soviet zone of occupation, while the KPD would seek to win the support of the German workers in both the Soviet and the Western zones. Once Germany was allowed to hold elections for a new parliament, Stalin hoped that the KPD would form a governing coalition with the Socialist and Liberal Parties, eventually taking control of the German government. This may well have been the reason that the USSR was the first occupying power to allow the formation of democratic parties in its zone in June 1945. In the autumn of 1945 the Russians were also ready to agree to setting up a central German transport authority and a **national federation of trade unions**, but both these proposals were defeated by French opposition to restoring a united Germany, which might again dominate Europe.

The creation of the Socialist Unity Party (SED)

To broaden the appeal of the German Communist Party (Kommunistische Partei Deutschlands, KPD), so that it would eventually appeal to Germans in all four zones, Stalin ordered his officials to force through the merger of the Social Democratic Party (SPD) with the KPD in the Soviet zone in Eastern Germany. After at least 20,000 Social Democrats had been interrogated and imprisoned and in some cases even murdered, the central executive of the SPD in the Soviet zone agreed in February 1946 to the formation of the new party that Stalin envisaged: the Socialist Unity Party (SED). At the end of April 1946 Stalin issued an important directive to his officials in the Soviet zone (Source D, page 42):

> **KEY TERM**
>
> **National federation of trade unions** A national organisation representing all the trade unions.

? What, according to Stalin's instructions in Source D, is the future task of the SED?

SOURCE D

At the end of April 1946 Stalin issued an important directive to his officials in the Soviet zone. The following is an extract from this directive, quoted in Willy Loth, *Stalin's Unwanted Child: The German Question and the Founding of the GDR*, Macmillan, 1998, p. 38.

From the standpoint of the Soviet Union, it is not yet time to establish central authorities nor in general to continue with a policy of centralisation in Germany. The first goal, organising the Soviet occupation zone under effective Soviet control, has been more or less achieved. The moment has thus now come to reach into the Western zones. The instrument is the United Socialist–Communist Party. Some time will have to elapse before the party is organised in an orderly fashion in Greater Berlin itself, and this process will take even longer in the Western zones. Only when the Soviet vision has been realised and the Unity Party has established itself in the Western zones, will the time have come to address once again the question of central administrations and of effective Soviet support for a policy of centralisation in Germany.

Reaction in Western Germany

The violence in Eastern German created fear and suspicion in Western Germany, preventing the party's success there. When SPD voters in the Western zones of Berlin were asked by the SPD leaders in Berlin to approve the merger of the two parties, it was rejected by 82 per cent. Soviet and KPD actions in Eastern Germany made many in Western Germany and in the Western zones of Berlin, as well as the Western allies, suspicious of Soviet intentions.

The problem of reparations

By the spring of 1946 the compromise over reparations, which had been negotiated in Potsdam, was already breaking down. As the Western zones, particularly the heavily populated British zone, were taking the majority of the German refugees, who had been expelled from the former German territories that had been ceded to Poland and Czechoslovakia at the end of the war (see the map on page 36), Britain and the USA were anxious to encourage a modest German economic recovery so that their zones could at least pay for their own food imports. Consequently, until their zones became self-supporting, they wished to delay delivering to the USSR the quotas from their own zones of machinery and raw materials that had been agreed at Potsdam (see page 35). There was even talk that the Soviet zone would have to deliver food to the hard-pressed Western zones.

In May, General Clay, the **military governor** of the US zone, in an attempt to bring the French into line and to force the Soviets to agree to treat Germany as an economic unity with its economy organised on a national rather than a zonal level, announced that no further reparation deliveries would be made until there was an overall plan for the German economy. To the Soviets it seemed that the Americans were bringing pressure to bear on them to agree to a reconstructed

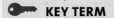

KEY TERM

Military governor
The head of a zone of occupation in Germany.

German economy within an international capitalist system. They feared that a united German capitalist economy would play an important part in a US-dominated global capitalist trading system. In June they responded to this threat by increasing production in their zone and transforming 213 key German firms into special Soviet-controlled companies, the total production of which was to go straight to the USSR.

The creation of Bizonia

When the Conference of Foreign Ministers returned to the question of Germany in July, Molotov, the Soviet foreign minister, insisted that the Germans should pay the USSR the equivalent of $10 billion in reparations. Byrnes again argued that reparations could only be paid once Germany had a **trade surplus** that would cover the cost of food and raw material imports. He then offered to unify the US zone economically with the other three zones. Only Britain, which was finding its zone a major drain on its fragile economy, accepted.

In retrospect, this was a major step in the division of Germany between East and West, although its significance was played down initially. When the British and US zones were merged economically in January 1947 to form what became called **Bizonia**, the Americans argued that, far from breaking the Potsdam Agreement, the amalgamation would create the economic preconditions for fulfilling the Potsdam Agreement. It was hoped that Bizonia would become so prosperous that, through interzonal trade, it would gradually attract and knit the French and Russian zones into a united national German economy. A more prosperous Germany would then be able to pay the reparations that had been demanded at Potsdam. In an attempt to convince the USSR that Bizonia was not an **embryonic state**, the offices responsible for food, finance and transport were deliberately located in different cities. The USSR suspected, however, that Bizonia was the first step towards creating a separate West German state.

Moscow Conference of Foreign Ministers, March–April 1947

The Moscow Conference was one of the turning points in the early history of the Cold War. The Soviets made a determined effort to destroy Bizonia by demanding that a new central German administration under Four-Power Control should be immediately set up. They ran into strong opposition from the British foreign secretary, **Ernest Bevin**, who feared that this would slow up the economic recovery of the British zone. In London, Bevin's officials had skilfully drawn up a plan for revising the Potsdam Agreement, which Bevin knew the Soviets could not accept. The USSR would, for instance, have to return some of the reparations that it had seized in its zone to help balance the budgets in the Western zones, and it would receive no coal or steel deliveries until the whole of Germany could pay for its own food and raw material imports. Bevin successfully managed to manoeuvre the USSR into a corner when he persuaded the Americans to agree that political unity could only come after economic unity. As this would mean a

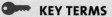

KEY TERMS

Trade surplus A surplus of exports over imports.

Bizonia Formed in January 1947 out of an amalgamation of the British and US zones of occupation.

Embryonic state Organisation that has some of the powers of a proper state, and is likely to grow into a fully fledged state.

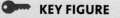

KEY FIGURE

Ernest Bevin (1881–1951) Labour politician, trade union leader and British foreign secretary 1945–51.

protracted delay in reparation deliveries, the Soviets had little option but to reject the proposal, which is exactly what the Western powers hoped they would do.

To the British and Americans, the Moscow Conference was what Willy Loth called a 'successful failure', in that it enabled them to press on with building up Bizonia. Nothing, however, was decided on the divisive issues of reparations, and the future of Germany was left to dominate the agenda of the next conference scheduled to meet in London in November (see page 62).

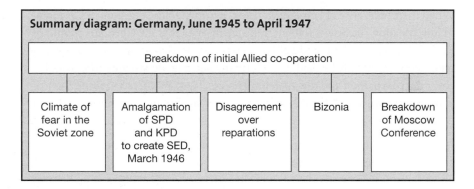

Summary diagram: Germany, June 1945 to April 1947

Breakdown of initial Allied co-operation

| Climate of fear in the Soviet zone | Amalgamation of SPD and KPD to create SED, March 1946 | Disagreement over reparations | Bizonia | Breakdown of Moscow Conference |

3 The Truman Doctrine, the Marshall Plan and the Soviet response

▶ *To what extent were the Truman Doctrine and Marshall Plan designed to contain Soviet power?*

▶ *What were the aims of the Marshall Plan and why did the USSR reject them?*

The Truman Doctrine and the Marshall Plan marked the real beginning of the Cold War and of US military and economic engagement in Western Europe. Together they helped ensure capitalism and democratic governments in much of western and southern Europe while limiting the political and economic influence of the Soviet Union and its satellite states. The Marshall Plan, particularly, was a major challenge to the USSR and forced it to consolidate its hold on Eastern Europe. Some revisionist historians such as Williams Appleman Williams and Gabriel Kolko see the Marshall Plan as further evidence of US provocation of the USSR (see page 57). This interpretation does, however, play down the perceived Soviet threat to western and southern Europe.

Origins of the Truman Doctrine

In June 1945 the Americans had assumed that Britain would continue to play a major role in the eastern Mediterranean, but by January 1947 Britain faced a crippling economic crisis. As a result of political unrest in India, Palestine and Egypt, and the long delay in completing the post-war peace treaties, Britain had to keep a large number of troops in Germany, Italy, the Middle East and Asia. This was, of course, enormously expensive, and by January 1947 Britain had used up the loan granted to it by the USA in 1945. The situation was made worse by the heavy blizzards and exceptionally cold weather that had brought British transport, industry and coal mining virtually to a halt for several weeks. On 21 February the British, in desperation, informed the Americans that their financial and military aid to both Greece and Turkey would have to cease on 31 March.

This was very unwelcome news to Washington, as civil war had broken out again in Greece in September 1946 when Stalin, contrary to his earlier policy in 1944 (see page 17), tolerated Yugoslav, Bulgarian and Albanian efforts to assist the Greek Communists against the British-backed Greek government with soldiers, equipment and money. Truman feared, above all, that the Communists might launch a similar uprising in Italy once Allied troops had left after the signing of the peace treaty (see page 39). He felt therefore that he had to act quickly to strengthen non-Communist forces in areas that were vulnerable to Soviet pressure, but to do this he required money, which could only be found by persuading **Congress** to vote for the necessary funds.

The announcement of the doctrine

On 12 March, in a deliberately dramatic speech designed to appeal to Congress, Truman stressed the seriousness of the international situation and how Europe was increasingly becoming divided into two mutually hostile blocs:

SOURCE E

From Truman's speech to Congress, 12 March 1947, quoted in G. Roberts, *The Soviet Union in World Politics*, Routledge, 1999, p. 22.

One way of life is based upon the will of the majority, and is distinguished by free institutions, representative government, free elections, guarantees of individual liberty, freedom of speech and religion, and freedom from political oppression. The second way of life is based upon the will of a minority forcibly imposed upon the majority. It relies upon terror and oppression, a controlled press and radio, fixed elections and the suppression of personal freedoms.

*I believe that it must be the policy of the United States to support free peoples who are resisting attempted subjugation by armed minorities or by outside pressures. I believe that we must assist free peoples to work out their own destinies in their own way … The seeds of **totalitarian regimes** are nurtured by misery and want. They spread and grow in the evil soil of poverty and strife. They reach their full growth when the hope of a people for a better life has died.*

 KEY TERMS

Congress The US parliament.

Totalitarian regimes Undemocratic regimes such as those in Soviet Russia or Nazi Germany, which sought to control every aspect of their people's lives.

What information does Source E reveal about the way Truman perceived the Soviet threat to the West?

Initially, Stalin dismissed this speech as an exercise in propaganda, but it soon became clear that it marked a new and important US policy initiative, which was to lead to what became called the Marshall Plan.

The Marshall Plan

Since 1945 the Americans had been pumping money into Western Europe in an attempt to prevent famine and total economic collapse. In 1947 influential US journalists and politicians were beginning to argue that only through political and economic integration could Western Europe solve the whole complex of problems facing it. This would create a large and potentially prosperous market, which would act as a barrier to the further spread of communism and perhaps, in time, even pull the Eastern European states out of the Soviet bloc. It would also build a political structure into which West Germany, or indeed the whole of Germany, could be integrated and so contained – as well as helping to boost the US economy.

General Marshall's offer

In June 1947, after extensive consultations in Washington, General **George Marshall**, the new US secretary of state, made his historic offer of an aid package for Europe. Source F is a key extract from this:

SOURCE F

From General Marshall's speech to Harvard University on 5 June 1947, quoted in *US Department of State Bulletin*, XVI, 15 June 1947, p. 1160.

It is already evident that before the United States Government can proceed further to alleviate the situation and help start the European world economy, there must be some agreement among the countries of Europe as to the requirements of the situation and the part those countries themselves will take in order to give proper effect to whatever action might be undertaken by this Government. It would be neither fitting nor efficacious for this government to undertake to draw up unilaterally a programme to place Europe on its feet economically.

The Paris negotiations

After Marshall's speech, the British and French called for a conference in Paris to formulate plans for the acceptance of US aid. Stalin suspected that the offer masked an attempt by the USA to interfere in the domestic affairs of the European states, but he sent Molotov to Paris to discuss further details with the British and French. The Soviets certainly wanted financial aid from the USA but without any conditions attached. Britain and France, however, argued that the European states should draw up a joint programme for spending the aid, rather than each individual state sending in a separate list of requests. On Stalin's orders, Foreign Minister Molotov rejected this and left the conference. Stalin feared that a joint programme would enable US economic power to

KEY FIGURE

George C. Marshall (1880–1959)

Chief of staff of US army 1939–45, US secretary of state 1947–9, defence secretary 1950–2.

What information does Source F convey about the conditions that were attached by the USA to the granting of Marshall Aid?

undermine Soviet influence in Eastern Europe by encouraging free trade and the exchange of ideas with the West and the growth of capitalism. Bevin, who had done much to engineer this break, as he did not want to run the risk of the USSR obstructing talks with the Americans, observed that Molotov's departure marked the beginning of the formation of a **Western bloc**.

On 16 July detailed negotiations on the Marshall Plan began in Paris, where sixteen Western European nations, including Turkey and Greece, were represented. Relevant information on Bizonia was provided by the occupation authorities. The Eastern European states were invited but were stopped by Stalin from attending. For the Western powers this simplified the negotiations, but even so, agreement was difficult to arrive at. Each Western European state had its own agenda. The French, for instance, wanted to ensure that their own economy had preference in receiving US aid over the economic needs of Bizonia. They were, however, ready to consider the formation of a **customs union**, as long as it enabled France to control the West German economy. The British, on the other hand, wished to safeguard their national **sovereignty** and were opposed to creating powerful **supranational** organisations.

By mid-August the Americans were disappointed to find that the Western Europeans had not come up with any radical plans for economic integration, and had only produced a series of national 'shopping lists'. Each country had merely drawn up a list of requests with its own needs in mind, rather than thinking supranationally. Jefferson Caffery, the US ambassador in Paris, complained that this simply re-created pre-war economic conditions with all the 'low labor productivity and maldistribution of effort which derive from segregating 270,000,000 people into 17 uneconomic principalities' – that is seventeen small countries with their own separate economies. As an American citizen he was dismissive of small historical countries that were fiercely proud of their independence.

The Western European states also asked for $29 billion, far more than Congress was ready to grant. To avoid the conference ending in failure, Bevin called an emergency meeting in Paris, which decided to let the Americans themselves propose where cuts in this sum could be made. The US officials immediately set up an **Advisory Steering Committee**, which attempted to bring the Europeans into line with essential US requirements, but by late September Washington had achieved only a limited success:

- Although the seventeen states promised to liberalise trade and France agreed to start negotiations for a customs union, these commitments were hedged around with qualifications aimed at protecting national independence.
- Germany's economic revival was declared essential, although it was to be carefully controlled to protect its neighbours.
- There was to be co-operation on the development of **hydroelectric sources**, pooling of railway wagons, and the setting up of production targets for coal, agriculture, refined oil and steel.

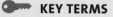

KEY TERMS

Western bloc An alliance of Western European states and the USA.

Customs union An area of free trade unhindered by national tariffs.

Sovereignty Independence. A sovereign state possesses the power to make its own decisions.

Supranational Transcending national limits.

Advisory Steering Committee A committee that would advise on priorities and the key decisions to be taken.

Hydroelectric sources Power stations that generate electricity through water power.

There was to be no supranational authority that could force the individual states to carry out these policies. At most, the seventeen states promised to set up a joint organisation to review how much progress was being made.

The Soviet response

Stalin's decision to put pressure on the Eastern European states to boycott the Paris conference marked the end of his attempts to co-operate with the USA and maintain the Grand Alliance. In September 1947 he invited the leaders of the Eastern European, French and Italian Communist parties to a conference at Szklarska Poręba in Poland to discuss setting up the Communist Information Bureau (Cominform), which would co-ordinate the policies and tactics of the Communist parties both in the satellite states and in Western Europe. Andrei Zhdanov, Stalin's representative, told the delegates that the world was now divided into two hostile camps: the **imperialist** bloc led by the USA, intent on 'the enslavement of Europe', and the 'anti-imperialist and democratic camp' led by the USSR. From this it followed that the whole policy of co-operating with moderate socialist and liberal parties would have to be abandoned and, where possible, Communist parties would have to take over power themselves and create societies whose economy and social system would be modelled on the Soviet system. From now on, as Martin McCauley has put it, 'there was to be only one road to socialism'.

KEY TERM

Imperialist Britain and France, who both still had extensive colonial empires. The Soviets also regularly called the Americans imperialists.

Summary diagram: The Truman Doctrine, the Marshall Plan and the Soviet response

Truman Doctrine, March 1947

Reasons for its announcement
- Britain unable to defend eastern Mediterranean
- Yugoslavs assisted Greek Communists

The Doctrine
- Truman offered US support to countries resisting Communist subversion
- Stressed need to improve economic conditions in Europe

The Marshall Plan
- Offer of aid package
- Funds distributed by supranational organisation

- Accepted by Western European states
- Rejected by USSR, which set up Cominform

4 The 'Iron Curtain': European states 1945–7

▶ *How correct was Churchill's assessment that an 'Iron Curtain' had descended across Europe?*

The 'Iron Curtain'

In a famous speech at Fulton in the USA on 5 March 1946 (see Source G), Churchill observed that 'from Stettin in the Baltic, to Trieste, in the Adriatic, an **Iron Curtain** has descended across the continent'.

How accurate was this analysis? Up to the spring of 1947 it can be argued, to quote the British historians G. Swain and N. Swain, that 'diversity rather than uniformity' still characterised the situation in Europe. Yugoslavia and Albania had their own Communist regimes, whose aggressive plans for a Balkan union and meddling in Greek domestic affairs Stalin at first attempted to control. Poland and Romania, both vital to the USSR's security, underwent Socialist revolutions and were in effect already Soviet satellites. In Hungary, Czechoslovakia, Finland and even Bulgaria, Stalin pursued a more moderate policy of influence rather than direct control. Yet with the escalation of the Cold War brought about by the Marshall Plan discussions and the creation of the Cominform, Stalin began to impose a much more uniform pattern on Eastern Europe. In Western Europe the intensifying Cold War polarised domestic politics, with the Communists on one side and non-Communists on the other. Communist parties were forced out of coalitions in France and Italy. Only in Finland did the situation remain unchanged.

KEY TERM

Iron curtain A term used by Churchill to describe how Stalin had separated Eastern Europe from the West.

SOURCE G

From Winston Churchill's speech at Fulton, Missouri, USA, on the 'Iron Curtain', 5 March 1946, quoted in R. Morgan, *The Unsettled Peace*, BBC Books, 1974, pp. 67–8.

From Stettin in the Baltic, to Trieste, in the Adriatic, an iron curtain has descended across the continent. Behind that line lie all the capitals of the ancient states of Central and Eastern Europe – Warsaw, Berlin, Prague, Vienna, Belgrade, Bucharest and Sofia. All these famous cities, and the populations around them, lie in the Soviet sphere, and all are subject in one form or another, not only to Soviet influence, but to a very high and increasing measure of control from Moscow. Athens alone … is free to decide its future … The Russian dominated Polish government has been encouraged to make enormous and wrongful inroads upon Germany … The Communist parties, which were very small in all these eastern states of Europe, have been raised to pre-eminence and power far beyond their numbers, are seeking everywhere to obtain totalitarian control. Police governments are prevailing in nearly every sense, and so far, except in Czechoslovakia, there is no true democracy … An attempt is being made by the Russians in Berlin to build up a quasi-Communist party in their zone of occupied Germany by showing special favours to groups of left-wing leaders.

According to Source G, why does Churchill argue that an 'Iron Curtain has descended across the continent'?

SOURCE H

From Stalin's interview with the Soviet newspaper, *Pravda*, 13 March 1946, quoted in M. McCauley, *Origins of Cold War, 1941–1949*, third edition, Longman, 2003, pp. 142–3.

… The following circumstances should not be forgotten. The Germans made their invasion of the USSR through Finland, Poland, Romania and Hungary. The Germans were able to make their invasion through these countries because at the time governments hostile to the Soviet Union existed in these countries. As a result of the German invasion the Soviet Union has lost irretrievably in the fighting against the Germans, and also through the German occupation and the deportation of Soviet citizens to German servitude, a total of about seven million people. In other words, the Soviet Union's loss of life has been several times greater than that of Britain and the United States of America put together. Possibly in some quarters an inclination is felt to forget about these colossal sacrifices of the Soviet people which secured the liberation of Europe from the Hitlerite [Nazi] yoke. But the Soviet Union cannot forget about them … And so what can there be surprising about the fact that the Soviet Union, anxious for its future safety, is trying to see to it that governments loyal in their attitude to the Soviet Union should exist in these countries? How can anyone, who has not taken leave of his senses, describe these peaceful aspirations of the Soviet Union as expansionist tendencies on the part of our state?

Poland

Why did Britain and the USA not intervene in Poland to stop the Communists from seizing power? To deflect Western criticism from his Polish policy, Stalin had set up a Provisional Government of National Unity in June 1945, which had been joined by **Stanisław Mikołajczyk**, the former leader of the government-in-exile in London. Stalin could not risk genuinely free elections since the Communist Party, as a result of its unpopularity, would inevitably suffer defeat. Mikołajczyk therefore resigned in protest from the provisional cabinet in August 1945, and in October 1946 he refused to allow his party, the Polish Peasants' Party, to join the Communist-dominated **electoral bloc**, which would present the electors with a single list of candidates who would all support a Communist-dominated government. He hoped that this boycott would trigger a political crisis that would force Britain and the USA to intervene.

In fact, the new **doctrine of containment** being worked out by Truman accepted unofficially that Poland was within the USSR's sphere of interest and that the USA would not intervene in its domestic affairs. Thus, when Mikołajczyk suggested that Britain and the USA should send officials to monitor the election in January 1947, both declined in the knowledge that there was little they could do to influence events in Poland. The results were a foregone conclusion. The bloc, which used terror and falsified electoral results with impunity, officially gained 394 seats, while the Peasants' Party gained a mere 28.

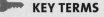

Although Władysław Gomułka, the leader of the Polish Communist Party, was dependent on Soviet assistance, he believed passionately that Poland had a unique history and could not just follow unquestioningly the Soviet example. He therefore viewed with dismay the creation of the Cominform, as he feared that it would force the Eastern European Communist parties to follow down to the last detail the Moscow model of socialism. Only under considerable pressure did he reluctantly accept it, and a year later Stalin had him removed from the leadership.

Romania

After the Potsdam Conference, at which it was decided that peace treaties could only be signed when governments recognised by the wartime allies had been established, Romania's King Michael called on Britain and the USA not to recognise the new government as it had been imposed by the Soviet Union in December 1945. As the Council of Foreign Ministers was about to begin negotiations on the Romanian peace treaty, Stalin decided to call on **Petru Groza**, the prime minister, to appoint two more non-Communists to the government. In reality, however, this made little difference. Groza was able to strengthen the National Democratic Front in March 1946 when the Romanian Socialist Party merged with the Communist Party. As in the Soviet zone of Germany, this effectively ensured Communist domination of the party. In May, the Front was further extended to include the National Popular Party, the National Peasant Party, as well as representatives from the Communist-organised trade unions, youth and women's organisations.

In November 1946, the Communist-dominated Front went to the polls. As in Poland, abuses did occur during the election: opposition newspapers were closed down and leading members of the opposition were murdered. It was therefore unsurprising that the Front won more than 80 per cent of the vote. Nevertheless, it did represent a broad spectrum of the population and would have won the national elections even without these aggressive and undemocratic tactics. The Front opposed the supporters of the former government, which had allied with Germany in the Second World War, and it also carried out popular social reforms such as the redistribution of land from the great landowners to the peasantry.

In February 1947, with the signature of the Paris Peace Treaties (see page 38), the ACC was dissolved. Under Soviet pressure, Romania refused Marshall Aid and joined the Cominform. In December 1947, King Michael was forced to abdicate and, in April 1948, a Communist people's republic was declared.

Bulgaria

Soviet techniques and policy were similar in Bulgaria, although Stalin hoped to avoid unnecessary friction with the Western powers until the peace treaty had been signed. In December 1945 he therefore forced the Communist-dominated

KEY FIGURE

Petru Groza (1884–1958)

Leader of the Ploughmen's Front and Romanian prime minister 1945–52.

Bulgarian government to include two members of the opposition, but when these began to demand changes in policy, Stalin advised the Communists to adopt a series of well-planned measures to smother the opposition. Yet, with an eye on the still unfinished peace treaties he remained anxious to mask the party's dictatorship. He even urged the sceptical Bulgarian Communists in September 1946 to set up a 'Labour Party' which would have 'a broader base and a better mask for the present period'.

In October elections took place for a national assembly. The opposition parties managed to win over one-third of the total votes, but Western hopes that this would form the basis of an effective parliamentary opposition were soon dashed. The Truman Doctrine and increasing US involvement in Greece meant that Bulgaria became a frontline state in the defence of communism. Consequently, Stalin allowed the Communists to liquidate the opposition. The Bulgarian Communist Party also took the creation of the Cominform as a cue for pressing on with its radical programme for nationalising industry, **collectivising agriculture** and creating a one-party state.

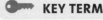

KEY TERM

Collectivising agriculture
Abolishing private farms in favour of large units run collectively by the peasantry along the lines of Soviet agriculture.

Yugoslavia

Yugoslavia occupied a unique position among the Soviet-dominated states in eastern and south-eastern Europe, as the Communist Party had effectively won power independently of the Soviet forces. The People's Front, a bloc of parties dominated by the Yugoslav Communist Party, won 90 per cent of the votes in the election of November 1945, and Tito was then able smoothly to implement a revolution based on the Stalinist model in the USSR.

In southern Europe, Tito had ambitious aims which clashed with British and US policy. Yugoslavia assisted Greek Communists in their attempts to seize power in Greece (see pages 23 and 45), while also claiming border territories from Italy – specifically Venezi Giulia and Trieste (see map on page 9) an important port on the Adriatic Sea. In May 1945, Yugoslav partisans occupied both territories after German troops were withdrawn, but were forced out of Trieste by British and US troops.

The USSR sympathised with Tito and argued that Trieste belonged historically, as well as geographically and economically, to the regions that now formed Yugoslavia, but Stalin was not ready to risk confrontation with Britain and the USA over these claims. In the end, an agreement was reached in the Paris peace negotiations in 1947 where Trieste was divided into two separate parts; one under Anglo-American control and the other under Yugoslav control.

Czechoslovakia and Hungary

Up to the autumn of 1947 Stalin appeared to be interested primarily in preserving a strong Communist influence in Czechoslovakia and Hungary rather than in complete domination.

Czechoslovakia

In Czechoslovakia, the post-war social revolution had been carried out by an alliance of socialists and Communists under the direction of President Beneš. Soviet troops had been withdrawn as early as December 1945. The elections in May 1946, in which the Communists won some 38 per cent of the vote, were carried out without any violence or efforts by the Communist Party to manipulate the vote. Although the Communist leader, Klement Gottwald, had established a tight grip on the Czech security forces, he had no plans for a coup and appeared to pin his hope on winning the 1948 election. Without the intensifying Cold War, Czechoslovakia might perhaps have remained a bridge between East and West, as Beneš had hoped, but the Marshall Plan and the subsequent creation of the Cominform effectively created a climate where this was impossible. The Czech cabinet voted unanimously in July to attend the Paris conference on the plan (see page 47), but the Soviet government insisted that the Americans, under cover of offering a loan, were trying to form a Western bloc and isolate the Soviet Union.

Czech proposals for compromise were ruthlessly dismissed. Jan Masaryk, the foreign minister, later told the British ambassador: 'I went to Moscow as the foreign minister of an independent sovereign state; I returned as a **lackey** of the Soviet government.' What this implied became clearer at Szklarska Poręba in September, when the secretary-general of the Czech Communist Party, Rudolf Slánský, told the conference that the reactionary forces would have to be expelled from the National Front. In February 1948 the Communist Party seized power in Czechoslovakia.

🔑 **KEY TERM**

Lackey An uncritical follower; a servant, who cannot answer back.

Hungary

It seemed in the autumn of 1945 that Hungary, like Czechoslovakia, was treated as a special case by Stalin. The elections of November 1945 were free, even though the Soviets could have influenced them easily. Two years later the press was still free, as was debate in parliament, the borders with the West were open, and most small- and medium-sized businesses were in private hands. Yet, until the signing of the peace treaty, Soviet influence was guaranteed through its dominating position on the Allied Control Commission, which was the real governing force in Hungary, and Stalin was able to insist on the Communist Party participating in the coalition government and controlling the vital Ministry of the Interior.

In the spring of 1947 the most powerful opposition to the Communists was shattered when the leader of the Smallholders' Party, Béla Kovács, was arrested by Soviet troops for conspiring against the occupation. Yet even this did not lead to an overwhelming Communist success in the August elections, when the left-wing bloc only won 45 per cent of the vote. As late as the autumn of 1947, it still seemed possible that Hungary might retain some independence, but it was increasingly being drawn into the Soviet bloc. On 8 December a treaty of friendship and co-operation was signed with Yugoslavia and, a month later, a mutual aid treaty with the USSR. In March 1948, as a result of Soviet pressure, the Hungarian Communist and Socialist parties merged. The following February, the Communist-dominated Hungarian People's Independence Front was formed, and in the elections of May 1949 only candidates from the Independence Front were allowed to stand.

France and Italy

In both Italy and France, there were strong Communist parties, which, as in the Eastern European states, had been members of coalition governments. The Cominform instructed them that they were to oppose their countries' support for the Marshall Plan.

France

After the liberation, the French government initially attempted to balance between the USSR and the Western powers. Indeed, many historians argue that France did not really join the Cold War on the side of Britain and the USA until the Moscow Conference of March 1947. However, the French historian, Annie Lacroix Riz, has shown that long before then France had in reality aligned itself with Britain and the USA. As early as October 1945 General de Gaulle was thinking of a Western European defence organisation with a US and possibly even a German contribution, despite his earlier determination to distance himself from the USA and Britain (see page 27); but when he fell from power, in 1946, the new government, a Communist, Socialist and Christian Democrat coalition, attempted to act as a bridge between East and West. Even then, though, to quote the French historian Georges-Henri Soutou, 'behind the scenes and in the utmost secrecy' the Christian Democrats and some of the Socialists attempted to draw nearer to the USA.

In March 1946 the French Socialist leader, Leon Blum, went to Washington to negotiate an American loan, and quite voluntarily accepted the US arguments for free international trade, which effectively meant France's inclusion in the capitalist Western world. At the Moscow Conference in March 1947 France openly aligned itself with the British and Americans, and two months later the Communists were expelled from the governing coalition. Initially, they remained allied with the Socialists, but in the autumn Stalin ordered them to stage a series of violent strikes against the Marshall Plan. This finally persuaded the Socialists to distance themselves from them and to accept the pro-US policy of the Christian Democrats.

Italy

There was a similar pattern of events in Italy. The Communists joined the coalition government in April 1945, and some Italian statesmen argued that Italy should try to balance between the USSR and the Western powers. Yet essentially, Italy, as Stalin himself conceded, had little option but to support the latter group, since it had been liberated and occupied by them. In December 1945 a new coalition government was created under Alcide de Gasperi, a Christian Democrat, who rapidly won US support for his economic policies. As East–West tension grew in 1946–7, the Italian government moved to the right, and in May 1947 the Communists were dismissed from the cabinet. This cleared the way for the government to accept the Marshall Plan and to align itself unambiguously with the West.

Finland

Finland again remained the exception to the pattern developing in the other Eastern European states. Its weak Communist Party received little help from the USSR. Why was this so? The British historian Adam Ulam argues that Finland escaped being integrated into the Soviet bloc merely by chance, as Zhdanov, the Soviet chairman of the Allied Control Commission, was away most of the time in Moscow. Yet, another historian, Jukka Nevakivi, argues that Stalin simply wanted to neutralise Finland. Once the peace treaty with Finland was concluded in 1947, which committed Finland to paying $300 million in reparations and ceding the strategically important naval base of Petsamo to the USSR (see the map on page 91), he was ready to leave them alone. Stalin seemed convinced that, unlike Poland, Finland was no threat to the USSR, and the threat of invasion through Finland into the Soviet Union was considered highly unlikely.

Finland's neutrality was emphasised in 1947 when its government declined an invitation to the Paris conference on the Marshall Plan, on the grounds that it wished 'to remain outside world political conflicts'. On the other hand, it did not become a member of the Cominform, and received financial assistance from the USA outside the Marshall Plan.

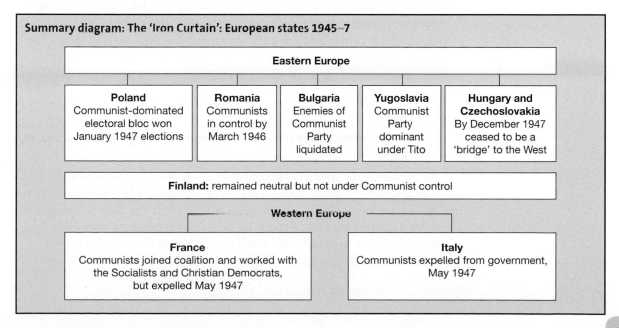

Summary diagram: The 'Iron Curtain': European states 1945–7

Eastern Europe

Poland	**Romania**	**Bulgaria**	**Yugoslavia**	**Hungary and Czechoslovakia**
Communist-dominated electoral bloc won January 1947 elections	Communists in control by March 1946	Enemies of Communist Party liquidated	Communist Party dominant under Tito	By December 1947 ceased to be a 'bridge' to the West

Finland: remained neutral but not under Communist control

Western Europe

France	**Italy**
Communists joined coalition and worked with the Socialists and Christian Democrats, but expelled May 1947	Communists expelled from government, May 1947

⑤ Key debate

▶ *Did the USA or the USSR start the Cold War 1945–7?*

The Cold War divided Europe until 1989. Why this happened and who was responsible are topics much debated by historians. To the conservative or traditionalist historians in the West, there is no doubt that it was Stalin; while revisionists look more sympathetically on the USSR and blame the USA and, to a lesser extent, Britain. With increased access to Soviet archives after 1990, historians from both 'the West' and the former Soviet bloc, such as Leonid Gibiansky, argue that Stalin's policy in Europe was more varied than had been originally assumed by Western historians.

Traditionalist interpretations

Traditionalist Western historians, such as Herbert Feis who wrote in the 1950s, firmly put the blame for starting the Cold War on Stalin. These historians argued that Stalin ignored promises given at the Yalta Conference in February 1945 to support democratically elected governments. Instead, over the next three years, he proceeded to put his own Communist puppets in power in the Eastern European states. Once it was clear that Britain and France were too weak economically and politically to defend Western Europe, the USA intervened and made the following key decisions which marked the beginning of the Cold War:

- creation of Bizonia
- Truman Doctrine of containment
- Marshall Plan.

This interpretation of the start of the Cold War depicted the USA responding defensively to aggressive Soviet moves. In the USA, the leading Cold War historian John Lewis Gaddis, writing after the end of the Cold War, gave a new slant to this interpretation by arguing that the Cold War was an unavoidable consequence of Stalin's paranoia, and was an extension of the way he dealt with opposition within the USSR.

EXTRACT 1

From 'Origins of the Cold War' by Arthur Schlesinger, *Foreign Affairs*, volume 46, 1967, pp. 22–52.

An analysis of the origins of the Cold War which leaves out those factors – the intransigence of Leninist ideology, the sinister dynamics of a totalitarian society and the madness of Stalin – is obviously incomplete. It was these factors which made it hard for the West to accept the thesis that Russia was moved only by a desire to protect its security and would be satisfied by the control of eastern Europe; it was these factors which charged the debate between universalism [the belief that mankind can only be saved through a particular belief – in this case Marxism–Leninism] and spheres of influence with apocalyptic [prophetic] potentiality.

Revisionist historians

Revisionist historians argued that the USA pursued policies that caused the Cold War in Europe. For instance, William Appleman Williams claimed in 1959 that the USA aimed to force the USSR to join the global economy and open its frontiers to both US imports and political ideas, which would have undermined Stalin's government. Ten years later another historian, Gabriel Kolko, summed up US policy as aiming at restructuring the world economically so that US business could trade, operate and profit without any restrictions.

EXTRACT 2

From William Appleman Williams, *The Tragedy of American Diplomacy*, Delta Books, 1962, pp. 206–7.

American leaders had … come to believe the theory, the necessity and morality of open door [free trade] expansion … As far as American leaders were concerned the philosophy and practice of open-door expansion had become in both its missionary and economic aspects, the view of the world …

Particularly after the atom bomb was created and used, the attitude of the United States left the Soviets with but one real option; either acquiescence in American proposals or be confronted with American power and hostility. It was the decision of the United States to employ its new and awesome power in keeping with the Open Door policy, which crystallized the Cold War.

Post-revisionist historians

Post-revisionist historians have the advantage of being able to use Soviet archive material. Historians like John Lewis Gaddis, Vladislav Zubok, Constantine Pleshakov and Norman Naimark have shown that local Communists in the Soviet zone in eastern Germany, Bulgaria, Romania and elsewhere, had considerable influence on policies which sometimes ran counter to Stalin's own intentions. They have also shown that Stalin's policy in Eastern Europe was more subtle than traditionally viewed. While he was certainly determined to turn Poland, Romania and Bulgaria into satellite states, regardless of what the West might think about the violation of democracy or **human rights**, he also had flexible views. For two years this allowed Hungary and Czechoslovakia to retain connections to the West and for Finland to remain a neutral non-Communist Western-style democracy.

 **KEY TERM**

Human rights Basic rights such as personal liberty and freedom from repression.

? Was the break-up of the
Grand Alliance in the
period 1945–7 a result
more of Soviet or US
policies?

EXTRACT 3

From John Lewis Gaddis, *The Cold War*, Allen Lane, 2006, p. 11.

*Stalin's post-war goals were security for himself, his regime and his ideology in
precisely that order. He sought to make sure that no internal challenges could
ever again endanger his personal rule, and that no external threats would ever
again place his country at risk. The interests of Communists elsewhere in the
world, admirable though these might be, would never outweigh the priorities of
the Soviet state as he had determined them. Narcissism, paranoia and absolute
power came together in Stalin: he was, within the Soviet Union and
international Communist movement, enormously feared – but also worshipped.*

Conclusion

Is it an exaggeration to say that Stalin pursued a relatively moderate line in
Eastern Europe up to 1947, and that his German policy was more a clumsy
attempt to neutralise Germany and gain the vital reparations needed by the
USSR, rather than a result of deep-laid plans to take control of territory occupied
by Germany during the Second World War? Historian Michael McGwire has
argued that Stalin was actively seeking to preserve what was left of the wartime
co-operation between Britain, the USA and the USSR and, as a consequence
of this, had by 1947 lost his chance to control Greece. By mid-1947, Stalin was
pushed on the defensive, first by the Truman Doctrine and then by the Marshall
Plan.

Does this mean that Truman in fact started the Cold War? The Truman Doctrine
and the Marshall Plan were certainly important stages reached in the escalation
of the Cold War, but the context in which the USA acted is also important. The
seismic events of early 1947 – Britain's near bankruptcy and withdrawal from
the eastern Mediterranean, growing economic paralysis in Germany, civil war
in Greece and China (see page 133) and the strength of the Communist parties
in Italy and France – galvanised the US government into announcing first the
Truman Doctrine and then the Marshall Plan. This was the turning point in the
immediate post-war period and provoked the USSR into tightening its grip on
Eastern Europe and creating the Cominform.

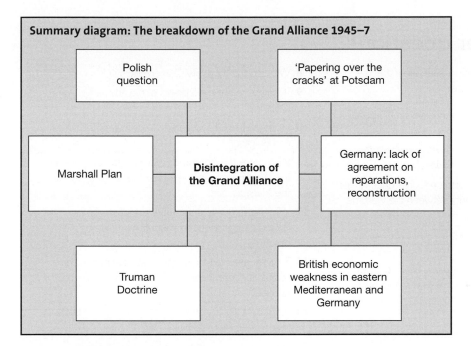

Summary diagram: The breakdown of the Grand Alliance 1945–7

- Polish question
- 'Papering over the cracks' at Potsdam
- Marshall Plan
- **Disintegration of the Grand Alliance**
- Germany: lack of agreement on reparations, reconstruction
- Truman Doctrine
- British economic weakness in eastern Mediterranean and Germany

Chapter summary

After the Second World War in Europe ended, the Grand Alliance between Britain, the USA and the USSR came under increasing pressure as all three powers had diverging aims. The abrupt termination of lend–lease supplies, disagreement over the United Nations and the control of nuclear weapons increased the tension between the three former allies. The Potsdam Conference temporarily produced compromise agreements on Germany and Poland. Four-Power Control in Germany rapidly exposed divisions between the powers. There was disagreement on reparations, and in January 1947 Britain and the USA took the first step towards the partition of Germany by establishing Bizonia.

The year 1947 was pivotal in the collapse of the Grand Alliance and the start of the Cold War. In March 1947, in response to a Communist rebellion in Greece, pressure on Turkey and Britain's growing economic weakness, Truman announced the Truman Doctrine. This was followed in June by the Marshall Plan, which offered financial aid to Europe. Fearing that the plan would enable the USA to interfere with the economies of Eastern Europe, Stalin created the Cominform and vetoed any acceptance of the Marshall Plan by the Eastern European states. The USSR also began to consolidate its grip on these states. In reaction to this, Western European states looked increasingly to the USA for economic aid and military protection. In this context, the question of who caused the Cold War is discussed in the key debate.

Refresher questions

Use these questions to remind yourself of the key material covered in this chapter.

1 What initial impact did Truman have on US policy towards the USSR?

2 To what extent did the Allies disagree about the constitution of the United Nations?

3 To what extent did the Potsdam Conference reveal fundamental disagreements between the wartime allies?

4 Why did the UN fail to gain control over nuclear weapons?

5 Why, despite worsening relations between the USSR and Britain and the USA, was it possible to negotiate the peace treaties with Italy and other minor Axis states in 1947?

6 Why could the occupying powers not agree on German reparations?

7 Why did the USA and Britain create Bizonia?

8 Why did the Moscow Conference fail?

9 What were the main points of the Truman Doctrine?

10 How did the USSR tighten its control of Romania and Bulgaria?

11 Why were the Americans disappointed by the way the West Europeans organised the carrying out of the Marshall Plan?

12 Why did Britain and the USA not intervene in Poland to stop the Communists from seizing power?

13 To what extent did Hungary and Czechoslovakia remain 'bridges' between Eastern and Western Europe?

14 How did the Communist Party in France and Italy react to the Marshall Plan?

15 Why was Finland able to retain its neutrality in 1946–7?

Question practice

ESSAY QUESTIONS

1 'The Marshall Plan may have saved Western Europe from communism but it also divided Europe.' Explain why you agree or disagree with this view.

2 To what extent was disagreement on Germany the cause of the breakdown of the Grand Alliance?

3 How successful was the USA's intervention to deal with the growing Soviet threat to Western Europe 1945–7?

4 Which of the following had the greater impact on preventing the four occupying powers from agreeing on German unity? i) The amalgamation of the SPD and KPD in April 1946. ii) Disagreement over German reparations. Explain your answer with reference to both i) and ii).

SOURCE ANALYSIS QUESTIONS

1 With reference to Sources G (page 49) and H (page 50), and your understanding of the historical context, which of these two sources is more valuable in explaining why the Cold War started after 1945?

2 With reference to Sources E (page 45), G (page 49) and H (page 50), and your understanding of the historical context, assess the value of these sources to a historian studying the factors that led to the creation of the 'Iron Curtain'.

CHAPTER 3

Conflict over Germany and consolidation of rival blocs

This chapter covers the key period from 1948 to 1955 during which two German states, the Federal Republic of Germany (FRG) and the German Democratic Republic (GDR), were created and the division of Europe was consolidated into a Soviet bloc and a Western bloc. This chapter examines these developments through the following themes:

★ The division of Germany

★ The rearmament of Western Europe 1948–52

★ The political and economic consolidation of the rival blocs

★ The 'Thaw' 1953–5

The key debate on *page 92* of this chapter asks the question: Was it inevitable that the division of Germany should deepen and become more permanent during the years 1948–55?

Key dates

1947	Dec. 15	Break-up of London Foreign Ministers' Conference	1951	April 18	European Coal and Steel Community (Schuman Plan) Treaty
1948	June 20	Currency reform in Western zones	1952	March 10	Stalin's note proposing a neutral united Germany
	June 24	Berlin Blockade started		May 27	European Defence Community (EDC) Treaty signed in Paris
1949	May 12	Berlin Blockade ended			
		COMECON formed	1953	March 5	Stalin died
	April 4	NATO set up		June 16–17	Strikes and riots in the GDR
	Aug.	FRG established	1955	May 5	The FRG became a sovereign state and joined NATO
	Oct. 12	GDR set up			
1950	June 25	Outbreak of Korean War		May 14	Warsaw Pact signed

1 The division of Germany

▶ *Why and how were the FRG and GDR created?*
▶ *Why did the Berlin Blockade fail to prevent the creation of the FRG?*

The London Conference of Foreign Ministers 1947

The foreign ministers of Britain, France, the USA and USSR met in London in November 1947 in yet another attempt to find a solution to the problem of what to do with Germany. However, by the time the conference opened in London, the chances of any agreement on Germany seemed remote. The USA vigorously supported the idea of **Western European integration** and was at least temporarily resigned to the division of Germany. The USSR still wished to avoid the partition of Germany, as this would result in the great industrial complex of the **Ruhr** becoming a part of a US-dominated Western European bloc.

The Soviets had tried hard to rally public opinion across Germany against the policy of the Western allies. **Walter Ulbricht**, the leader of the SED (see page 41), was instructed to organise a 'German People's Congress for Unity and a Just Peace'. Representatives from all parties throughout Germany were invited to attend its meetings on 6–7 December 1947 in Berlin. The intention was then to send a delegation to the London Conference to support the Soviet demand for the formation of a German central government. Roughly one-third of the 2225 delegates came from the West, but these were overwhelmingly Communists from areas like the Ruhr and the big industrial towns. The movement did not therefore genuinely reflect West German opinion, and the British foreign secretary, Ernest Bevin, refused to allow its delegation permission to enter Britain.

The London Conference broke up on 15 December amid bitter recriminations. The Soviets accused Britain and the USA of violating the Potsdam Agreement and of denying the USSR its fair share of reparations, while the Western powers rejected Soviet proposals for forming a German government, which would govern a united Germany, as they feared the Soviets would gain control of it. All hope of Four-Power Control now disappeared, and instead, for Britain, France and the USA, the alternatives of a Western alliance, closer economic co-operation in Western Europe and the creation of a West German state appeared to be the only practical options.

The decision to create a West German state

The failure of the London Conference of Foreign Ministers in December 1947 strengthened the Western allies in their resolve to form a separate West German

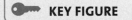

state. A second London conference was then held from February to June 1948 where Britain, France, the USA and the **Benelux states** met to discuss the establishment of this new nation.

At the conference, US and British plans met with considerable hostility from France, which dreaded the revival of a Germany with the potential to invade France yet again. French fears were gradually eased by a US pledge to keep troops stationed in Western Europe to maintain peace and prevent a revival of an aggressive Germany. Britain and the USA also promised to control tightly the new German government that they were resolved to establish. The production of the great industrial centre of the Ruhr, for example, was to be regulated by the **International Ruhr Authority**, which would be controlled by the Western allies. West Germans would also have to accept the **Occupation Statute** which would give Britain, France and the USA far-reaching powers over trade, foreign relations, economic issues and disarmament. On 7 June, Germans in the Western zones were granted permission to create a constitution for a democratic, **federal** West Germany.

Currency reform

On 20 June, the Western allies, without consulting the Soviet Union, introduced a new currency for Western Germany, the *Deutschmark*, or German mark. Four days later, the Soviets responded by introducing a new currency for their Eastern German zone, the *Ostmark*, or East mark. With the introduction of new currencies, two separate German states began to take shape.

The Soviet response: the Berlin Blockade

The Soviets believed that they could force the Western allies to abandon their plans for a West German state by applying pressure to West Berlin, which was controlled by the Western allies but separated from the rest of Germany due to its location in the Soviet zone in Eastern Germany (see the map on page 36). West Berlin was totally dependent on the rail and road links running through the Soviet-controlled zone for its supplies of food and new materials from Western Germany. Starting in March 1948, Soviet forces began to restrict the movement of people and goods between West Berlin and Western Germany.

The blockade begins

The Soviets reacted to the introduction of the *Deutschmark* into West Berlin on 23 June 1948 by blockading West Berlin. They argued that the blockade was a defensive measure to stop the Soviet zone being swamped with the devalued *Reichsmark*, which the new *Deutschmark* was replacing in Western Germany and West Berlin. Rail and road links to the west, as well as the supply of electricity which came from East Berlin, were cut.

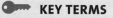 **KEY TERMS**

Benelux states Belgium (Be), the Netherlands (Ne) and Luxembourg (Lux).

International Ruhr Authority An organisation to establish how much coal and steel the Germans should produce and ensure that a percentage of its production should be made available to its western neighbours. It was replaced in 1951 by the European Coal and Steel Community.

Occupation Statute A treaty defining the rights of Britain, France and the USA in West Germany.

Federal A country formed of several different states that enjoy considerable autonomy in domestic affairs.

Reichsmark German currency before 1948; it lost most of its value after Germany's defeat in the Second World War.

Figure 3.1 A map showing how the airlift worked. Radar beacons regulated the flow of the aircraft before they entered corridors to Berlin. What does this map indicate about West Berlin's vulnerability to the blockade?

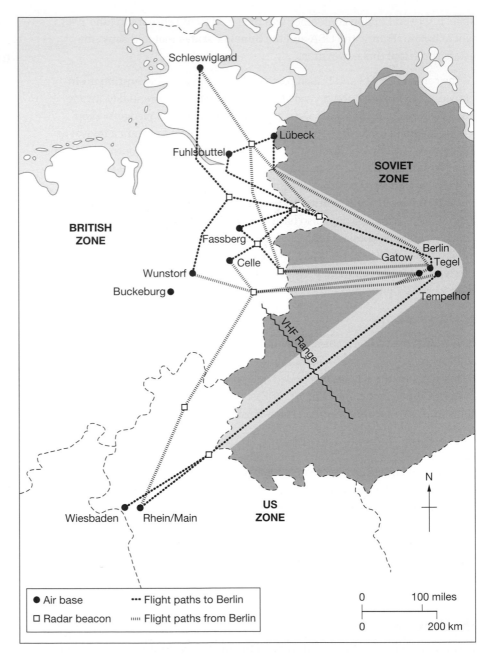

The Western response: the Berlin airlift

The Western response was confused and unsure. The French were convinced that West Berlin could only hold out for a matter of weeks, while, to quote the historian Avi Schlaim, the US administration 'seemed almost paralysed by uncertainty and fear'. It was Bevin who again provided the initial leadership of the alliance, and suggested forceful countermeasures. Essentially, he was determined to maintain the Western position in Berlin and press on with setting

SOURCE A

West Berlin children watch a US plane, loaded with food, come in to land in August 1948. Pilots would often drop sweets to the waiting children below.

What information is conveyed by Source A? **?**

up a West German state, while at all costs avoiding war. He rejected suggestions by General Clay, the US military governor, that an armed convoy should force its way through to West Berlin, because this could easily have provoked a clash with Soviet forces. Instead, he convinced the Americans that West Berlin could be supplied by an **airlift** made possible by aircraft flying along the three 'corridors', or flight paths, allocated to the Western allies by the Soviets in 1945 (see the diagram on page 64). He also responded enthusiastically to US requests to transfer 60 B-29 bombers to East Anglia. It was assumed at the time that these carried atomic bombs, but in fact this was a bluff, as the modified B-29s, which could carry them, only arrived in Britain in 1949. Nevertheless, this gesture probably did deter the Soviets from trying to interfere with the airlift, although they, too, wanted to avoid war.

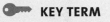 **KEY TERM**

Airlift The transport of food and supplies by air to a besieged area.

By the end of July, British and US planes were managing to fly into West Berlin an average of 2000 tons of food and raw materials a day. Yet if stocks were to be built up for the coming winter, 5000 tons would have to be flown in on a daily basis.

The Moscow talks

As it was very uncertain whether these totals could be maintained, the three Western powers were ready to explore the possibility of reaching an agreement over Berlin. On 2 August their ambassadors met Stalin in Moscow. Interpreting their approach as a sign of weakness, he was uncompromising over his demands. According to the Soviet record of the meeting on 2 August:

? According to Source B, what were Stalin's proposals for solving the Berlin Crisis?

SOURCE B

From the official Soviet record of a meeting of 2 August 1948, quoted in 'The Soviet Union and the Berlin Crisis' by M. Narinski, in F. Gori and S. Pons, editors, *The Soviet Union and Europe in the Cold War, 1945–53*, Palgrave Macmillan, 1996, p. 68.

Comrade Stalin spoke of two factors – the special currency in Berlin and the decisions of the London Conference. He thought that it was those decisions which gave rise to the restrictive measures under discussion … Comrade Stalin said that … simultaneously with the rescinding of the restrictions on transport applied by the Soviet Military Administration, the special currency [the Deutschmark*] … introduced by the three powers into Berlin should be withdrawn and replaced by the currency circulating in the Soviet zone … That was the first point. Secondly, assurance should be given that application of the London Conference's decisions would be postponed until representatives of the four powers had met and negotiated on all the basic questions concerning Germany.*

The Western powers would not reverse their decision to create a West German state, but they were ready to agree to the circulation of the *Ostmark* in the whole of Berlin, subject to the financial control of the four powers. Yet, as further discussions between the military governors of the four zones in September showed, the Soviets wanted total control of the currency. If they were to abandon the blockade, at the very least they intended, as one Soviet official observed:

? According to Source C, what were Soviet intentions in Berlin?

SOURCE C

From the recollections of a senior Soviet official, quoted in 'The Soviet Union and the Berlin Crisis' by M. Narinski, in F. Gori and S. Pons, editors, *The Soviet Union and Europe in the Cold War, 1945–53*, Palgrave Macmillan, 1996, p. 69.

… to restore the economic unity of Berlin, to include all Berlin in the economic system of the Soviet zone and also to restore unified administration of the city. That would have served as a basis for winning over the population of West Berlin, and would have created the preconditions for completely ousting the Western powers from Berlin.

These talks broke down on 7 September because neither side would give way. As the Soviets were convinced that the airlift to West Berlin could not be sustained during the winter, they decided to play for time and avoid any compromise. Consequently, all the efforts of the United Nations (UN) to mediate during the winter of 1948–9 failed.

 **KEY TERM**

C-54 Large US transport plane.

End of the blockade

By the end of January 1949, however, it became clear that Stalin's gamble was failing. The winter of 1948–9 was exceptionally mild and, thanks to the effective deployment of the large American **C-54** planes, which flew to Berlin from bases in the British zone, the average daily tonnage for January was 5620. By April this had reached 8000 tons a day and about 1000 aircraft were able to use the air corridors to Berlin at any one time (see the diagram on page 64). In February, the Western powers also declared the *Deutschmark* to be the sole legal currency in West Berlin and stopped all Western exports to the Soviet zone, which increased the pressure on the zone's economy.

Stalin, who was not prepared to go to war over Berlin, had little option but to cut his losses. In an interview with a US journalist on 31 January he made a considerable concession when he indicated that he would make the lifting of the blockade dependent only on calling another meeting of the Council of Foreign Ministers. The Americans responded to this and talks began between the Soviet and US representatives on the UN Security Council in New York. In early May they finally reached agreement that the blockade would be called off on 12 May and that eleven days later a Council of Foreign Ministers should meet in Paris to discuss both the future of Germany and the Berlin currency question. On neither issue did the Council produce a breakthrough, but the four powers approved the New York agreement on lifting the blockade and agreed to discuss how the situation in Berlin could be normalised, although on this no agreement was secured until 1971 (see page 171).

Formation of the two German states

The future shape of Germany was effectively decided by the end of 1948. Stalin had failed to deter the Western allies from pressing ahead with their plans for establishing the Federal Republic of Germany (FRG) and in the end he had little option but to create a Communist East Germany, the German Democratic Republic (GDR), as a counterweight to the FRG.

The Federal Republic of Germany (FRG)

The West German constitution was approved in the spring of 1949 by the three Western occupying powers, and elections for the new parliament (*Bundestag*) took place in August. A month later when parliament met, **Konrad Adenauer** became the first West German chancellor. The FRG was, however, far from being independent. The Occupation Statute, which came into force in September, replaced the military government in the former Western zones with a **High Commission**. This still gave Britain, France and the USA the final say on West German foreign policy, security questions, exports and many other matters that an independent state is free to decide on for itself.

The German Democratic Republic (GDR)

In the winter of 1948–9 the Soviets were reluctant to set up a separate East German state if there was still a chance of stopping British and US plans for West Germany and of one day creating a neutral pro-Soviet Germany. Stalin was prepared to give the Soviet zone a greater degree of independence, but

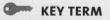

KEY FIGURE

Konrad Adenauer (1876–1967)

Former lord mayor of Cologne 1917–33, leader of the Christian Democrat Party and chancellor of FRG 1949–63.

KEY TERM

High Commission A civilian body charged with the task of defending the interests of the Western allies in Germany.

for the moment this was just a temporary step that would not block eventual German unity. He feared that the creation of an East German state would make the division of Germany final.

Throughout the spring and summer of 1949 Walter Ulbricht and the other leaders of the SED claimed that only their party was working for national unity, in contrast to the **splitters** in the West, whom he alleged were deliberately plotting to divide Germany. To emphasise this claim, in March 1948 the SED set up a 'German People's Council' (*Volksrat*) of 400 delegates, a quarter of whom were Communists from the Western zones, to draft a constitution for a united German state. If a unified Germany proved impossible to create, then this constitution would form the basis of a new East German state. In May, Wilhelm Pieck, the chairman of the SED, pointed out that once a West German state was set up, the Soviet zone would inevitably have to 'develop its own independent state structure. It did not matter whether the Western Powers tore Germany apart … a month earlier or a month later. The important thing was to be prepared for every eventuality.'

By March 1949 the SED was ready for this 'eventuality'. The constitution of the future East German state had been drafted and approved by the People's Council. On paper at least, it did not seem to be so very different from West Germany's. In reality, however, it was, as the historian Peter Merkl observed, a **make-believe constitution** camouflaging a one-party dictatorship. In May a new People's Congress was elected. The voters, as in the other Soviet-dominated countries in Eastern Europe, had been presented with just one list of candidates, all of whom represented the views of the SED.

At the end of May the congress met and approved the draft constitution, but Moscow, where the real power lay, kept the SED in suspense. The Soviets believed that there was still a slim chance of stopping the setting up of the FRG. However, once the West German elections, in which the KPD won only 5.7 per cent of the votes, had taken place in August, Stalin realised that there was no longer any alternative to forming the GDR, even though for him it was an exercise in damage limitation, which would ensure that the Soviet zone did not become sucked into a united Western-orientated Germany. On 12 October the government of the new state was formed and the Soviet military occupation of the zone came to an end, although a Soviet Control Commission was set up, which, like the Allied High Commission in the West, retained considerable reserve powers.

Berlin

The division of Germany ensured that Berlin remained a divided city within a divided state within a divided continent. At the end of November 1948 the Germans in West Berlin, in response to threats and intimidation from the SED, set up their own city government with an elected assembly, which had an overwhelming anti-Communist majority. Britain, France and the USA permitted

West Berlin to send representatives to sit in the West German parliament in Bonn but, as the city was still legally under Four-Power Control, they had no voting rights.

There was, as yet, no physical barrier between East and West Berlin. Nevertheless, the Soviet sector of Berlin became the capital of the new GDR. The frontier was still open in the city. The Berlin Wall was not built until August 1961 (see page 113).

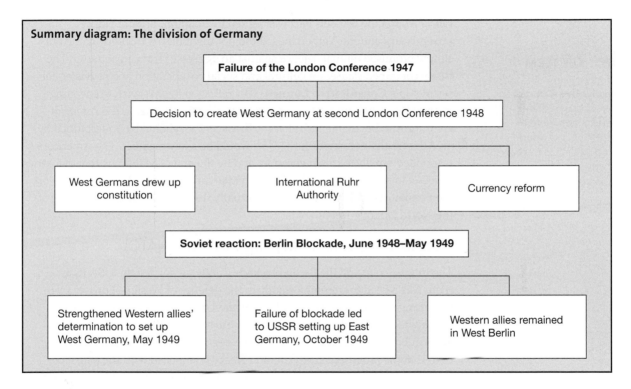

Summary diagram: The division of Germany

Failure of the London Conference 1947

Decision to create West Germany at second London Conference 1948

West Germans drew up constitution

International Ruhr Authority

Currency reform

Soviet reaction: Berlin Blockade, June 1948–May 1949

Strengthened Western allies' determination to set up West Germany, May 1949

Failure of blockade led to USSR setting up East Germany, October 1949

Western allies remained in West Berlin

2 The rearmament of Western Europe 1948–52

▶ *How was Western military power strengthened 1948–52?*

▶ *Why did it take so long for the European Defence Community treaty to be signed?*

The Brussels Pact and 'Western Union'

The creation of a West German state was still viewed with deep mistrust and fear by France and many other European states. In an effort to calm their anxieties, the British came up with a plan for a defensive alliance against

Germany, but which, in reality, as Paul-Henri Spaak, the Belgian prime minister, pointed out, 'was meant as a screen behind which to consider defences against Russia', as occupied Germany was hardly in a position to threaten its neighbours. The Communist seizure of power in Prague on 22 February 1948 (see page 53) had been a powerful factor in persuading the French to join an alliance system directed primarily against the USSR rather than Germany. The French government was also reassured by the US decision to keep troops in West Germany for the foreseeable future.

On 17 March the Brussels Pact was signed by Belgium, Britain, France, Luxembourg and the Netherlands. It did not mention the USSR by name but simply promised mutual defence against an aggressor from any quarter. The treaty contained clauses on cultural and social co-operation and provision for setting up a **Consultative Council**. This reflected Bevin's wish to encourage general Western European co-operation as a further barrier to the spread of communism. Bevin intended that the Brussels Pact should be underpinned by an Atlantic alliance in which the USA would be a key member. The Americans responded rapidly to this suggestion, and by the end of March the first of a series of secret meetings between British, Canadian and US officials began to explore the possibility of such an alliance. Eventually this was to lead to the signing of the North Atlantic Treaty.

The North Atlantic Treaty Organisation (NATO)

The Prague coup and the Berlin Blockade finally persuaded the USA that there was a need to commit formally to the defence of Western Europe. From the spring of 1948 through to early 1949, the USA gradually developed the framework for a North Atlantic–Western European military alliance with its allies in Europe. Over the course of these negotiations it became increasingly clear that the proposed North Atlantic Treaty interlocked with the plans for creating a West German state since it eased fears of a revitalised German state, particularly for France.

To persuade the US Congress to agree to commit troops to the defence of Europe, President Truman stressed that the treaty did not oblige the USA to go to war without the consent of Congress. In the end, Article 5 of the North Atlantic Treaty contained the rather imprecise wording that each treaty member 'will take such action as it deems necessary, including the use of armed force, to restore and maintain security in the North Atlantic area'. The Western European states, particularly France, found this too vague, but decided to use Article 3, which called for 'continuous and effective self-help and mutual aid', to involve the USA ever more closely in the defence of Western Europe.

The North Atlantic Treaty was signed on 4 April 1949 for an initial period of twenty years. It included Canada, the USA, the Brussels Pact Powers, Norway, Denmark, Iceland, Italy and Portugal, and it came into force in August 1949.

SOURCE D

From the North Atlantic Treaty, available at the NATO website (www.nato.int/ cps/en/natolive/official_texts_17120.htm).

The Parties to this Treaty … are determined to safeguard the freedom, common heritage and civilization of their peoples, founded on the principles of democracy, individual liberty and the rule of law.

They seek to promote stability and well-being in the North Atlantic area. …

Article III: In order more effectively to achieve the objectives of this treaty, the Parties, separately and jointly, by means of continuous and effective self-help and mutual aid, will maintain and develop their individual and collective capacity to resist armed attack. …

Article V: The Parties agree that an armed attack against one or more of them in Europe or North America shall be considered an attack against them all and consequently they agree that, if such an armed attack occurs, each of them, in exercise of the right of individual or collective self defence recognized by Article 51 of the Charter of the United Nations, will assist the Party or Parties so attacked by taking forthwith, individually and in concert with other Parties such action as it deems necessary including the use of armed force, to restore and maintain the security of the North Atlantic area.

Any such armed attack and all measures taken as a result thereof shall immediately be reported to the Security Council.

> According to Source D, what did NATO require of its member states? **?**

The growing Soviet threat to the West

Despite the foundation of NATO in April 1949, there was a strong feeling in the Western alliance in the winter of 1949–50 that it was losing ground to the Soviet Union. In September the USSR had successfully exploded its first atomic bomb, while a month later China fell to the Communists. Stalin also rapidly began to expand the Red Army. In 1948, tank production plans called for an annual increase from 1150 to 4350 tanks, and production of artillery was to quadruple.

Meanwhile, Western European integration was developing only slowly. NATO was still in its infancy, and lingering fears of German domination among the Western European states stopped the USA from building up the new Federal Republic's economic and military strength to a point where it could play a major role in the defence of Western Europe. Until the FRG was fully integrated economically and militarily into Western Europe there was a real danger that Stalin might be able to win the Germans over by offering them unity and markets stretching from the River Oder, which formed the border between the GDR and Poland (see the map on page 36), to the Pacific Ocean. If the West Germans, who now had their own parliament, voted for neutrality and reunification with the GDR, short of using military force, the Western allies would have to accept it. In such a situation, the danger for the USA and its allies would be that a neutral Germany, with its economic resources and population of 80 million, would be open to Soviet influence and pressure.

The impact of the Korean War

The Korean War changed the situation dramatically. The invasion of South Korea by Communist North Korean troops on 25 June 1950 (see page 139) appeared to many in Western Europe and the USA to be a prelude to a new global conflict in which the Soviets would finally overrun Western Europe. It was assumed that North Korea acted under Stalin's orders and this fear was reinforced when East Germany's leader, Ulbricht, not only supported North Korean aggression, but appeared to recommend similar action as a way of unifying Germany. The creation of a new East German **paramilitary police force** of some 60,000 men gave some substance to these threats.

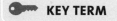

KEY TERM

Paramilitary police force
Police force that is armed with machine guns and armoured cars.

? What information is conveyed by Source E about Adenauer's assessment of the East German threat?

SOURCE E

On 17 August 1950 Chancellor Adenauer raised the question of security at a conference with the three Allied High Commissioners. From Konrad Adenauer, *Memoirs, 1945–1950*, Weidenfeld & Nicolson, 1965, pp. 274–5.

I had proposed the creation of a federal police force to the High Commissioners at the end of June 1950 … By the middle of August I was convinced on the basis of confidential information that French resistance might be overcome if I made another attempt to do so.

I raised the subject of security at a conference with the High Commissioners of [sic] 17 August 1950 … I begged the High Commissioners to intercede with their governments for some demonstration of military strength that might restore people's confidence in the possibility of resistance … My second request was that the Federal Government should be ready to build up a defence force … to offer effective resistance to an attack by the People's [GDR] Police.

I noted that Pieck and Ulbricht had repeatedly declared their intention of 'liberating' West Germany, and if these statements were taken in conjunction with military preparation currently being carried out by the Soviet Zone [GDR] police, there could be no doubt about their purpose.

The European Defence Community

In light of the Korean War and Ulbricht's statements, West German rearmament was viewed as essential to strengthen the defences of Western Europe. France, however, continued to have reservations about creating a strong and independent FRG. Consequently, on 24 October 1950, the French prime minister, René Pleven, proposed the formation of the European Defence Community (EDC); this was known as the Pleven Plan. Its purpose was to create a European army under supranational control with a European minister of defence responsible to a European Assembly which would be appointed by the participating governments. To ensure that the FRG was kept under control, its troops would join not in divisions (units of about 10,000 troops) but instead in battalions (much smaller units composed of only about 800 troops).

The Spofford Compromise

Militarily, the first version of the Pleven Plan was unworkable. It was essentially a French plan aimed more at controlling German rearmament than at military effectiveness. The British refused to join and only Belgium and Luxembourg showed any real interest, while the USA felt that it was military nonsense. However, after prolonged discussions, a workable compromise was realised that would ultimately enable German troops to be recruited. Charles Spofford, the deputy US representative on NATO's Atlantic Council, suggested that, while the political problems caused by the EDC proposal were being sorted out, certain practical steps to strengthen defences in Western Europe, 'upon which there already exist large measure of agreement', should be taken immediately. This was accepted by both France and Britain and the other NATO members, and from this emerged the Spofford Compromise. This proposed that, parallel with the creation of a European army, NATO itself would create an integrated force in Europe. In it would serve, for the time being, medium-sized German units, which would be subject to tight supervision by the Western allies.

Strains within NATO, December 1950 to June 1951

At first it seemed as though the Spofford Compromise had broken the deadlock over German rearmament. Preliminary negotiations about establishing the EDC began in Paris in February 1951, and at the same time Adenauer began to discuss plans with the Western allies for creating twelve West German divisions for NATO.

Rearmament as a political issue within the FRG

In West Germany, the Social Democrat Party bitterly attacked Adenauer's intention to join the EDC on the grounds that this would permanently divide Germany. He therefore attempted to negotiate for more independence with the Western allies in order to convince his electorate that rearmament would lead to the FRG being given equality of treatment by its former occupiers. This, of course, frightened French public opinion, which would not allow their government to make any more concessions to the Germans.

Disagreements about Korea and China

The escalating conflict in Korea put further pressure on the Alliance. When troops from the Communist People's Republic of China (PRC) came to the assistance of North Korea in November 1950, Western Europeans were alarmed by rumours that the USA would retaliate by dropping nuclear bombs on the PRC, and feared that this would lead to an all-out war and the withdrawal of US troops from Europe. Britain's prime minister, Clement Attlee, with the support

Appease To conciliate a potential aggressor by making concessions.

Republican Party Founded in 1854. Essentially an American conservative party.

Democratic Party Founded in 1828. Essentially a liberal or left-of-centre party.

Ratify When an international treaty has been signed, it can come into effect only after the parliaments of the signatory states have ratified (that is, approved) it.

Hydrogen bomb A nuclear bomb hundreds of times more powerful than an atomic bomb.

Joe McCarthy (1908–57)

Judge and Republican senator in the USA.

of the French government, tried to persuade the USA to open negotiations with the PRC. President Truman refused on the grounds that he could not **appease** communism in Asia while opposing it in Europe, but he did reassure Attlee that the atomic bomb would not be used.

Growing anti-communism within the USA

Once the PRC had sent troops into North Korea, it was clear that the war would continue into the indefinite future. This strengthened the **Republican Party** in the US Congress, which believed that the USA should take a more aggressive stance against both the USSR and the PRC. This forced Truman, a **Democrat**, to make rearmament his government's overriding priority so that the Korean War could be ended and further action as called for by Republicans would not be necessary. Truman was also under pressure from Senator **Joe McCarthy**, who accused several members of his administration of being Communists. Within the context of the escalating war in Korea, this led to a 'witch hunt' against alleged Communists in the USA.

Franco-German agreement on the EDC

In October 1951, as a result of US pressure, detailed negotiations on the EDC started in Paris. Simultaneously, talks began in Bonn, the capital of the FRG, between the High Commissioners and Konrad Adenauer, on replacing the Occupation Statute with a treaty which recognised the FRG's new status as a semi-independent state. Both sets of negotiations proved complicated and continued slowly until May 1952.

In Bonn, the negotiations centred on how much independence the Western allies were ready to give the FRG. In Paris, the key issue was still French determination to prevent Germany from becoming a major military power again. France vetoed German membership of NATO and insisted on restricting the size of German units that could be integrated into the EDC. The General Treaty that replaced the Occupation Statute was signed on 26 May 1952, and the EDC Treaty a day later in Paris. Afterwards, there was a long, unsuccessful struggle to have the treaties **ratified** by the national parliaments of France and West Germany.

Financing Western European rearmament

As we have seen, the Korean War and the Soviet development of the atomic bomb forced Truman to make rearmament his government's overriding priority in Europe. The USA began to develop the **hydrogen bomb** shortly after the outbreak of the Korean War and tripled military spending. Marshall Aid was at first diverted to those Western European industries that were vital for rearmament and then, in 1951, stopped altogether in favour of a direct military assistance programme. The sheer expense of rearmament threatened to destabilise NATO at a time when the threat from the Soviet bloc appeared to be growing.

The economic and political costs of rearmament

In Western Europe, NATO states increased their expenditure on rearmament from $4.4 billion in 1949 to $8 billion in 1951. This initially triggered a boom in industrial production, but expensive raw materials such as coal, copper and rubber had to be imported in considerable quantities, causing inflation and serious **balance of payments** problems. Between July 1950 and June 1951, inflation caused a significant increase in the cost of living. Costs rose by twenty per cent in France and ten per cent in Italy, Britain and the FRG, while wages did not increase as significantly.

There was also evidence that the shift in investment from civilian to defence production and the higher taxes to pay for this were undermining political stability. In Britain, a serious split developed in April 1951 in the Labour cabinet over the cost of rearmament, while in the French and Italian elections of May and June 1951 both Communists and the conservative nationalist parties made a strong showing against incumbent governments. In the FRG, there were ominous signs that the extreme right appeared to be making a comeback in the state elections in Lower Saxony.

Guns and butter

The **Organization for European Economic Co-operation (OEEC)** was convinced that Western Europe faced a great economic crisis that could only be solved by a second Marshall Plan. While it was unrealistic to expect any help on this scale from the USA as it was spending vast sums on its own rearmament programme, the OEEC and NATO did co-operate in a successful attempt to ensure that rearmament did not stifle the economic recovery of Western Europe. In August, the OEEC called for a dramatic 25 per cent expansion of Western Europe's industrial production over the coming five years. It proposed financing both rearmament and increased consumer goods production. This was summarised as a policy of the production of both **guns and butter**. Steadily growing demand for industrial goods and vehicles helped to make this plan successful. For the next twenty years, Western Europe enjoyed a period of unparalleled prosperity which in turn encouraged further economic and political integration and consolidated the Western bloc.

Stalin's response to rearmament

Stalin attempted to counter the threat of NATO and German rearmament in two ways. He:

- launched the Communist led World Peace Movement, which campaigned for disarmament and world peace
- offered the FRG the prospect of joining a neutral united Germany.

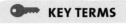 **KEY TERMS**

Balance of payments
The difference between the earnings of exports and the cost of imports.

Organization for European Economic Co-operation (OEEC)
Set up in 1948 to administer the Marshall Plan.

Guns and butter A phrase used initially in the US press in 1917 to describe the production of nitrates for both peaceful and military purposes; now usually used to describe the situation when a country's economy can finance both increased military and consumer goods production.

The World Peace Movement

In November 1949, Cominform (see page 48) was given the task of mobilising a Soviet-backed peace movement. At a time when rearmament was causing severe strains on the Western European economies, Stalin intended to use the peace movement to appeal to the fears of many in Western Europe, who dreaded the outbreak of a third world war. He hoped that this would lead to a backlash against NATO and Adenauer's government in the FRG.

In 1949, with assistance from Cominform, the World Committee for the Partisans for Peace was created to organise the Peace Movement. In early 1951, it handed this task to a World Peace Council elected by the Soviet-dominated Congress of the Partisans of Peace. In March 1950, the Council launched its Stockholm Appeal, which demanded the banning of the atomic bomb and the condemnation as war criminals of whichever government used it first in conflict. The campaign was supported mainly by Soviet bloc countries. NATO governments viewed it with considerable suspicion. The British prime minister, Attlee, for instance, called it 'a bogus forum of peace with the real aim of sabotaging national defence'. Because of its strong links with the USSR, it had little impact on NATO states.

The Stalin note of March 1952

From the autumn of 1950 until the spring of 1952, Stalin put forward a series of initiatives aimed at achieving a united but neutral Germany. In March 1952, in a note to the Western allies, he made a far-reaching proposal for free elections in Germany supervised by a commission of the four former occupying powers. This would lead to the establishment of an independent Germany. The new, reunified Germany would be neutral, and so would not be able to join the EDC or NATO. It would also not be burdened with reparations and would have a small army.

Was Stalin really serious with this offer? Many West Germans believed that Adenauer should have responded more positively to Stalin's initiative. They were convinced that it was a 'missed opportunity', an opinion that has been echoed by revisionist historians, of whom R. Steininger and Willy Loth are the most persuasive. Adenauer, however, like the Americans and the British, wanted to see the FRG firmly integrated into the West and not replaced by a unified neutral Germany, which would be vulnerable to Soviet pressure.

Thus, Stalin's initiative was never fully explored by the Western powers. In July 1952, Ulbricht was given the go-ahead for an accelerated socialisation programme in East Germany, which suggested that Stalin had now finally given up the idea of sacrificing the GDR to stop the rearmament of the FRG.

The leadership of the GDR's Socialist Unity Party (SED) went to Moscow in April 1952 to discuss the response of the Western allies to Stalin's note. Stalin was reported by one of the SED leaders as saying:

SOURCE F

From 'Stalin's Plans for Post-War Germany' by Wilfried Loth, in F. Gori and S. Pons, editors, *The Soviet Union and Europe in the Cold War, 1943–53*, Palgrave Macmillan, 1996, p. 31.

'Comrade Stalin considers that irrespective of any proposals that we can make on the German question, the Western powers will not agree with them and will not withdraw from Germany in any case. It will be a mistake to think that a compromise might emerge or that the Americans will agree with the draft of the peace treaty. The Americans need their army in West Germany to hold Western Europe in their hands. They say that their army is to defend [the Germans]. But the real goal of this army is to control Europe. The Americans will draw West Germany into the Atlantic Pact. They will create West German troops. Adenauer is in the pocket of the Americans … in reality there is an independent state being formed in West Germany. And you must organize your own state. The line of demarcation between East and West Germany must be seen as a frontier and not as a simple border but a dangerous one. One must strengthen the protection of this frontier.'

According to Source F, why was Stalin's proposal for free elections in Germany rejected? ?

SOURCE G

What information is contained in Source G that is important for a historian? ?

The SED celebrating its second party conference in July 1952.

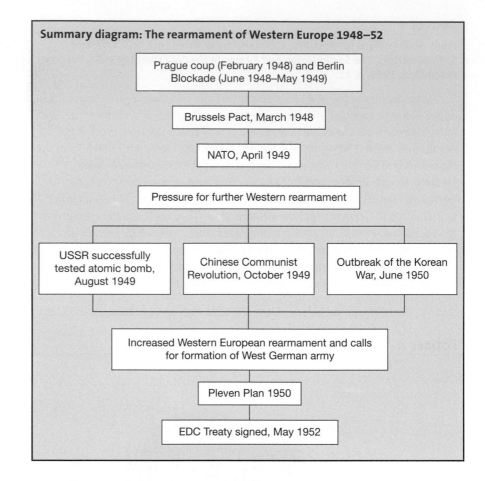

Summary diagram: The rearmament of Western Europe 1948–52

Prague coup (February 1948) and Berlin Blockade (June 1948–May 1949)

Brussels Pact, March 1948

NATO, April 1949

Pressure for further Western rearmament

USSR successfully tested atomic bomb, August 1949

Chinese Communist Revolution, October 1949

Outbreak of the Korean War, June 1950

Increased Western European rearmament and calls for formation of West German army

Pleven Plan 1950

EDC Treaty signed, May 1952

③ The political and economic consolidation of the rival blocs

▶ *How did the polarisation of Europe into two rival blocs accelerate during the years 1950–2?*

▶ *How did the USSR strengthen its grip on the Eastern bloc?*

Western economic integration

Western integration was determined by two key factors. On the one hand, the Americans intended, as the historian Michael Hogan has argued, to rebuild Western Europe in the image of the USA; they hoped that a European political and economic union would create a United States of Europe. The US government was convinced that once an economically integrated and politically united Western Europe existed, it would rapidly become as wealthy as the USA. This would:

- deter people from wanting Communist government
- significantly boost world trade
- provide valuable markets for US exports
- eventually draw the Eastern European states out of the Soviet bloc.

On the other hand, France and the smaller European states saw Western political and economic integration as providing the key to harnessing the great industrial resources of the FRG to the defence of Western Europe against communism and the USSR, without running the risk of resurrecting a strong Germany.

Britain, however, refused to commit itself to further integration with Europe and, instead, insisted on cultivating its close links with the USA and the British Commonwealth. The British government put forward the alternative strategy of using NATO as a means of rearming West Germany and of aligning it firmly with the Western powers within NATO, rather than within an integrated Western European political and economic framework. France was unconvinced by this argument. It feared that within NATO, West Germany would be able to develop its vast economic strength unchecked and, once the Cold War was over, France would once again be confronted with a strong Germany, which had invaded it twice already in the twentieth century.

The European Coal and Steel Community

In May 1950 France's foreign minister, Robert Schuman, announced a plan to create the European Coal and Steel Community (ECSC). The Schuman Plan, as it was called, would enable the Western allies to exploit Germany's coal and steel resources for their own rearmament programmes without running the risk of simultaneously building a strong and independent West Germany. It was received enthusiastically by Adenauer, the West German chancellor, as he realised that only through integration could West Germany forge a partnership with the Western allies and gain security from the Soviet threat. Italy and the Benelux states also welcomed it, but Britain, not wishing to lose control of its own coal and steel industries (which the Labour government had only just nationalised), was not willing to join.

The ECSC was formed in July 1952 and replaced the International Ruhr Authority (see page 63) with a new supranational organisation, controlled by the six member states: the Benelux countries, France, Italy and the FRG. The ECSC regulated all their coal and steel industries, guaranteeing that the economic needs of each member for these vital raw materials would be met. The ECSC laid the foundations for Western European economic, and ultimately political, integration. Together with the military security that NATO provided, it immeasurably strengthened the Western bloc.

The consolidation of the Eastern bloc 1948–52

From 1948, Communists dominated the governments of what became known as Eastern bloc states. Theoretically, each state within the Soviet bloc remained independent, but all, with the exception of Yugoslavia, adopted identical cultural, military, economic and social policies. To further encourage and support closer relations between the various Communist states, the Soviets created two supranational organisations: Cominform and COMECON.

Cominform

Cominform, the Communist Information Bureau (see page 48), was established in September 1947 to promote ideological unity among the Communist parties in Europe. All the Soviet bloc Communist parties joined, as did the French and Italian parties. Its main tasks were to complete the **Sovietisation** of the Soviet satellite states, to co-ordinate the activities of the Communist parties in both the Soviet bloc and throughout the world, and to combat what was termed **Titoism**.

COMECON

The Council for Mutual Economic Assistance (COMECON) was founded in 1949 by the USSR, Bulgaria, Czechoslovakia, Hungary, Poland and Romania, and joined in 1950 by the GDR. Its main task was to integrate the economies of Eastern Europe with the USSR's, but initially the organisation existed only in name. It was not until 1954 that a secretariat was established and only in 1959 was the organisation given more authority and became better organised. Although there was no effective economic integration in the Soviet bloc until after 1959, the individual states broadly followed the Soviet pattern of economic development:

- Agriculture was collectivised.
- Centralised economies were established.
- **Five-Year Plans** laid the foundations for large-scale industrialisation and the development of **heavy industry**.

Soviet control of Eastern Europe

The only effective ties strengthening the bloc were the network of **bilateral** treaties of friendship, co-operation and mutual assistance signed between the USSR and the individual satellite states, and also between these states themselves. Each of these treaties contained the following agreements:

- a mutual defence agreement
- a ban on joining a hostile alliance, such as NATO
- recognition of equality, sovereignty and non-interference in each other's internal affairs (although in practice this did not deter the USSR from intervening in the domestic policies of its satellites).

KEY TERMS

Sovietisation Reconstructing a state according to the Soviet model.

Titoism Communism as defined by Tito in Yugoslavia.

Five-Year Plans Plans to modernise and expand the economy over a five-year period.

Heavy industry Coal, iron and steel production.

Bilateral Between two states.

Stalin achieved obedience to the Soviet line by frequently summoning the leaders of the Eastern bloc states to Moscow, and also through the direct participation of Soviet ambassadors and advisers in the internal affairs of the satellites. In the background, of course, there was always the threat of the Red Army. The armed forces of the satellite states, unlike the NATO armies, formed a completely integrated system centred in Moscow. Each army was issued with Soviet equipment, training manuals and armaments. Even the style of uniform was identical. The **Stalin cult** was also a unifying factor in the Eastern bloc. He was celebrated everywhere as the builder of socialism in the USSR and the liberator of Eastern Europe. To survive in this period local politicians had, in the words of R.L. Hutchings, to be 'more like Stalin than Stalin himself', and the societies and economies of the satellite states had to be based on the Soviet model.

The Yugoslav–Soviet split

By 1949, not only was Europe divided into two blocs, but within the Eastern bloc there also emerged a split between the USSR and Yugoslavia. Although Tito, the Communist ruler of Yugoslavia, had been publicly praised in September 1947 as one of the USSR's most loyal and effective allies, Stalin had reservations about him. Stalin was particularly critical of Yugoslav attempts to play an independent role in the Balkans.

In the course of the winter of 1947–8, the friction between the Soviets and the Yugoslavs increased as Tito alarmed Stalin with talk of forming a Balkan Federation which would include Greece, Bulgaria and Romania. The leaders of both Bulgaria and Romania responded enthusiastically to these proposals. Tito also stationed Yugoslav troops in Albania to protect Greek Communist guerrilla camps without consulting either Stalin or Enver Hoxha, the Communist Albanian leader. Stalin feared that Tito's activities would not only make the Yugoslav Communist Party the strongest force in the Balkans, which the USSR would be unable to manipulate, but also provoke the USA at a time of escalating tension over Germany.

The break with Stalin

Communist Party officials from Bulgaria and Yugoslavia were summoned to Moscow in February 1948. Stalin specifically vetoed the stationing of Yugoslav troops in Albania and, instead of the wider federation favoured by Tito, proposed a smaller Bulgarian–Yugoslav union. The two states were required to commit themselves to regular consultations with Soviet officials on foreign policy questions in an effort to prevent independent action. Tito, however, refused to subordinate his foreign policy to the Soviet Union and rejected union with Bulgaria on these terms. He feared that, given Soviet influence there, the union would merely be a way for the Soviets to take control of the Yugoslav government. Stalin reacted to this open defiance of his leadership by

KEY TERM

Stalin cult The propaganda campaign vaunting Stalin as the great ruler and saviour of the USSR.

withdrawing Soviet advisors and personnel from Yugoslavia, and accused its leaders of being political and ideological criminals.

Stalin pressured other Eastern bloc states to support the Soviet decision to isolate Yugoslavia and in June 1948, at the second Cominform meeting, the entire Eastern bloc, along with Western European Communists, expelled Yugoslavia from the organisation. Yugoslavia was the first Communist state to act independently of the Soviet Union and defy Stalin.

Soviet attempts to remove Tito

Initially Stalin hoped that the Yugoslav Communist Party would overthrow Tito, but Tito rapidly purged the Party of pro-Cominform suspects. Soviet attempts to assassinate Tito were also unsuccessful, as were attempts to apply economic pressure through a **trade embargo**. Finally, Stalin started to apply military pressure by concentrating troops on Yugoslavia's borders. According to a Hungarian general who fled to the West, plans were actually made for a Soviet invasion of Yugoslavia, but abandoned when the outbreak of the Korean War indicated that the USA and NATO might respond in force.

Tito and the West

These threats led Tito to turn to the West for assistance. Tito abandoned his support for Greek Communist rebels and in return received arms and financial assistance from Britain and the USA. Close links developed between the **CIA** and the Yugoslav secret service. In 1954 Yugoslavia, along with Greece and Turkey, both of whom were NATO members, signed the Balkan Mutual Defence Pact aimed at the USSR and its allies.

Yugoslavia also distanced itself ideologically from the USSR. Tito broke with the Soviet model of **centralised control of the economy**, and instead in 1950 began to experiment with workers' self-management of factories. This, in theory, enabled the workers to manage and operate their own factories through elected workers' councils. Prices were no longer fixed by the government after 1952 and businesses were able to export their products without government involvement. The state did, however, retain control of the banking system and industrial investment.

Western attempts to destabilise the Soviet bloc

Tito's break with the USSR in 1948 demonstrated that the unity of the Soviet bloc was more fragile than it appeared to many observers. This encouraged NATO to explore various ways of weakening the USSR's position in Eastern Europe:

🔑 KEY TERMS

Trade embargo
A suspension of trade.

CIA The Central Intelligence Agency was established by the USA in 1947 to conduct counterintelligence operations abroad.

Centralised control of the economy Control of a country's economy from the centre, as in Stalinist Russia.

- The USA and Britain gave military and economic assistance to Yugoslavia (see above).
- Between 1949 and 1952 there was a series of unsuccessful operations by the USA and Britain to remove Albania's Communist leader Enver Hoxha, as a step towards replacing its Soviet-sponsored government.
- Attempts were made to undermine Soviet authority by constantly filing complaints to the UN about human rights abuses in the Eastern bloc.
- Eastern European refugees were helped financially, so as to encourage others to flee from the Soviet bloc.
- Radio Free Europe, which broadcast anti-Soviet propaganda to Eastern European states, was sponsored by the US government.

All these measures were aimed at weakening Soviet power in Eastern Europe over the long term. Neither the USSR, nor the USA and its NATO allies, were ready to risk war. It was the Far East where the triumph of communism in China posed new and dangerous challenges to the USA and the European colonial powers (see Chapter 5).

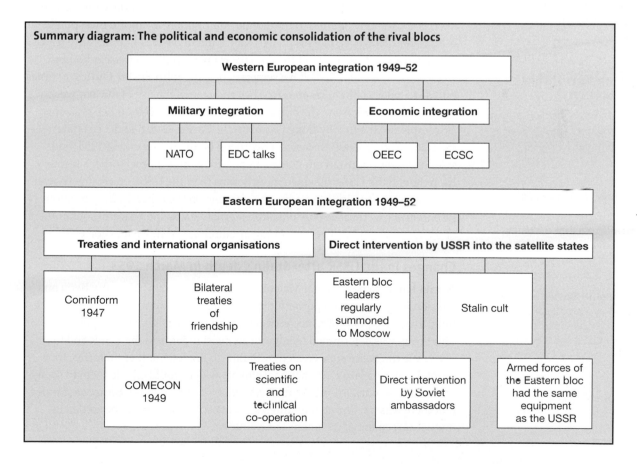

Summary diagram: The political and economic consolidation of the rival blocs

4 The 'Thaw' 1953–5

▶ *How did the Western powers react to changes in Soviet foreign policy?*

▶ *What were the aims of the new leaders in the USA and USSR?*

The new leaders 1953

In 1953, there was a change of leadership in the USSR and the USA. General **Dwight D. Eisenhower** won the presidential election in November 1952 in the USA, and a collective leadership took the place of Stalin's one-man dictatorship in the Soviet Union after his death on 5 March.

President Eisenhower

President Eisenhower promised to take a much tougher line towards the USSR and even spoke of freeing the people in Eastern Europe from Soviet control. He considered using nuclear weapons in Korea in 1953 and Indo-China a year later, and cavalierly referred to the atomic bomb simply as 'another weapon in our arsenal'. However, like his predecessor Truman, he was not in reality ready to risk a nuclear war, aware of the damage even a few Soviet nuclear bombs would do to the USA. He and his secretary of state, **John Foster Dulles**, at times pursued a policy of **brinkmanship**. They threatened the use of nuclear weapons but then drew back from 'the brink' of using them. On 1 November 1952, the USA exploded the first hydrogen bomb in the Pacific Ocean and a year later the USSR also successfully tested a hydrogen bomb. By the end of 1955, both sides had long-range aircraft able to drop these bombs on each other's territory. Even though the USA possessed more bombs than the USSR, each superpower was in a position to inflict catastrophic damage on the other. In this situation, Eisenhower saw that the only practical alternative was the peaceful containment of Soviet power in Europe, rather than attempting to remove it by force.

Changes in the USSR after Stalin's death in March 1953

Nikita Khrushchev, Georgi Malenkov, Vyachlav Molotov, Lavrenty Beria and Nikolay Bulganin shared power for three years after Stalin's death. At the same time, they were political rivals, each hoping to secure sole supreme power. This group was determined to improve living standards in the USSR and to dismantle the police state created by Stalin. To implement these reforms, they needed a more relaxed international climate which would enable them to spend less on armaments. In August 1953, Malenkov declared in the **Supreme Soviet** that there was 'no disputed or unresolved question that cannot be settled by mutual agreement of the interested countries'.

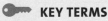

KEY FIGURES

Dwight D. Eisenhower (1890–1969)

Supreme commander of Allied troops in France 1944, Commander of NATO 1950–1; president of the USA 1952–61.

John Foster Dulles (1888–1959)

US diplomat and secretary of state 1952–9.

Nikita Khrushchev (1894–1971)

First secretary of the Russian Communist Party 1953–64 and premier 1958–64.

KEY TERMS

Brinkmanship Appearing to approach the brink of nuclear war to persuade the opposition to concede.

Supreme Soviet Set up in 1936 by Stalin. It consisted of two bodies: the Soviet of the USSR and the Soviet of Nationalities. Each Soviet republic had a Supreme Soviet or parliament, as did the overall USSR.

The West and *détente*

Given this desire for *détente* by the Soviet leadership, not only was a settlement in Korea and Indo-China possible, but it also appeared as though the question of German unity might be reopened and potentially resolved.

Eisenhower's response 1953

On 16 April 1953, Eisenhower announced that any improvement in Soviet–US relations would depend on free elections in Eastern Europe. In May, Winston Churchill, who had become prime minister of Britain again in October 1951, suggested a four-power conference in which plans for German reunification and demilitarisation would be discussed. This proposal was unpopular with the West German Chancellor Adenauer, Eisenhower and indeed with Churchill's own government. They all feared a neutral Germany would be established that would then be vulnerable to pressure from the USSR and ultimately removed from the Western European economic and military systems – this had consistently been the fear of Western governments since the end of the war. However, such was the desire for peace throughout Western Europe that both Adenauer and Eisenhower reluctantly had to agree to discuss a possible agenda for talks at a preliminary conference of foreign ministers, although this did not meet until December in Bermuda.

The USSR and the GDR, April to June 1953

In early 1953, the Soviet Foreign Office made proposals for German unity, submitting them to the USA, Britain and France. It suggested a provisional government be created of politicians from both German states and the removal of all foreign troops of occupation.

The crisis in the GDR

As a member of COMECON (see page 80), the GDR had reorganised its economy following the model of the USSR. In 1951 its first Five-Year Plan was launched with the intention of doubling the GDR's industrial output. By 1952, this aim was achieved in the production of iron, steel and chemicals. Ulbricht was, however, determined on yet more increases. In July 1952, workers' individual production targets were suddenly raised by ten per cent, while at the same time there were sharp rises in the price of food and public transport. Farmers were also threatened with collectivisation of agriculture along Soviet lines.

By spring 1953, tension was further increased by the arrest of leading non-Communist politicians. Church leaders warned of the possibility of a major catastrophe, while even within the GDR's Communist Party, the SED, there were indications that many were ready to challenge the government's economic plans, which were causing growing resentment in the country. Increasing numbers of East Germans fled into West Berlin and then to the rest of the FRG through **Berlin's open frontier**. As many of these were professionals, skilled workers and farmers, their departure deprived the GDR economy of vital human resources (see Source H below).

Soviet concern

The growing crisis in the GDR deeply embarrassed the new Soviet leadership. If an anti-government revolt erupted, Soviet troops would have to intervene, which would threaten the USSR's new policy of *détente*. In May 1953, the **Presidium** of the Soviet Council of Ministers met to consider the problem. Beria, the head of the Soviet secret police, now called the KGB, began to reassess the value of the GDR to the Soviet bloc. It was proving an expensive and unstable state to support, as well as an area of friction with the Western bloc. Backed by Deputy Prime Minister Malenkov, he urged his more cautious colleagues in the Presidium to propose to the USA, Britain and France that a united, neutral Germany be formed. He argued that to achieve reunification on such terms, Germany would be willing to pay substantial reparations to the USSR.

Although Beria and Malenkov failed to win over other Soviet ministers who still clung to the idea of working slowly and cautiously towards a unified and Communist Germany, they did agree to summon Ulbricht to Moscow on 2 June. In the interests of *détente*, he was ordered to pursue a more conciliatory approach so that various groups within the GDR were not antagonised, and to abandon his programme for rapid socialisation. These concessions, however, came too late and he failed to scale down the high production targets that had been set for the workers. Some contemporaries believed that by leaving the ten per cent increase in production targets in place, Ulbricht was deliberately provoking an uprising in the GDR, so that armed intervention by the USSR would be triggered. This would make it all the more difficult to reunite Germany and would therefore enable the GDR to survive as a Soviet satellite, thus keeping Ulbricht in power.

SOURCE H

From a document given to Ulbricht and two of his colleagues by the Soviet leadership when they visited Moscow on 2 June 1953. Quoted in 'Cold war Misperceptions: The Communist and Western Responses to the East German Refugee Crisis in 1953' by V. Ingimundarson, *Journal of Contemporary History*, volume 28, 1994, p. 473.

The pursuit of a wrong political line in the German Democratic Republic has produced a most unsatisfactory political and economic situation. There are signs of bitter dissatisfaction – among broad masses of the population, including the workers, the farmers, and the intellectuals – with the political and economic policies of the GDR. The most conspicuous feature of this dissatisfaction is the mass flight of East German residents to West Germany. From January 1951 through April 1953, 447,000 people have fled alone. Working people make up a substantial number of the defectors. An analysis of the social composition of defectors reveals the following: 18,000 workers;

According to Source H, what were the economic conditions within the GDR in 1953?

9,000 medium and small farmers, skilled workers, and retirees; 17,000
professionals and intellectuals; and 24,000 housewives. It is striking that 2,718
members and candidates of the SED and 2,619 members of the FDJ [Free
German Youth Movement] were among the defectors to West Germany in the
first four months of 1953.

The East German Uprising

A series of strikes and riots broke out throughout East Germany on 16 June
1953. Workers demanded increased pay, more political freedom and the
re-establishment of the German Social Democratic Party, which had been
amalgamated with the KPD in 1946 to create the SED (see page 41). By the
following day, waves of spontaneous and uncoordinated strikes, demonstrations
and riots had erupted across the whole of the GDR. Crowds collected outside
prisons and state and party offices and called for the resignation of the
government; but only in two cities, Görlitz and Bitterfeld, were there determined
efforts to take over the city governments. In East Berlin, 100,000 people
demonstrated on the streets.

The government, distrusting the loyalty of its own police forces, appealed to
the Soviets to intervene. On 17 June, Soviet troops backed by tanks moved to
suppress the uprising. Sporadic demonstrations and riots continued throughout
the summer and 125 were people killed, nineteen of them in East Berlin.

The consequences for German unity

The uprising took both the Soviets and the Western allies by surprise, and has
been called by the historian Christian Ostermann 'one of the most significant
focal points in the history of the Cold War'.

US reaction

Despite his pledge during the presidential election to liberate Eastern Europe
from Soviet control, Eisenhower did not interfere with the Soviet suppression of
the East German Uprising. The US government hoped that the sight of Soviet
troops on the streets of East Berlin would fuel West German fears of the USSR
and persuade the voters to re-elect Adenauer in the September 1953 elections.
Yet there was a danger that if the USA was seen to do nothing to help the East
Germans, there could, as C.D. Jackson, Eisenhower's advisor for psychological
warfare, said, 'be a terrible let down in East and West Germany, which will
seriously affect the American position and even more seriously affect Adenauer's
position'.

Eisenhower's advisors launched a two-pronged strategy. The USA would
respond to pressure of public opinion in West Germany for intervention in
East Germany by calling for a Foreign Ministers' Conference on the future
of Germany. At the same time, through provocative broadcasts from its radio

SOURCE I

East German workers hurl stones at Soviet tanks on 17 June 1953. This picture was published in the press throughout the non-Communist world and came to symbolise the spirit of revolt against Soviet rule.

In what ways could Source I be used by the enemies of Soviet rule in Eastern Europe?

stations in West Berlin, it would do all it could to prolong the unrest in East Germany. This policy certainly strengthened support for Adenauer in the FRG; he won the election in September by a much larger margin than he had in the previous election.

The Berlin Conference, 25 January to 18 February 1954

By the time the foreign ministers of Britain, France, the USA and USSR met in Berlin in early 1954, all hope of making any progress on reuniting Germany had ended. Beria, who of all the Soviet politicians had been the most anxious to find a solution to the problems caused by a divided Germany, had been arrested and executed by his political rivals on the grounds that his 'treachery' had led to the East German Uprising. In Berlin, both the USSR and the Western allies produced mutually unacceptable plans for German unity, which each side rejected. The USSR feared that the Western proposal of holding free elections in Germany would lead to a massive anti-Communist vote, while the Western powers feared that a neutral disarmed Germany, not integrated into NATO or the EDC, would be vulnerable to Soviet influence. The question of German reunification thus remained deadlocked.

French rejection of the EDC, August 1954

On 15 May 1953, the EDC and the General Treaty (see page 74) were both ratified by the West German parliament, but the EDC was rejected by the French National Assembly on 30 August 1954. This reopened the whole question of West German rearmament and the FRG's entry into NATO, which was vital for the defence of Western Europe.

FRG's entry into NATO, May 1955

The immediate priority of Britain and the USA was to secure the FRG's entry into NATO. France's fears of a rearmed Germany were overcome by Adenauer's agreement to limit the West German army to the size envisaged in the EDC treaty and the FRG's renunciation of nuclear weapons. Britain's commitment to keep four divisions of troops supported by aircraft in West Germany also reassured France. In October 1954, a fresh settlement was reached that recognised the sovereignty of the FRG and its membership of NATO. The Western allies again committed themselves to work towards a united, federal Germany integrated into a democratic (Western) Europe. Until this happened, their troops would remain in the FRG and Berlin would remain under Four-Power Control. On 5 May 1955, the treaty came into force and four days later the FRG joined NATO and also became a member of the Western European Union.

These treaties effectively completed the post-war settlement of Western Europe. Yet they also deepened the division of Europe. While the possibility was kept open for German unification, in reality the integration of the FRG into NATO made unity in the foreseeable future unlikely. The very success of the FRG's integration intensified what the historian Christoph Klessmann has called 'the reactive mechanism' of the Cold War: the more the FRG was integrated into the West, the more tightly bound was the GDR into the Soviet bloc.

The Warsaw Pact Treaty

On 14 May 1955, the USSR and Eastern European states signed the Warsaw Pact; the GDR eventually joined in January 1956. The Pact committed its members to consult on issues of mutual interest and to give all necessary assistance in the event of an attack on any one of them in Europe. Essentially, the treaty was signed for political rather than military reasons as a response to the FRG's entry into NATO, but it still kept open the option of a neutral Germany by declaring that if a 'general European treaty of Collective Security' was signed, the Warsaw Pact would lapse.

? What, according to
Source J, was the Warsaw
Pact a direct response to?

SOURCE J

From the introduction to the Warsaw Pact Treaty, which was signed in May 1955, quoted in Roger Morgan, *The Unsettled Peace*, BBC Books, 1974, p. 75.

... the situation created in Europe by the ratification of the Paris agreements, which envisage the formation of a new military alignment in the shape of 'Western European Union', with the participation of a re-militarized Western Germany and the integration of the latter in the North Atlantic bloc ... increases the danger of another war and constitutes a threat to the national security of peaceable states.

Being persuaded that in these circumstances the peaceable European states must take the necessary measures to safeguard their security and in the interests of preserving peace in Europe ... have decided to conclude the present Treaty of Friendship Cooperation and Mutual Assistance ... .

Article III: [They] shall immediately consult with one another, whenever in the opinion of any one of them, a threat of armed attack on one or more of the parties to the Treaty has arisen ...

Article V: The contracting parties have agreed to establish a joint command of the armed forces ...

The 'Geneva spirit' and its limitations

In May 1955, Khrushchev and Bulganin, who had now emerged as the leaders of the USSR, accepted an invitation from the Western allies to meet in Geneva, Switzerland. This would be the first major summit conference since Potsdam in 1945 (see page 34). The British prime minister, Anthony Eden, envisaged this to be the first of several summits, which would aim to reduce tension between the Soviet and Western blocs.

The Geneva Conference

When the leaders of Britain, France, the USA and USSR met in July, they agreed on the following agenda:

- the reunification of Germany
- European security
- disarmament
- the development of contacts between East and West.

While conversations were conducted in an atmosphere of *détente*, the limits to the new spirit of coexistence, or 'Geneva spirit', were quickly reached. The USSR agreed to evacuate Austria, which had been divided into four zones in 1945, provided it remained neutral and did not join NATO. There was, however, still deadlock between the two sides over the future of Germany. Nor was progress made on disarmament or arms control, although it was agreed that the foreign ministers of the major powers should meet again to discuss the questions of Germany, security and disarmament.

Adenauer's visit to Moscow, September 1955

In September 1955, Adenauer visited Moscow to negotiate the return of the last German prisoners-of-war and to establish normal diplomatic relations with the USSR. Far from leading to a breakthrough in the German question, the division between the two Germanys widened still further. To reassure the GDR of continued Soviet support, the USSR acknowledged the GDR as an independent state in its own right. Adenauer, worried that an exchange of ambassadors with the USSR might be interpreted to mean that his government recognised the legal existence of the GDR, announced the **Hallstein Doctrine**. This stated that the FRG would consider the recognition of the GDR by any state, other than the USSR, as an unfriendly act which would lead to an immediate break in diplomatic relations.

> **KEY TERM**
>
> **Hallstein Doctrine** Named after Walter Hallstein, state secretary in the FRG's Foreign Ministry.

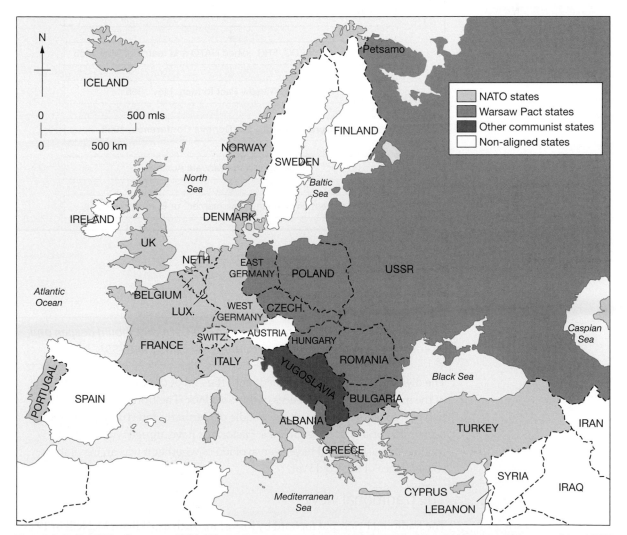

Figure 3.2 Cold War Europe in 1955. What information is conveyed by the map about the division of Europe in May 1955?

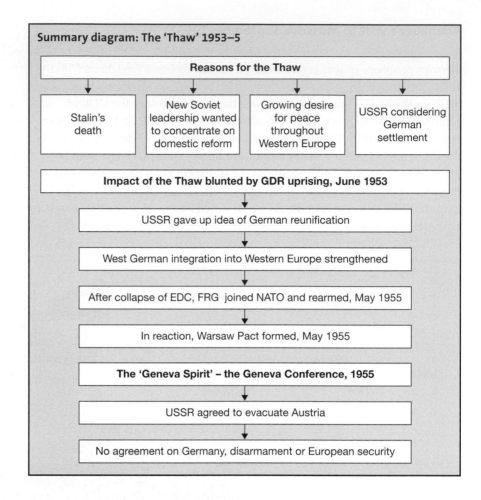

Summary diagram: The 'Thaw' 1953–5

Reasons for the Thaw

- Stalin's death
- New Soviet leadership wanted to concentrate on domestic reform
- Growing desire for peace throughout Western Europe
- USSR considering German settlement

Impact of the Thaw blunted by GDR uprising, June 1953

USSR gave up idea of German reunification

West German integration into Western Europe strengthened

After collapse of EDC, FRG joined NATO and rearmed, May 1955

In reaction, Warsaw Pact formed, May 1955

The 'Geneva Spirit' – the Geneva Conference, 1955

USSR agreed to evacuate Austria

No agreement on Germany, disarmament or European security

⑤ Key debate

▶ *Was it inevitable that the division of Germany should deepen and become more permanent during the years 1948–55?*

The division of Germany remained, until the end of the Cold War in 1989, one of the most visible consequences of the Cold War. The frontiers between the two hostile blocs ran through the middle of Germany, interrupting historic economic, social and political links. Historians have argued whether this traumatic division could have been avoided or whether it was an inevitable consequence of the Cold War.

The traditional view

The traditional view put forward by historians such as William McNeill in 1953 and Herbert Feiss in 1957 argues that Stalin as a Marxist–Leninist did harbour ambitions to turn Germany, or at least the Soviet zone, into a Marxist state. Consequently, the creation of the SED in 1946 and Soviet policies within the Soviet zone in Germany were merely preliminary steps to achieve that aim. Ultimately this triggered the division of Germany.

Martin McCauley succinctly sums up this view:

EXTRACT 1

From Martin McCauley, *Origins of the Cold War, 1941–1949*, Pearson, 2003, pp. 10–11.

According to … [this traditional view] the well springs of the Cold War are to be found in Marxism-Leninism with its doctrine of class struggle leading to revolution on a world scale … They take it for granted that the Soviets always sought ways of undermining the authority of non-Communist powers so as to expand the Communist world. … Not content with eastern and south-eastern Europe, the USSR attempted to draw the whole of Germany into the Soviet orbit and by fomenting strikes and social unrest in western and southern Europe and in Asia sought to expand Communist influence in those regions as well.

Opposition to the orthodox view

The revisionist views question the idea of Stalin having a Marxist programme and argue that his policy was in reality more flexible and also that it was often a defensive response to Allied initiatives. For instance, the historians Ann Deighton and J. Farquharson both stress the role of Britain in the partition of Germany. They show that economic weakness led Britain to support the creation of the Bizone and to press for the creation as soon as possible of a self-governing West Germany. Britain could no longer afford to subsidise its zone in Germany.

EXTRACT 2

From David Williamson, *A Most Diplomatic General. The Life of General Lord Robertson of Oakridge*, Brassey's, 1996, p. 107.

Bevin [the British foreign secretary] went to Moscow quite prepared to break with the Russians over Germany. His officials had drawn up a radical plan which became known as the 'new Potsdam' or Bevin Plan. This laid down conditions for the revision of the Potsdam agreement, which they knew Russia would not be able to accept. Not only would Russia have to return some of the reparations, which she had illegally taken from her own zone to help balance Anglo-American deficits, but also contribute to the bills of the western powers and receive no steel or coal deliveries until Germany was self sufficient.

The decision by the Western allies to set up the FRG led to the creation of the GDR. Revisionist German historians such as Rolf Steininger and Willy Loth stress that Stalin did not intend to divide Germany, but was more interested in obtaining a neutral Germany, which would not threaten the USSR. Both these historians argue that Stalin's offer of a united neutral Germany in March 1952 was genuine and should have been explored. This has been hotly disputed by many other German historians such as Hans-Peter Schwarz and Gerhard Wittig. For Stalin the creation of a potentially independent West German state was a serious blow. East Germany has been described by Loth as his 'unwanted child'. Until his death, Stalin, so Loth and Steininger argue, saw the GDR as only a temporary structure that he would be happy to dismantle, if he could somehow create a neutral Germany independent of a US-dominated Western Europe.

Consequently, by moving so quickly to set up a separate West Germany and a North Atlantic security system, were Britain, France and the USA responsible for the division of Germany and the partition of Europe into two blocs? The eminent US diplomat George Kennan warned in September 1948 that this policy would lead to 'an irrevocable congealment of the division of Europe into two military zones: a Soviet zone and a US zone. Instead of the ability to divest ourselves gradually of the basic responsibility for the security of Western Europe, we will get a legal perpetuation of that responsibility.'

From the reaction to this advice in London, Paris and Washington, it was obvious that most Western Europeans and their governments preferred a divided Germany and a Western Europe protected by a US military presence to the uncertainties and risks to which a neutral unified Germany would have exposed them. It was also by no means clear that Stalin would in reality have tolerated a genuine independent and neutral Germany.

Revisionists and the June uprising in the GDR

Revisionist historians, particularly Loth and Ostermann, are also interested in Soviet policy towards the GDR in the months after Stalin's death, and argue that Beria and Malenkov were serious in their desire to reunite the two Germanys, provided the security of the USSR could be guaranteed. They argue that this promising initiative was destroyed by the East German Uprising, which led to Soviet military intervention and renewed Cold War tension in Germany. By intervening militarily, the Soviets played into the hands of Ulbricht, who had a vested interest in the survival of the GDR. At this point, then, according to their arguments, it was Ulbricht rather than the Kremlin that perpetuated the division of Germany (see page 87).

Post-revisionist views

The views of many of the early revisionist historians, such as Gabriel Kolko and William Appleman Williams, were often inspired by anti-Americanism and opposition to the Vietnam War (see page 158). The post-revisionists, writing either after the end of the Cold War or in its final stages, were able to take a more balanced view, which in some ways comes nearer to the 'orthodox' view of the 1950s.

John Lewis Gaddis

Gaddis comes down on the side of arguing that, while Stalin may very briefly have flirted with the idea of tolerating an independent united Germany, he was determined to keep the USSR's grip on a socialist East Germany, which was firmly integrated into the Soviet bloc. Gaddis, however, does agree that briefly Beria really did champion the idea of 'selling' the GDR to the West Germans, and that it was Ulbricht who sabotaged that proposal. He is also sceptical as to whether the West would ever have accepted the creation of a united neutral Germany.

Geir Lundestaad

Lundestaad took issue with Williams and Kolko, as they saw the USA as the 'aggressor' and therefore divider of Germany and Europe. After studying the sources in the Western European archives he argued that the Americans, far from imposing their power on Western Europe, in fact created an **empire by invitation**. Lundestaad argues that it was the Western Europeans, particularly the West Germans, who 'invited' the USA to construct what amounted to an empire in Western Europe in order to defend it against communism. He stresses how anxious the Western Europeans were, for instance, to support NATO and to rely on US military superiority. In the final analysis the West Germans were not ready to risk reunification with the GDR as long as the USSR remained Communist.

> 🔑 **KEY TERM**
>
> **Empire by invitation**
> The Western Europeans were in effect asking to be put under US protection and so become a part of a US 'empire' or a US-dominated region.

Conclusion

Was agreement over Germany possible? Germany in 1945, despite the appalling bomb damage, was still potentially the great industrial powerhouse of Europe. The Western allies were fortunate enough to control the Ruhr. Could they risk losing this economic power to an unstable neutral Germany? By the same token, could the USSR risk a united Germany becoming integrated into Western Europe?

EXTRACT 3

From David Reynolds, 'The European Dimension of the Cold War' in M. Leffler and D. Painter, editors, *Origins of the Cold War*, Routledge, 1994, p. 136.

Even if the wartime allies had been willing to limit their geopolitical and ideological aspirations, however, the problems of Germany made a secure sphere of influence agreement –mutual tolerance of eastern and western blocs – an unlikely eventuality. The aftermath of Hitler's war was too profound, too unsettling. For the western powers the economic dislocation of Germany and the emergence of Communism, whatever Stalin's immediate policy, were unacceptable. For the Soviet Union, any attempt to rehabilitate Germany, its mortal enemy, were equally intolerable. The struggle for the mastery of Germany lay at the heart of the grand alliance and also of the Cold War.

> ? How far do the historians quoted in Extracts 1–3 agree or differ in the reasons they give for the division of Germany?

Chapter summary

By June 1948 Four-Power Control in Germany had broken down, and the Western allies decided to create the FRG. To stop this, Stalin blockaded West Berlin. The blockade was broken by the airlift, and called off in May 1949. In August the FRG's first government was formed. In response, the GDR was created in October, but Berlin remained under Four-Power Control. The division of Germany intensified the Cold War. The Western powers rearmed, created NATO and began the process of Western European integration. The USSR responded by tightening its grip on the Soviet bloc through COMECON (see page 80) and Cominform. Only Yugoslavia was able to establish a regime which, although Communist, was independent of the USSR. It received covert financial and military aid from the USA. In 1952, Stalin proposed German reunification, provided Germany remained neutral, but the Western allies rejected this because they feared a neutral Germany would be vulnerable to Soviet pressure. In 1953 unity again seemed momentarily possible, but any chance of this was ruined by the June uprising. In 1955 the FRG joined NATO and in response the Communist states formed the Warsaw Pact. Perhaps earlier the division of Germany could have been avoided, but now it seemed permanent.

Refresher questions

Use these questions to remind yourself of the key material covered in this chapter.

1 How was French opposition to the establishment of the FRG overcome at the London Conference?

2 Why did the Western allies persist with setting up the FRG?

3 To what extent was the GDR set up in response to the FDR?

4 What impact did the division of Germany have on Berlin?

5 What was the real intention of the Brussels Pact?

6 Why was the North Atlantic Treaty signed and to what extent was it a compromise between European and US wishes?

7 How were the economic problems caused by the rearmament programmes of 1950–1 overcome?

8 What did the French hope to achieve with the Schuman Plan and how did it help to end the bad feeling between France and Germany?

9 What was the political and economic significance of the ECSC?

10 How successful were Western attempts to destabilise the Soviet bloc in the period 1948–55?

11 What was the response of the USSR to the growing crisis in the GDR?

12 What was the significance of the East German Uprising for Germany?

13 What were the consequences of the French rejection of the EDC?

14 To what extent was the Warsaw Pact a consequence of West Germany's membership of NATO?

15 What was the importance of the 'Geneva spirit' in international affairs?

Question practice

ESSAY QUESTIONS

1 'The Berlin Blockade was a monumental error by Stalin.' Explain why you agree or disagree with this view.

2 To what extent was Europe divided into two mutually hostile blocs by 1950?

3 How successful was Western European rearmament by 1955?

4 Which of the following had the greater impact on preventing the reunification of Germany? i) The FRG's membership of NATO. ii) East German membership of the Warsaw Pact. Explain your answer with reference to both i) and ii).

SOURCE ANALYSIS QUESTIONS

1 With reference to Sources E (page 72) and F (page 77), and your understanding of the historical context, which of these two sources is more valuable in explaining the military integration of Western Europe after 1949?

2 With reference to Sources B (page 66), E (page 72) and J (page 90), and your understanding of the historical context, assess the value of these sources to a historian studying the factors that consolidated the division both of Europe and of Germany.

CHAPTER 4

The Khrushchev era and the 'Second Cold War'

This chapter covers the eventful period when the Soviet leader, Nikita Khrushchev, was trying to consolidate the USSR's grip on Eastern Europe, while also attempting to 'destalinise', or liberalise, conditions within it. It focuses on the following interlinked events and their impact on East–West relations:

★ The year of crises: 1956

★ The aftermath of the Hungarian and Suez Crises

★ The Berlin Crisis 1958–61

★ The Cuban Missile Crisis 1962

★ Assessment: the 'Second Cold War'

Key dates

1956	Feb. 25	Khrushchev attacked Stalin at the Twentieth Party Congress	1960	May 1	US U-2 spy plane shot down over USSR
	June	Riots in Poland		May 16–17	Paris Summit broke down
	Nov. 4	Hungarian Rising defeated	1961	Aug. 13	Frontier between East and West Berlin closed
1957	March 25	Treaty of Rome signed			
1958	Nov. 27	Khrushchev's Berlin ultimatum	1962	Sept. 13	USA warned USSR on installation of missiles in Cuba
1959	Jan.	Castro seized power in Cuba		Oct.–Nov.	Cuban Missile Crisis

1 The year of crises: 1956

▶ *Why did destalinisation cause serious crises within the Soviet bloc?*

The year 1956 was a pivotal year in the Cold War. In the spring it seemed that the USSR would continue with the policy of *détente* and liberalisation, but in the autumn Soviet leaders were confronted with the dilemma that would recur several times before the end of the Cold War: how far could they afford to relax Soviet control over Eastern Europe? If concessions led to demands for ever-greater political freedom, at what point would Soviet troops intervene to maintain control?

It was also in 1956 that the foreign policy of the USSR became more global. Stalin had shown little interest in the **Developing World**. The new Soviet leadership, however, was more anxious to gain influence in the former colonies, which had now become independent of their European rulers. Khrushchev realised that the USSR could exploit anti-colonialism to weaken the West. In December 1955, Khrushchev and Bulganin, during a tour of India, Burma and Afghanistan, stressed Soviet willingness to co-operate with the Developing World and lost no opportunity to repeat, as Lenin had done before them (see page 8), that their main enemy was colonialism and imperialism.

Destalinisation

Destalinisation had a big impact on the relations between the USSR and its satellite states. It appeared to promise a return to the policy of 'different roads to socialism', which Stalin briefly tolerated between 1945 and 1947 (see page 49). The pace of destalinisation accelerated after the fall of Beria (see page 86). His secret police network, which had spies throughout Eastern Europe, was dissolved, and politicians such as Gomułka in Poland and Kadar in Hungary were released from prison and returned to public life. This raised expectations in the satellite states that they would be given more independence from Moscow.

Khrushchev's speech at the Twentieth Party Conference

A further wave of destalinisation followed after Khrushchev's famous speech at the Twentieth Party Conference in February 1956 denouncing Stalin and recognising the rights of the satellite states to find their 'national ways to socialism'. Although the speech was supposed to be secret, the US security service, the CIA, acquired a copy and ensured that it was broadcast to Eastern Europe. By raising hopes of political change, this contributed to the unrest in Poland and Hungary later in the year.

Yugoslavia

Expectations of reform were further increased by the improvement in relations between the USSR and Yugoslavia, which was 're-admitted' to the Socialist bloc after Khrushchev and Bulganin had visited Belgrade in May 1955. The blame for the break in 1948 was attributed fairly and squarely to Stalin (see page 81). Khrushchev was, of course, primarily interested in bringing back Yugoslavia into the Soviet sphere of influence, while Tito, the Yugoslav leader, ambitiously believed that, as a result of his experience in defying Stalin, he was a role model for the new generation of Soviet leaders and would now become a leading figure in the Soviet bloc. In June 1956, after talks in Moscow, Khrushchev and Tito issued a communiqué in which they agreed that 'the path of socialist development differs in various countries and conditions, that the multiplicity of forms of socialist development tends to strengthen socialism and that any tendency of imposing one's opinions on the ways and forms of socialist

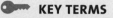

KEY TERMS

Developing World States that had been former colonies but which were now free and independent of both the USSR and the West. Used to be called the Third World.

Destalinisation The attempts to liberalise the USSR after the death of Stalin in 1953.

development is alien to both'. This was an optimistic doctrine assuming that the satellite states wished to remain within the Soviet bloc. What would happen, however, if one or more of these states decided to take a controversial road to socialism, with which the USSR did not agree? Would it intervene militarily or run the risk of seeing the Soviet bloc disintegrate?

The Polish Crisis, June to October 1956

The limits to this doctrine of allowing the Eastern European states to develop socialism in their own way were tested first of all in Poland in the autumn of 1956. At the end of June riots broke out in Poznań when the local factory workers protested about the imposition of increased work targets. They were put down with heavy casualties, but to overcome the bitterness this caused, the Polish Communist Party turned again to its popular former leader, Gomułka, who had just been released from prison. The Soviet government, fearing that he would seek to restore Polish independence, sent a high-powered delegation to Warsaw on 19–20 October, and ordered the Red Army units stationed in Poland to advance on the city in an attempt to stop his election. Gomułka refused to be cowed and his election went ahead (Source A).

Faced with the prospect of having to fight the Poles at a time when the situation in Hungary was rapidly deteriorating (see below), Khrushchev wisely withdrew the troops and chose to believe Gomułka's assurances that Poland would remain a loyal member of the Warsaw Pact. As the Soviet leader was to observe, 'finding a reason for an armed conflict now would be very easy, but finding a way to put an end to such a conflict would be very hard'.

What information is conveyed in Source A about Soviet–Polish relations in 1956?

SOURCE A

From Khrushchev's comments to the Central Committee of the USSR on the political situation in Poland and Hungary, 24 October 1956. Quoted in 'Hungary and Poland, 1956: Khrushchev's CPSU CC Presidium Meeting on East European Crises, 24 October, 1956' with introduction, translation and annotation by Mark Kramer, Cold War International History Project (www.wilsoncenter.org/program/cold-war-international-history-project).

On 24 October Khrushchev told a Central Committee meeting in Moscow that the discussions between the delegations ranged from being very warm to rude. Gomułka several times emphasised that they would not permit their independence to be taken away and would not allow anyone to interfere in Poland's internal affairs. He said that if he were leader of the country he would restore order promptly.

The Hungarian Rising

Just as the worst of the Polish Crisis was over, the USSR was faced in Hungary with the most serious challenge to its power since the Second World War. As part of his destalinisation campaign Khrushchev had, with Tito's backing, put pressure on the Hungarian Communist Party in July to replace its old-style Stalinist leader, Mátyás Rákosi, with the more liberal Ernö Gerö. Tito had considerable ambitions in Hungary, as he hoped that an independent Communist regime would emerge in Budapest that would look to Belgrade rather than Moscow and so strengthen his overall influence within the Soviet bloc.

The appointment of Imre Nagy

In the early autumn the pressures for further change, which Tito encouraged, continued to grow. A turning point was reached on 23 October 1956 when a large demonstration in Budapest, called in support of the Polish reformers, escalated out of control. Protestors demanded the withdrawal of Soviet troops and a new government under **Imre Nagy**, an independent-minded Communist who advocated reforms similar to those Tito had introduced in Yugoslavia (see page 82). They attacked the state radio station and, in an attempt to avert further violence, Gerö gave way and appointed Nagy as prime minister.

In response to these demonstrations, the USSR initially mobilised 30,000 troops backed with tanks and artillery. Khrushchev, however, tried to reconcile his pledges to concede greater independence to the satellite states with Soviet security needs. On 30 October, he issued the 'Declaration on the Principles of Development and a Further Strengthening of Friendship and Co-operation between the USSR and other Socialist Countries'. This attempted to provide a **legal and mutually agreed framework** for Soviet military bases in Eastern Europe. This did not, however, stop Nagy from threatening the basis of Soviet power in Eastern Europe by announcing his intention to withdraw Hungary from the Warsaw Pact. If this happened, Hungary would effectively become independent of the USSR and Poland, and the other satellite states would most likely follow.

Heavy fighting between the Hungarians and Soviet troops erupted in the countryside in north-west Hungary and, by 28 October, the rebels were in control of most of Hungary outside Budapest.

US policy

The USA's Radio Free Europe, a radio station sponsored by the US government to broadcast anti-Soviet and pro-US propaganda, encouraged Hungarians to revolt. They were led to believe that NATO would intervene to provide protection from the USSR, although that was in reality unlikely. US President Eisenhower, fearing that the USSR might be willing to risk nuclear war rather than lose Hungary, made it absolutely clear to the Soviet leaders that NATO

KEY FIGURE

Imre Nagy (1896–1958)
Hungarian Communist, and prime minister 1953–5 and October–November 1956. Executed 1958.

KEY TERM

Legal and mutually agreed framework A legal agreement, freely negotiated, that would allow the USSR to maintain bases in Hungary.

would not intervene to save Nagy. He instructed Secretary of State John Foster Dulles to announce publicly on 27 October 1956 that the 'US had no ulterior purpose in desiring the independence of the satellite countries' and would not 'look upon these nations as potential military allies'.

The Suez Crisis

KEY FIGURE

Abdul Nasser (1918–70)

He played a key role in the overthrow of the Egyptian monarchy 1952; undisputed leader of Egypt 1954–70.

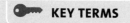

KEY TERMS

Nationalise To take ownership of privately owned industries, banks, and so on, by the state.

Zionist A supporter of the foundation of a Jewish state in the historic land of Israel.

Soviet policy during the Hungarian Rising cannot be fully understood without also looking at the Suez Crisis. The USSR had been so successful in cultivating good relations with **Colonel Nasser**, the Egyptian leader, that the Americans decided to bring him to heel by cancelling their loan for building the Aswan Dam in July 1956. This merely prompted Nasser to turn to the USSR for finance and to **nationalise** the Suez Canal, which was owned by an Anglo-French company, so that he could get further revenue from tolls that the ships had to pay when using the canal.

Anglo-French collusion with Israel

Nationalisation of the Suez Canal gave Britain, France and Israel an excuse to topple Nasser. All three states wanted to remove him from power. For the British and French, he was a determined enemy of their remaining colonial influence in North Africa and the Middle East. For the Israelis, Nasser represented a dangerous threat as he was intent on ending what he saw as the 'European **Zionist** occupation of Palestine'; that is, the new state of Israel, and, to strengthen itself, Israel wished to gain control of more territory, specifically Egypt's Sinai Peninsula.

On 16 October 1956, Britain, France and Israel created a joint plan for invading Egypt. Israeli troops would invade Egypt through the Sinai and advance towards the Canal. Britain and France would intervene in the conflict between Israel and Egypt by sending a force of 80,000 troops to protect the Canal, using the 1954 Anglo-Egyptian Agreement to justify their action. When Israel attacked on 29 October, Britain and France immediately demanded withdrawal of both the Israeli and Egyptian forces from the Canal, although Egypt had not been the aggressor and had lost control of most of the Sinai. When Nasser refused, British planes bombed Egypt's airfields on 31 October.

The Suez Crisis and Hungary

Khrushchev was convinced that Nasser would be quickly removed and that Soviet influence in the Middle East would suffer a disastrous blow. If this was combined with further setbacks in Hungary, Soviet power and prestige might never recover.

On 4 November, Soviet troops advanced into Hungary and, after a few days of fierce fighting, a new government loyal to the USSR under János Kádér was installed.

SOURCE B

Russian officers in Budapest, November 1956, advance threateningly towards a Western photographer.

What does Source B reveal about Soviet attitudes towards Western journalists? **?**

US intervention

Much to Khrushchev's surprise, Nasser was saved by the Americans, who viewed the Suez War as an attempt by Britain and France to prop up their disintegrating empires in the Middle East and Africa. The British had assumed they would get US support, but Eisenhower, in the middle of an election campaign, refused to give this. Not only did the Americans condemn the attack in the United Nations (UN), but they also refused a loan to Britain. Through massive diplomatic and financial pressure on London and Paris, Eisenhower managed to halt the fighting on 6 November, just at the point where the British and French troops were near to capturing the whole length of the Suez Canal.

The main reason why the USA had halted the Suez conflict was that it was determined to prevent Soviet attempts to increase their influence among Arab nationalists and to avoid criticism of their lack of intervention in Hungary. Khrushchev had already proposed a joint USA–USSR peacekeeping operation along the Suez Canal under control of the UN and threatened to send troops to enforce the peace even if the USA did not participate. Dulles and Eisenhower therefore felt that the USA had to choose between supporting Anglo-French colonialism and aligning with Arab nationalism. By choosing the latter, they believed that the USA would be able to counter Soviet influence in the Middle East and the Developing World more effectively.

The Soviet missile threat

Khrushchev cleverly exploited this split in the Western alliance and on 5 November threatened nuclear missile attacks on Britain, France and Israel if they did not stop the war. Although it was known at the time by **Western intelligence** that the USSR did not yet possess the rockets to propel such missiles, the ceasefire on the following day made it look as if it was the Soviet ultimatum rather than US financial pressure that had saved Egypt. Khrushchev himself was thus able to take the credit in the Middle East and the Communist world for having defeated the British and French 'imperialists'.

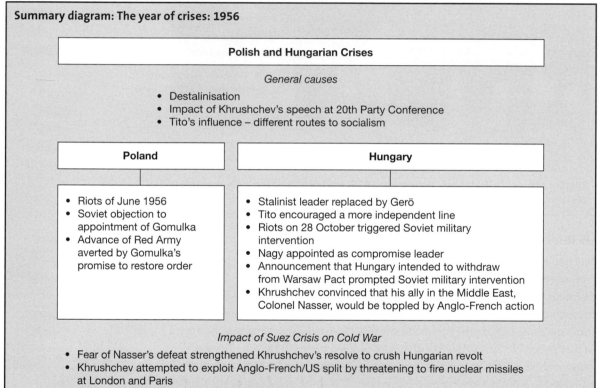

Summary diagram: The year of crises: 1956

Polish and Hungarian Crises

General causes
- Destalinisation
- Impact of Khrushchev's speech at 20th Party Conference
- Tito's influence – different routes to socialism

Poland
- Riots of June 1956
- Soviet objection to appointment of Gomulka
- Advance of Red Army averted by Gomulka's promise to restore order

Hungary
- Stalinist leader replaced by Gerö
- Tito encouraged a more independent line
- Riots on 28 October triggered Soviet military intervention
- Nagy appointed as compromise leader
- Announcement that Hungary intended to withdraw from Warsaw Pact prompted Soviet military intervention
- Khrushchev convinced that his ally in the Middle East, Colonel Nasser, would be toppled by Anglo-French action

Impact of Suez Crisis on Cold War
- Fear of Nasser's defeat strengthened Khrushchev's resolve to crush Hungarian revolt
- Khrushchev attempted to exploit Anglo-French/US split by threatening to fire nuclear missiles at London and Paris
- USSR's position in Middle East strengthened
- Khrushchev encouraged to develop policy of nuclear diplomacy

2 The aftermath of the Hungarian and Suez Crises

▶ *What were the consequences of the 1956 crises for the Soviet and Western blocs?*

The Soviet bloc

The Polish and Hungarian Crises had shown how difficult it was for the Soviet government to encourage the satellite states to reform without creating a demand for their transformation into genuine democratic regimes. They also highlighted the problems the Soviet bloc had in the post-Stalinist era in agreeing on common policies, as there was no framework for regular consultations.

Moscow Conference of international Communist leaders

Khrushchev attempted to remedy this at the conference attended by the international Communist leaders at Moscow in October 1957. Although opposed by the Poles and the Yugoslavs, this conference passed a motion recognising the USSR as 'the first and mightiest' of the socialist countries, while still acknowledging the legitimacy of the principle of 'different roads to socialism'. It also made very clear that a Communist leader under pressure could appeal to the Soviet bloc for 'mutual aid', which in effect meant military assistance to counter any major disturbances. An element of diversity was still tolerated and considerable economic help was given to the satellite states by the USSR, but it was understood that they must in all essentials stick to the Soviet political and economic model. Almost inevitably, this doctrine led to a fresh break with Tito, who now joined with India and Egypt to form the **non-aligned movement** of neutral states.

Khrushchev's position strengthened

One of the important legacies of the Hungarian and Suez Crises was that Khrushchev's position was greatly strengthened in the USSR. Dulles, the US secretary of state, had perceptively warned that he was 'the most dangerous person to lead the Soviet Union since the **October Revolution**'. Dulles felt that, whereas Stalin attempted to calculate carefully the consequences of his actions, Khrushchev was prepared to take dangerous risks to achieve his ends.

After his propaganda success in the Suez Crisis, Khrushchev was convinced that the mere threat of nuclear weapons would enable him to force the West to make concessions in Berlin and elsewhere. His policy of **nuclear diplomacy** gained more credibility when the USSR launched the world's first **intercontinental ballistic missile (ICBM)** in August 1957, and followed it up by sending a satellite, the *Sputnik*, into orbit in October. As the historian John Lewis Gaddis

KEY TERMS

Non-aligned movement Not allied with either the USSR or the West.

October Revolution The second Russian Revolution, in October 1917, in which the Bolsheviks seized power.

Nuclear diplomacy Negotiations and diplomacy supported by the threat of nuclear weapons.

Intercontinental ballistic missile (ICBM) Missile capable of carrying nuclear warheads and reaching great distances.

Sputnik This satellite weighed 84 kilograms and was able to orbit the Earth. In Russian the word means 'fellow traveller', or supporter of the USSR.

has observed, '[This] brought the Cold War quite literally close to home. One needed no Geiger counter to measure this new manifestation of potential political danger.' One needed merely to look at the sky on a clear night 'to see the sunlight reflecting off the spent rocket casing as it tumbled slowly in orbit over one's own house'. The USSR followed up this success by putting the astronaut Yuri Gagarin into space in April 1961: a few weeks ahead of the USA's Alan Shepard.

Although the overall military balance still favoured the West, Khrushchev deliberately exaggerated the extent of the Soviet successes in order, as he wrote in his memoirs, 'to exert pressure on American militarists – and also influence the minds of more reasonable politicians – so that the United States would start treating us better'. In fact, it was not until 1960 that the USSR had four ICBMs equipped with nuclear warheads (see page 111). Meanwhile the USA was developing Polaris submarines. By 1962 eight of these were at sea and were able to fire 144 nuclear missiles.

NATO

What were the consequences of the 1956 crises for the Western bloc? The immediate damage done to NATO by the Suez Crisis was quickly repaired, as was the Anglo-American special relationship; yet in continental Western Europe as a whole, a certain distrust of US policies lingered. Once the Soviets were in a position to threaten the US east coast cities with their new ICBMs, the European leaders wondered whether the Americans would still defend Western Europe from a possible Soviet attack. Rather than see New York and Washington destroyed, would they not do a deal with the Soviets and surrender Western Europe or at least West Germany?

These fears were strengthened by several contemporary developments. The Americans and British were reducing their **conventional forces** in Europe and equipping those that remained with **tactical nuclear weapons**. In October 1957 Adam Rapacki, the Polish foreign minister, also put forward plans for a **nuclear-free zone** in Central Europe, which Adenauer, the chancellor of the FRG, believed was a 'Russian trap' leading to the reunification of a neutralised Germany. Adenauer feared that a neutral united Germany could easily be overrun by the USSR. Not surprisingly, therefore, Adenauer became more responsive to French plans in early 1958 for developing a Franco-German-Italian nuclear bomb that would be independent of the British and Americans.

Doubts about the USA's loyalty to its European allies also influenced Adenauer's thinking about the future of the new European Economic Community (EEC), and his attitude to General de Gaulle, who returned to power in France in May 1958. The two statesmen had very different plans for its future. Adenauer wanted it to develop into a closely integrated community linked to the USA, while de Gaulle hoped that it would become an association of independent states, completely free from US influence, and under French leadership. If, however, the Americans decided to pull out of Europe or sacrifice West Berlin to the USSR, de Gaulle's vision of Europe was the only alternative Adenauer could fall back on.

The EEC and EFTA

The European Economic Community (EEC) was set up by the Treaty of Rome, which was signed with general US approval by the FRG, France, Italy and the Benelux states in March 1957. Its aim was to create a common market or customs union within twelve years, while also gradually forming a more integrated political structure. British plans for setting up a much larger free trade zone were turned down by the leaders of the six powers on the grounds that they would not provide an effective basis for European economic and political co-operation. This led to Britain forming the European Free Trade Association in 1960 with Denmark, Norway, Sweden, Switzerland, Austria and Portugal. Thus, a major economic split in Western Europe developed just at the time that it was about to face renewed pressure from the Soviet bloc.

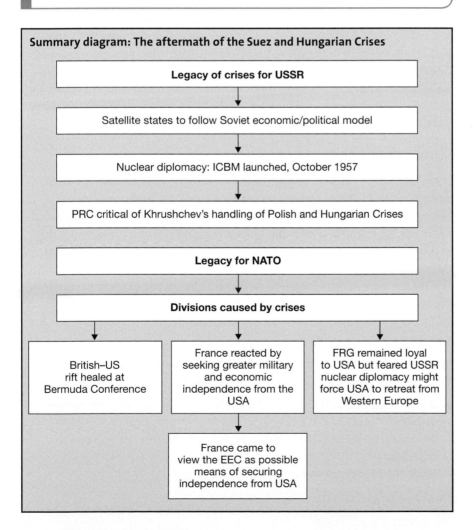

Summary diagram: The aftermath of the Suez and Hungarian Crises

Legacy of crises for USSR

↓

Satellite states to follow Soviet economic/political model

↓

Nuclear diplomacy: ICBM launched, October 1957

↓

PRC critical of Khrushchev's handling of Polish and Hungarian Crises

Legacy for NATO

↓

Divisions caused by crises

- British–US rift healed at Bermuda Conference
- France reacted by seeking greater military and economic independence from the USA
- FRG remained loyal to USA but feared USSR nuclear diplomacy might force USA to retreat from Western Europe

↓

France came to view the EEC as possible means of securing independence from USA

③ The Berlin Crisis 1958–61

▶ *What was Khrushchev intending to achieve by triggering a crisis over Berlin?*

The first stages

In the autumn of 1956 the GDR had acted, in contrast to Poland and Hungary, as a loyal ally of the USSR. Yet the GDR, despite joining the Warsaw Pact in 1956 (see page 89), remained a fragile and artificial state totally dependent on Moscow and on the presence of twenty divisions of Soviet troops stationed within its frontiers. It was confronted by a prosperous West Germany, the miraculous economic recovery of which inevitably attracted many of its youngest and most ambitious citizens.

Through the open frontier in Berlin, it was still possible to flee from the drab life of socialist planning and rationing to the bright lights of the FRG, and both Adenauer and the USA did everything to encourage this. Between 1945 and 1961 about one-sixth of the whole East German population had fled westwards. One way of stopping this exodus was dramatically to improve the standard of living in the GDR, but to achieve this it was essential to stop skilled workers and professionals quitting in large numbers to the FRG. This meant that something had to be done about the status of West Berlin.

Khrushchev's aims

By the autumn of 1958 Khrushchev was increasingly confident that the USSR could force the USA into making concessions over West Berlin, and indeed perhaps over the whole German question. By grossly exaggerating the extent of Soviet nuclear power and by putting pressure on West Berlin, he was sure that he could squeeze concessions from the Western allies without the risk of war. He graphically observed: 'Berlin is the testicles of the West … every time I want to make the West scream I squeeze on Berlin.' Also, as the Chinese Communist leaders pointed out, if the GDR could not be turned into a viable state able to hold its own with the FRG, the whole prestige of international communism was at stake.

Apart from strengthening the GDR, what other aims had Khrushchev in mind? He also hoped to:

- stop or at least delay the decision by NATO to equip the FRG with nuclear weapons
- show his critics within the USSR and China that he was not 'soft on the imperialists'
- divide the Western powers

- force them to accept the USSR as a political and military equal and to come to the conference table to draw up a German peace treaty. This would involve the Western powers' withdrawal from Berlin and their recognition of the division of Germany and of the GDR's post-war frontiers with Poland.

In the words of a US historian, Hope Harrison, 'Khrushchev always saw and used West Berlin … as a lever to compel the West to recognize the post-war *status quo* and the existence of East Germany.'

The Berlin ultimatum, November 1958

The long and dangerous crisis began on 10 November when Khrushchev called for a peace treaty with the two German states (Source C).

On 27 November Khrushchev followed this up with a six-month ultimatum demanding the demilitarisation of West Berlin, the withdrawal of Western troops, and its change of status into a **free city**. If the Western allies refused to sign a peace treaty with the two German states, Khrushchev threatened to conclude a peace agreement just with the GDR and to recognise its sovereignty over East Berlin. This would then enable it to control access to West Berlin and interfere at will with traffic using the **land corridors** from the FRG. The Western allies would thus be compelled to deal with GDR rather than Russian officials and so in effect recognise the sovereignty of the GDR, which would shatter the Hallstein Doctrine (see page 91). He was, however, as we shall see, to have second thoughts about putting quite so much power into the hands of Walter Ulbricht, the leader of the GDR.

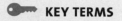

KEY TERMS

Free city Self-governing city not incorporated into a state.

Land corridors Roads, railways and canals, which the Soviets had agreed in 1945 could be used to supply West Berlin.

SOURCE C

From Khrushchev's speech of 10 November 1958, quoted in R. Morgan, *The Unsettled Peace*, BBC Books, 1974, p. 78.

Is it not time for us to draw appropriate conclusions from the fact that the key items of the Potsdam Agreement concerning the maintenance of peace in Europe and consequently throughout the world, have been violated, and that certain forces continue to nurture German militarism, prompting it in the direction in which it was pushed before the Second World War, that is against the East?

The time has obviously arrived for the signatories of the Potsdam Agreement to renounce the remnants of the occupation regime in Berlin, and thereby make it possible to create a normal situation in the capital of the German Democratic Republic. The Soviet Union, for its part, would hand over to the sovereign German Democratic Republic the functions in Berlin that are still exercised by Soviet agencies. This, I think, would be the correct thing to do.

According to Source C, what was Khrushchev actually proposing?

SOURCE D

? What is the value of Source D to a historian studying Khrushchev's role in the Berlin Crisis?

Khrushchev wagging his finger to make a point. Khrushchev's speeches at summit conferences and the United Nations during the long Berlin Crisis were both threatening and aggressive.

The Western reaction 1959–60

Although the Western allies rejected the ultimatum, Khrushchev was successful in forcing them to the conference table to discuss the 'German question'. In February 1959 they agreed that a foreign ministers' conference should meet in Geneva in the summer. Khrushchev was also delighted to see splits beginning to appear in the Western alliance. In the preceding months Adenauer viewed with increasing concern statements from London and Washington signalling a desire for compromise and concession, and inevitably drew closer to de Gaulle, who urged a much tougher line against the Soviets. He was particularly alarmed by the decision of British Prime Minister Harold Macmillan to visit Moscow in February and by Eisenhower's invitation to Khrushchev to visit the USA in the coming autumn.

The Geneva Conference, May to August 1959

KEY TERM

Confederation A grouping of states in which each state retains its sovereignty. Hence, much looser than a federation.

At the Geneva Conference both sides put forward proposals for German unity, but no agreement was secured. The Western powers came up with their usual demand for free elections, while the USSR suggested that the two Germanys should form a **confederation**, which would only very slowly evolve into a united state. However, as the Soviets did succeed in persuading the West to discuss the Berlin problem as a separate issue, Khrushchev believed that his threats were paying off, and he continued the pressure, renewing the ultimatum in June.

Summit meetings, September 1959 to May 1960

Why was so little progress made in solving the Berlin Crisis in 1959–60? Between 1959 and 1961 there were more summits than at any time since the Second World War. When Khrushchev visited Eisenhower at Camp David, the holiday residence of the US president, in September 1959, the mood was friendly but, to quote the US historian John Lewis Gaddis, the two leaders 'got no further than an agreement to disagree'. Over the next two years Khrushchev alternated periods of *détente*, when he temporarily allowed the ultimatum to lapse again, with spells of acute crisis during which further threats were devised, to force the West into making concessions over the status of Berlin and the future of Germany.

Khrushchev's actions were not without success. Behind the scenes in London and Washington, and at times even in Paris, various schemes for creating a nuclear-free zone in Central Europe, recognising Poland's western frontiers and the GDR, were considered. Adenauer meanwhile was desperate to stop any of these plans from reducing the FRG to a neutral second-rate state, but by May 1960, when the Paris Summit was due to open, he had no idea what Eisenhower and Macmillan might be about to propose. Thus, for him at least, it was 'a gift from heaven', as the German historian Klessmann has called it, when Khrushchev used the shooting down of a US spy plane over the USSR as an excuse to cancel the Summit, and wait until a new US president was elected in the autumn.

> ### U-2 spy planes and the arms race
>
> In 1956 the US air force bought 53 Lockheed U-2 spy planes. Based in Japan, Turkey and Britain, they were able to fly over Soviet territory and photograph military bases, missile factories and launch pads. By 1961 Soviet technology had caught up with the U-2s, and on 1 May a Soviet anti-aircraft missile shot down a plane that had been sent to see whether there were missile bases in the Urals. These flights established that, for all Khrushchev's boasting, the Soviets possessed in the spring of 1961 very few ICBMs and no launching platforms for them. Indeed, the USSR had only four ICBMs based on a site near Archangel.

The construction of the Berlin Wall

Khrushchev's hopes that the new US president, John F. Kennedy, would make the concessions that Eisenhower had refused, proved unrealistic. Yet his response to Soviet threats to West Berlin hinted at a possible solution to the Berlin problem.

President Kennedy and Berlin

While Kennedy dramatically increased US forces in Europe, he also urged negotiation on the German question and pointedly stressed in a television

John F. Kennedy

1917	Born into a wealthy Irish American family in Massachusetts
1940–3	Served in the US Navy; his boat was rammed and sunk by a Japanese destroyer
1953	Elected to the Senate as a Democrat
1960	Won presidential elections by a narrow margin and became the first Roman Catholic president in the USA's history
1961	Allowed a disastrous invasion of Cuba by exiles – the Bay of Pigs incident
	Met Khrushchev in Vienna and was told that the USA was on the 'wrong side of history'
	Indicated that the USA would protect West Berlin by force if necessary
1962	Successfully brought the Cuban Missile Crisis to an end
1963	Assassinated in Dallas, Texas

After Kennedy had met Khrushchev for the first time in Vienna in June 1961, he remarked: 'He just beat the hell out of me. I've got a terrible problem. If he thinks I'm inexperienced and have no guts, until we remove those ideas, we won't get anywhere with him.' Kennedy was worried about the USA losing the Cold War and believed that the USSR was in a strong position to gain support in the Developing World. He built up the US armed forces and was determined that the USA should send a man to the moon by 1970.

In the Cuban Missile Crisis, historians have traditionally seen him as a hardliner, who in the last resort was ready to risk war, but in fact secret tape recordings of his key advisory body, which were taken with the permission of Kennedy during the crisis, show that he took the lead in pressing for a compromise.

broadcast on 25 July 1961 (see Source F) that the USA was essentially interested in defending free access to West Berlin from the FRG, rather than maintaining the existing status of Berlin as a whole. He was, in fact, indicating that the USA and NATO would fight to preserve the freedom of West Berlin, but would not intervene to stop the GDR from closing the frontier between East and West Berlin.

Until the autumn of 1960 Khrushchev determined the course of the Berlin Crisis. Ulbricht, who certainly stood to benefit from a successful outcome, was little more than a spectator. Khrushchev still hoped to use Berlin as a means to solve the German problem as a whole, and despite his bluster, acted cautiously. However, in desperation, as the numbers of refugees to the West dramatically increased during the years 1960–1, Ulbricht pressed Khrushchev to sign a separate peace treaty with the GDR, at one juncture sarcastically observing: 'You only talk about a peace treaty, but don't do anything about it.'

In the end Khrushchev was compelled to act by the growing economic crisis in the GDR. In April 1960 the remaining independent farmers were forced into collective farms. The immediate economic impact of this was disastrous: crop yields plummeted and within months there were serious shortages of bread, butter and meat. This led to an ever-increasing number of people fleeing to West Germany. In 1960, 199,000 fled and in the six months up to June 1961, a further 103,000. There was also widespread unrest in factories.

SOURCE E

Building the Berlin Wall, August 1961.

What information is conveyed by Source E about the construction of the Berlin Wall?

Around the beginning of August, Khrushchev decided that the border between East and West Berlin would be closed. This decision was confirmed at a meeting of the Warsaw Pact states in Moscow on 3–5 August 1961, and in the early morning of 13 August the operation was efficiently and swiftly carried out. The border was sealed with barbed wire, and when no Western countermeasures followed, a more permanent concrete wall was built.

Significance of the Berlin Wall

The first Berlin Crisis ended in complete failure for Stalin (see page 67). Like Stalin, Khrushchev failed to force the Western allies to withdraw troops from West Berlin or to compel them to negotiate peace treaties with the two German states. On the other hand, with the construction of the Berlin Wall, he achieved a limited but important success for Soviet policies. The existence of the GDR was now assured, and ultimately the FRG would be forced to drop the Hallstein Doctrine and recognise its independence. By tolerating it, the Western powers, in effect, recognised East Germany. As the historian Hermann Weber observed, East German Communists were to look back on 13 August 1961 as 'the secret foundation day of the GDR'. With the Berlin Wall in place, the people of East Germany had no option but to remain in the GDR. This enabled Ulbricht to develop what he called the New Economic System which was eventually supposed to revolutionise the GDR's economy and gain enthusiastic acceptance for socialism.

Learning to live with the Berlin Wall 1961–3

The prolonged crisis over Berlin effectively ended with the Wall, although this was not immediately obvious at the time. The Soviet Union renewed nuclear testing and on 30 October 1961 exploded an enormous bomb of over 50 megatons, which it was calculated could destroy an area considerably larger than Wales. There was also continued tension along the Wall in Berlin. US troops were ostentatiously practising tearing down simulated walls, while on 27 October Soviet and US tanks stood almost muzzle to muzzle for several hours at **Checkpoint Charlie**. Khrushchev was determined to keep up the pressure on West Berlin. In October, for instance, he told the Soviet foreign minister, Gromyko, and the Polish leader, Gomułka, that 'we should … exploit the weakness of the enemy. We should strive to remove the official representatives from West Berlin.'

In a series of talks with the Soviet leaders over the next year Kennedy attempted to lower the tension by exploring the possibility of an agreement over Berlin, which would guarantee the rights of the Western allies, while recognising what he called the 'legitimate interests of others'. By this, of course, he meant the USSR and GDR. Inevitably, Adenauer regarded these negotiations with great suspicion and dreaded that Kennedy would end up sacrificing West Berlin. Consequently, he drew even closer to Gaullist France, signing in January 1963 the Franco-German Treaty of Friendship and supporting the French veto on Britain's application to join the EEC (see page 166).

In October 1962 the Cuban Missile Crisis (see below) temporarily forced the Berlin question into second place and rallied the Western powers around Kennedy. After the crisis, discussions on Berlin continued, but the need to find a settlement was no longer so urgent. Having come so close to nuclear war in Cuba, Khrushchev shied away from another confrontation in Berlin and accepted that for the time being the Wall had consolidated the GDR. The Soviet government also began to reassess its policies and priorities in light of the lessons learned in the Cuban Missile Crisis. As far as they affected Europe, these policies will be analysed in Chapter 6.

SOURCE F

From US President Kennedy's 'Report to the Nation in July 1961', 25 July 1961. *Department of State, Documents on Germany, 1944–1985*, US Department of State Publication, no. 9446, Office of the Historian, Bureau of Public Affairs, Washington, DC, 1986, pp. 763–4.

We are there [in Berlin] as a result of our victory over Nazi Germany, and our basic rights to be there deriving from that victory include both our presence in west Berlin and the enjoyment of access across East Germany. These rights have been completely confirmed … But in addition to those rights is our commitment to sustain – and defend, if need be – the opportunity for more than two million people [in West Berlin] to determine their own future and choose their own way of life.

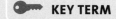

KEY TERM

Checkpoint Charlie
One of the few official crossing points between East and West Berlin. It is now a museum.

? According to Source F, why was the USA determined to keep troops in West Berlin?

Thus our presence in West Berlin, and our access thereto, cannot be ended by any act of the Soviet Government ... An attack in that city will be regarded as an attack upon us all ...

We cannot and will not permit the Communists to drive us out of Berlin either gradually or by force.

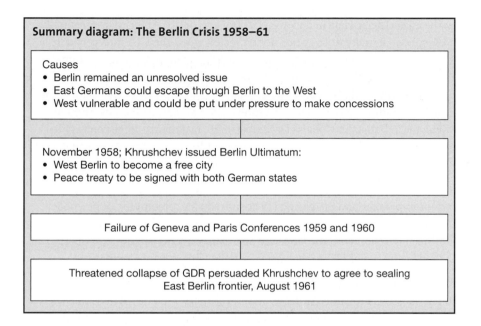

Summary diagram: The Berlin Crisis 1958–61

Causes
- Berlin remained an unresolved issue
- East Germans could escape through Berlin to the West
- West vulnerable and could be put under pressure to make concessions

November 1958; Khrushchev issued Berlin Ultimatum:
- West Berlin to become a free city
- Peace treaty to be signed with both German states

Failure of Geneva and Paris Conferences 1959 and 1960

Threatened collapse of GDR persuaded Khrushchev to agree to sealing East Berlin frontier, August 1961

 # The Cuban Missile Crisis 1962

▶ *What were the origins of the Cuban Missile Crisis?*

▶ *Why did the Cuban Missile Crisis not result in war between the USA and the USSR?*

The US historian John Lewis Gaddis wrote in 1997:

SOURCE G

From John Lewis Gaddis, *We Now Know*, Oxford University Press, 1997, p. 261.

[The crisis over Cuba was] the only episode after World War II in which each of the major areas of Soviet–American competition intersected: the nuclear arms race to be sure, but also conflicting ideological aspirations, 'third world rivalries', relations with allies, the domestic political implications of foreign policy, the personalities of individual leaders. The crisis was a kind of funnel – a historical singularity if you like – into which everything suddenly tumbled and got mixed together. Fortunately no black hole lured at the other end ...

According to Source G, what was the cause of the Cuban Missile Crisis?

Although the Cuban Missile Crisis was a direct confrontation between the USA and the USSR, involving neither NATO nor the Warsaw Pact, it had a profound impact on the Cold War in Europe. Both sides came to the brink of war but drew back from a nuclear conflict. After the crisis the Cold War changed, and gradually evolved into what some historians call the **long peace**.

The causes of the crisis

In the 1950s the Soviets had viewed Central and South America as essentially a US sphere of interest. They had not protested when the CIA intervened in 1954 to topple the allegedly pro-Communist President Árbenz in Guatamala. However, the USA's domination did cause a growing resentment among South American intellectuals and nationalists, and was one of the factors that influenced **Fidel Castro** to launch a **guerrilla war** against the government of Fulgencio Batista in Cuba in December 1956. By January 1959, contrary to expectations, his forces were able to take over the government in Havana.

At this stage Castro was an anti-American nationalist but not a Communist. It was probably growing opposition from the Cuban middle classes to his economic policies and increasing US hostility to his attempt to adopt a policy of non-alignment in the Cold War that drove him into adopting Marxism–Leninism. Friction with the USA was also caused by his seizure of property owned by the major US firms, particularly the United Fruit Company.

As relations with the USA deteriorated during the summer of 1959, Castro began to put out feelers towards Moscow, and in February 1960 he invited Anastas Mikoyan, deputy chairman of the Soviet Council of Ministers, to visit Havana. Mikoyan returned to Moscow with a glowing account of the Cuban Revolution, which reminded him of the heroic early days of the Russian Revolution. In July, Khrushchev threatened the USA with a missile attack if it dared invade Cuba and suggested that Washington declare the end of the **Monroe Doctrine**.

The Bay of Pigs incident

The growing links between Cuba and the USSR persuaded Eisenhower to authorise the CIA to start planning Castro's removal. In April 1961, four months after Kennedy came to power, a force of about 1400 Cuban exiles landed south of Havana at Playa Girón on the Bay of Pigs. It was hoped that this would spark off a popular uprising against Castro, but Castro, in anticipation of such a move, imprisoned thousands of suspects. At the last moment Kennedy also cancelled both bombing raids by the US air force and a landing by US marines. Consequently, Castro had no trouble in defeating the invasion. As John Lewis Gaddis has observed, the Bay of Pigs incident was 'a monumental disaster for the United States … comparable only to the humiliation the British and French had suffered at Suez five years earlier' (see page 103).

Although Khrushchev was delighted by this humiliation, he nevertheless saw it as a warning that the Americans would inevitably try to topple Castro again. In this he was correct. The CIA continued to devise plans for Castro's assassination, and large-scale military manoeuvres took place in the Caribbean Sea in the spring and summer of 1962 in anticipation of an invasion.

The Soviet decision to place missiles on Cuba

In August 1962 Khrushchev negotiated without the knowledge of the USA the Soviet–Cuban accord with Castro. Over the next few weeks the Soviets began secretly to deploy medium-range nuclear missiles on Cuba. These would be defended by 40,000 Soviet troops, anti-aircraft batteries, short-range battlefield rockets and MIG-21 fighter planes.

There were two key reasons for this highly dangerous operation:

- To gain a base from which the USA could be threatened by medium-range Soviet missiles. This would correct the strategic imbalance caused by the construction of US missile bases in Turkey and Western Europe and go some way towards closing the **missile gap** between the USSR and the USA.
- Castro also wanted to defend the revolution in Cuba. The Soviets saw the revolution as a major success for Marxism–Leninism, and its defeat would, as Mikoyan told Castro, 'throw back the revolutionary movement in many countries'.

On 4 October the Soviet ship *Indigirka* arrived at the port of Mariel in Cuba with enough nuclear warheads to equip at least 158 strategic and nuclear weapons.

The crisis comes to a head: 14–28 October 1962

On 14 October a US U-2 spy plane discovered the missiles. President Kennedy was informed two days later and initially the news was kept quiet from the US public. The options open to the US government were explored by a small crisis committee, the **ExComm**. It dismissed launching a surprise air attack as too risky, while an appeal to the UN was ruled out as it would take too long, especially as further reconnaissance flights indicated that the Soviets already had four medium-range missile sites operational. Instead, plans were drawn up for a possible invasion of Cuba by US forces and an ultimatum was to be sent to Moscow demanding that the missiles be withdrawn.

Quarantine zone

In the meantime the US Navy set up a quarantine zone 1200 kilometres (800 miles) from the Cuban coast. Once they entered this area Soviet ships would be stopped and searched for weapons due to be delivered to Cuba. On the advice of the British ambassador this was reduced to 800 kilometres (500 miles).

On 22 October Kennedy announced on US television the news of the existence of Soviet missiles on Cuba and that he had ordered the naval blockade of the island. He also made clear that if any nuclear missile was fired from Cuba, he would order a massive nuclear attack on the USSR. Khrushchev initially was

---

🔑 KEY TERMS

Missile gap Where one side has a temporary lead over the other in nuclear weapons.

ExComm The Executive Committee of the US National Security Council.

SOURCE H

What information does Source H convey about the causes of the Cuban Missile Crisis?

An aerial reconnaissance photograph showing a medium-range ballistic missile launch site in Cuba, October 1962.

determined to complete the missile sites in Cuba and ordered the Soviet ships to challenge the blockade. It looked as though a naval confrontation was inevitable.

Soviet decision to withdraw the missiles

On 26 October, in response to an appeal for negotiations from U. Thant, the UN secretary-general, and fearing an imminent US air attack on Cuba, Khrushchev informed the Americans that he would withdraw the missiles. In return, he demanded a guarantee that the USA would not invade Cuba. However, once he realised that this made him look weak in the eyes of his political rivals, in a second message on 27 October he insisted that the removal of missiles from Cuba was dependent on the dismantling of US **Jupiter missile** bases in Turkey. To appease US public opinion Kennedy responded to the first letter officially, but secretly he agreed to remove the fifteen Jupiter missiles from Turkey once the Cuban Crisis was over. He stressed, however, that if the Soviets made this offer public, it would be withdrawn.

Effectively this ended the crisis, and all the Soviet missiles and troops were withdrawn from Cuba by 20 November.

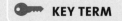 **KEY TERM**

Jupiter missile A liquid-fuelled, surface-deployed missile, which was already out of date by 1962.

SOURCE I

From Khrushchev's message to Kennedy, 27 October 1962, quoted in Priscilla Roberts, editor, *Cuban Missile Crisis: The Essential Reference Guide*, ABC-CLIO, 2012, p. 213.

You are disturbed over Cuba. You say that this disturbs you because it is 90 miles [145 km] by sea from the coast of the United States of America. But Turkey adjoins us … Do you consider, then, that you have the right to demand security for your own country and the removals of the weapons you call offensive, but do not accord the same right to us? You have placed destructive missile weapons, which you call offensive in Turkey, literally next door to us …

I think it would be possible to end this controversy quickly and normalize the situation …

I therefore make this proposal: We are willing to remove from Cuba the means which you regard as offensive … Your representatives will make a declaration to the effect that the United States, for its part, considering the uneasiness and anxiety of the Soviet state, will remove [the missiles] from Turkey …

> According to Source I, how is Khrushchev proposing to end the missile crisis?

The aftermath of the crisis

In the short term, President Kennedy's prestige increased enormously. He was promoted as the one who had called Khrushchev's bluff. His concession that the Jupiter missiles would be withdrawn from Turkey in return for the removal of the missiles from Cuba remained a secret until after his death. Khrushchev's retreat met with bitter criticism from Mao and Castro, who accused him of surrendering to the USA. It weakened his position within the USSR. Yet his fall in October 1964 (see page 166) was more the result of domestic politics and power struggles than a consequence of the Cuban Missile Crisis.

Cuba

The Soviet decision to remove the missiles was seen as a betrayal by Castro and convinced him that Cuba would have to develop its own independent revolutionary strategy. By the mid-1960s, Castro actively assisted revolutionary movements in the Developing World, not only to support the spread of communism but also to distract the USA so that it would not renew pressure on Cuba.

The USSR

The overwhelming superiority of the USA in nuclear weapons, as shown during the nuclear crisis, came as a shock to the Soviet leadership. The USSR was determined to achieve parity in nuclear weapons with the USA and began an ambitious programme for the construction of ICBMs (see page 165). The total command of the seas by the USA which enabled it to establish so effectively the quarantine zone around Cuba also persuaded the USSR to build a large navy, which in the future would enable it to project its power globally.

Reduction in international tension

The Cuban Missile Crisis brought both the USA and USSR to the brink of nuclear war. The crisis neither ended the Cold War nor stopped the nuclear arms race between the USA and USSR, but it did lead to an understanding by both sides that nuclear war would lead to what became known as 'mutually assured destruction' or MAD. Increasingly, both sides began to give priority to plans for controlling the proliferation of nuclear weapons and their testing (see page 164). In 1963, a **hotline** was established which linked the Soviet and US leaders. The intention behind this was that both leaders could directly contact each other instead of relying on contacts through the UN or their own diplomats, and therefore rapidly defuse crises that might lead to nuclear war.

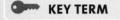 **KEY TERM**

Hotline A direct communications link between US and Soviet leaders.

Summary diagram: The Cuban Missile Crisis 1962

Causes

- Castro's revolution in Cuba
- Deterioration in US–Cuban relations
- Failure of Bay of Pigs invasion
- Secret Soviet–Cuban accord, August 1962: medium-range missiles installed and defended by Soviet troops

US reaction to discovery of Soviet missile pads, 14 October 1962

- Kennedy's ultimatum, 22 October
- Quarantine announced
- Threat of massive US retaliation if missiles were fired from Cuba

Khrushchev's reaction: two conflicting messages

1. Promised withdrawal from Cuba provided USA did not invade Cuba
2. Withdrawal subject to later dismantling of US Jupiter missiles in Turkey

Kennedy's response

Accepted first publicly, but privately agreed to second

Consequences of Crisis

- Kennedy's prestige increased
- Khrushchev criticised by Mao, Castro and rivals in USSR
- Cuba developed revolutionary strategy in Developing World, independent of USSR
- USSR determined to achieve nuclear parity with USA and build surface fleet
- USSR and USA agreed to hotline and plan to control proliferation of nuclear weapons

5 Assessment: the 'Second Cold War'

▶ *How accurate is it to describe the whole period 1956–63 as the 'Second Cold War'?*

Deterioration in East–West relations

In 1955 it seemed that the Cold War in Europe, if not over, had at least stabilised. The Soviets had pulled out of Austria (see page 90) and there was much talk about the Geneva spirit. Yet over the next six years no progress was made towards *détente*, as relations between the Warsaw Pact states and the North Atlantic Alliance deteriorated to a level not seen since the Berlin Blockade of 1948–9. Do the reasons for this lie with Khrushchev or were there deeper causes?

A major cause of European instability was the failure of the USSR to set up in Eastern Europe what the Americans managed to create in Western Europe: 'an empire by invitation' (see page 95). The destalinisation policies of 1953–6 were attempts to create more popular regimes that did not depend on terror and the Red Army to survive, and to allow the peoples of Eastern Europe some input into influencing their own politics. Yet the Polish riots and the Hungarian revolt of 1956 showed how hard it was to get the balance between liberalisation and the maintenance of essential control. This was to remain one of the main dilemmas facing the Soviet leadership for the next 33 years.

To the brink and back?

Until 1961 the division of Germany and the unsolved problem of Berlin also remained a major destabilising factor in Europe. The root of the problem was the chronic economic weakness of East Germany, which could only be remedied by closing the inner Berlin frontier. This would prevent the flight of desperately needed skilled workers from East to West where they could earn more money. However, this measure would violate the Potsdam Agreement (see page 34) and cause a major crisis involving the USA and its allies. Both German states depended for their existence on their superpower protector. As neither the USA nor the USSR could allow its part of Germany to collapse or be absorbed by the rival bloc, the two German leaders, Ulbricht and Adenauer, had at times immense influence over the foreign policy of Moscow and Washington, respectively. Thus, Adenauer did much to stop Eisenhower from effectively exploring the possibilities of a Berlin settlement in the period 1958–60, while recent research by Hope Harrison (*Driving the Soviets up the Wall, 1953–1961*, 2005) has shown that it was pressure from Ulbricht that finally propelled Khrushchev into building the Berlin Wall.

The crises of 1956 and 1958–61 were triggered by instabilities within the Soviet bloc and Central Europe, but they were made far more dangerous by Khrushchev's high-risk 'nuclear diplomacy'. In 1956, by threatening to bombard Britain, France and Israel with nuclear missiles, even when in reality the USSR had not yet developed the military capacity to do this, he was able to pose as the saviour of Egypt. He did not hesitate to use the ultimate threat of nuclear weapons as a bargaining counter in both the Berlin and Cuba Crises. Yet, as we have seen, much of this was only 'bluff and bluster'. In that sense Khrushchev very much presided over a period of acute tension which perhaps could be called a Second Cold War.

In other ways, however, the Khrushchev years set the pattern for the next three decades in Europe. The Berlin Wall, however cruel in its division of a city and prevention of families and friends from seeing each other, did at last stabilise the GDR and with it Central Europe. It also enabled both superpowers, as Gaddis has put it, to 'break loose' from their German allies and explore the possibility of *détente* in Europe. Paradoxically, Khrushchev was also the father of *détente*. Despite his brinkmanship over Berlin and Cuba he aimed for peaceful economic and ideological competition with the West. After the Cuban Crisis, Soviet policy settled down, as we shall see later, to a dual policy of achieving *détente* in Europe and nuclear equality with the USA, while also exploiting anti-Western movements in the Developing World.

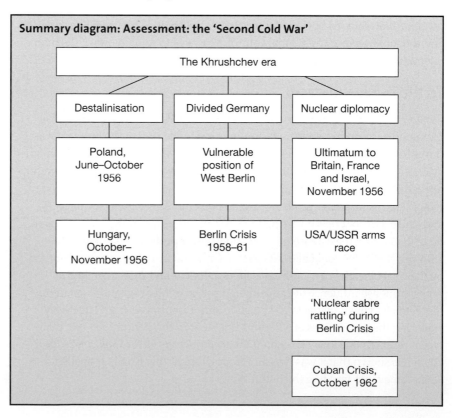

Summary diagram: Assessment: the 'Second Cold War'

Chapter summary

Khrushchev attempted to liberalise the Soviet regimes in Eastern Europe, but the Hungarian Rising terminated this experiment and resulted in Soviet military intervention. The Suez Crisis in November 1956 enabled him to pose as the champion of developing, non-aligned states and to take the credit for the failure of the Anglo-French attempt to topple Nasser.

The division of Germany and the unsolved problem of Berlin still remained a major problem. The cause of this was the GDR's economic weakness, which could only be remedied by preventing the flight of skilled workers to the FRG. Ultimately, Khrushchev sanctioned the Berlin Wall, which led to the consolidation of the GDR.

In Cuba, the USSR exploited Castro's break with the USA to install medium-range nuclear missiles which could threaten the security of the USA. Kennedy responded vigorously and the subsequent crisis was one of the most dangerous of the Cold War. Conflict was avoided by Khrushchev's agreement to dismantle the missiles in exchange for a guarantee from Kennedy that the USA would not invade Cuba, as well as a secret promise that NATO's nuclear missiles would be removed from Turkey.

Refresher questions

Use these questions to remind yourself of the key material covered in this chapter.

1 What was the significance of Khrushchev's speech at the Twentieth Party Conference?

2 Why did the USSR face a challenge to its authority in Hungary and Poland?

3 In what ways did the Suez Crisis influence Soviet action in Hungary?

4 Why did Dulles think that Khrushchev was such a dangerous Soviet leader?

5 How did the Western allies respond to Khrushchev's ultimatum regarding Berlin in 1958?

6 Why was so little progress made in solving the Berlin Crisis in 1959–60?

7 Why did Ulbricht want to seal off East Berlin from West Berlin?

8 Why did Khrushchev agree to the construction of the Berlin Wall?

9 Was the construction of the Berlin Wall a major success for the Soviet bloc?

10 Why, despite the construction of the Berlin Wall, did tension remain high in Europe until 1963?

11 Why did the US-backed invasion of Cuba fail?

12 Why did Khrushchev decide to site medium-range Soviet missiles on Cuba?

13 Why did the Cuban Missile Crisis not result in war between the USA and the USSR?

14 How near to war did the USA and USSR come during the years 1958–62?

15 Was there a 'Second Cold War'?

Question practice

ESSAY QUESTIONS

1 'However cruel, the construction of the Berlin Wall stabilised the situation in Germany.' Explain why you agree or disagree with this view.

2 To what extent did the Hungarian Uprising of 1956 affect international relations?

3 Assess the consequences for the Soviet bloc of Khrushchev's policy of destalinisation.

4 Which of the following had the greater impact on causing the escalation of the Cuban Crisis? i) The Bay of Pigs incident. ii) The Soviet decision to place missiles on Cuba. Explain your answer with reference to both i) and ii).

SOURCE ANALYSIS QUESTIONS

1 With reference to Sources C (page 109) and F (page 114), and your understanding of the historical context, which of these two sources is more valuable in explaining the development of the Berlin Crisis 1958–61?

2 With reference to Sources C (page 109), F (page 114) and I (page 119), and your understanding of the historical context, assess the value of these sources to a historian studying the aims and diplomacy of the USA and USSR during 1958–62.

CHAPTER 5

The spread of communism in Asia

While the Cold War divided Europe, it did not lead to the outbreak of a 'hot war'. In Asia, on the other hand, the spread of communism led to large-scale hostilities in Korea and Indo-China and guerrilla conflict in Malaya. This chapter investigates the spread of communism in Asia during this period through the following themes:

★ Japan and the Cold War 1945–52

★ The triumph of communism in China 1945–50

★ The Korean War 1950–3

★ South-East Asia 1945–54

Key dates

1945	Aug.	Soviet invasion of Manchuria
		Japan surrendered and occupied by USA
1946	June	Chinese Civil War resumed
	Nov.	Guerrilla warfare began in Vietnam
1949	Oct.	People's Republic of China (PRC) proclaimed
1950	Feb.	USSR–PRC Treaty

1950	June	Outbreak of Korean War
	Oct.	PRC entered Korean War
1951	Sept.	Japanese Peace Treaty signed
1953	July	Korean War ended
1954	May	Điện Biên Phủ
	July	Geneva Accords
1957		Malayan independence

① Japan and the Cold War 1945–52

 **KEY TERMS**

▶ *How did the US occupation of Japan from 1945 to 1952 increase Cold War tensions?*

The defeat of Japan in the Second World War eliminated a power that had dominated east Asia since the early twentieth century. Japanese occupation of the former European colonies such as **Malaya**, **French Indo-China** and the **Dutch East Indies** in 1941–2 weakened colonial governments and led to the formation of independence movements, many of which were associated with communism and called for an end to imperialism.

Malaya A British colony that became Malaysia and Singapore.

French Indo-China A French colony consisting of today's Laos, Cambodia and Vietnam.

Dutch East Indies A Dutch colony that became Indonesia.

The US occupation of Japan

In Europe, the Soviet Union destroyed Germany's army, but remained uninvolved in the concurrent war in Asia and the Pacific until August 1945. At the Yalta Conference it was agreed that the USSR would declare war on Japan three months after the surrender of Germany in order to assist a likely US invasion of Japan (see page 25). In return, Stalin was promised, by Churchill and Roosevelt, the restoration of the economic rights which Russia had enjoyed in north-east China and Manchuria before 1905.

The combination of the dropping of atomic bombs on the Japanese cities of Hiroshima and Nagasaki on 6 and 9 August (see page 37) by the USA and the Soviet invasion of Manchuria led to the unconditional surrender by Japan on 15 August. Soviet troops advanced through Manchuria to the 38th parallel in Korea (see the map on page 143) and at the end of August Japan was placed under Allied military occupation under the command of US General **Douglas MacArthur**. The USA successfully resisted Soviet demands to divide Japan, like Germany, into separate Allied zones. Only in December 1945 was the inter-Allied Council for Japan formed, but it had no real power to make decisions about the future of Japan. MacArthur retained the key power to control and administer Japan and needed only to consult with the Allied Council. The USA provided most of the troops occupying Japan and was therefore able to dominate the country, dictating all policies.

US policy in Japan 1946–52

In 1947, US policy in Japan, as in Germany, became less repressive, both because the Cold War in Europe had intensified and because in China the Nationalist Government was increasingly threatened by Communist forces (see page 133). The emphasis was now on transforming Japan into an economic ally of the USA and a market for its exports. In 1948, a new plan for the development of the Japanese economy was unveiled and financial assistance was granted to rebuild Japanese industry, despite Soviet protests that this would restore Japan's military strength. The USA intended to strengthen Japan's economy so that it would help prevent the formation of Communist governments elsewhere in South-East Asia by encouraging regional trade and increasing prosperity. US policy towards Japan was one of the reasons that led to the signing of the Treaty of Friendship and Mutual Assistance between Communist China and the USSR in February 1950 (see Source A).

KEY FIGURE

Douglas MacArthur (1880–1964)

Supreme commander South-West Pacific 1942–5, military ruler of Japan 1945–50 and UN commander-in-chief in Korea 1950–1.

The Treaty of Peace with Japan

On 4 September 1951, the Treaty of Peace with Japan, which came into force in April 1952, was signed in San Francisco between Japan and its former adversaries in the Second World War. Its key terms were:

- the termination of military occupation
- the surrender of Japanese claims to territory, rights or property in Korea, Taiwan or China
- the right of the USA to continue to use the island of Okinawa as a military base
- agreement that Japan would provide compensation to Allied civilians and prisoners-of-war who had lost property or suffered as a result of Japanese internment and human rights abuses
- that reparations by Japan would be made to states affected by the war, including Vietnam, the Philippines, Burma and Indonesia.

The USSR attended the San Francisco Conference but refused to sign the treaty. Soviet Deputy Foreign Minister Andrei Gromyko protested that the treaty aimed to transform Japan into a US military base while drawing Japan into a military alliance against the USSR. Gromyko was partly right. Japan was indeed in the US sphere of influence; only four days after the treaty, a bilateral agreement was signed between Japan and the USA which permitted the USA to station troops in Japan for the purpose of defending it against a possible attack from the newly created People's Republic of China (see page 135). Unlike the Federal Republic of Germany, Japan, was not, however, developed into a military power.

SOURCE A

From the translation of the 'Treaty of Friendship and Mutual Assistance' signed between the USSR and the People's Republic of China on 14 February 1950, in *US National Intelligence Estimate 58*, 10 September 1952.

Article 1: Both Contracting Parties undertake jointly to adopt all necessary measures at their disposal for the purpose of preventing the resumption of aggression and violation of peace on the part of Japan or any other state that may collaborate with Japan directly or indirectly in acts of aggression. In the event of one … [Party] being attacked by Japan or any state allied with her and thus being involved in a state of war, the other … Party shall immediately render military and other assistance by all means at its disposal …

Article 2: The two Contracting Parties undertake, in a spirit of friendship and mutual agreement to bring about the earliest conclusion of the peace treaty with Japan jointly with the other powers which were allies during the Second World War.

What is the importance of Source A in understanding the reaction of the USSR and Communist China to US plans to create a pro-Western and independent Japan?

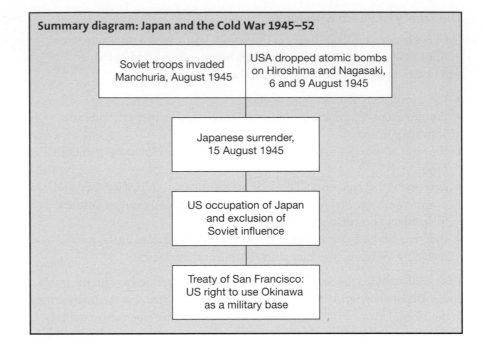

Summary diagram: Japan and the Cold War 1945–52

Soviet troops invaded Manchuria, August 1945	USA dropped atomic bombs on Hiroshima and Nagasaki, 6 and 9 August 1945

Japanese surrender, 15 August 1945

US occupation of Japan and exclusion of Soviet influence

Treaty of San Francisco: US right to use Okinawa as a military base

② The triumph of communism in China 1945–50

▶ *What were the aims of the USSR and USA in China 1945–9?*

The triumph of Communist forces in China under Mao Zedong dramatically altered the character of the Cold War. The USSR gained a new and potentially powerful ally in eastern Asia which could now put pressure on the USA and its allies.

Nationalists and Communists in China 1927–45

The Chinese Civil War between the Nationalists led by General **Chiang Kai-shek** and the Communists led by Mao Zedong broke out in 1927. When Japan launched a large-scale invasion of China in 1937, the **CCP** and **KMT** formed an uneasy anti-Japanese alliance which lasted until Japan's defeat in August 1945. At the Cairo Conference of 1943, Chiang was recognised by Britain and the USA as China's leader and a key ally in their war against Japan. The KMT, however, suffered a series of devastating defeats at the hands of the Japanese in the spring and summer of 1944, which, combined with high inflation and governmental corruption in the areas it controlled, undermined Chiang's claims to be China's national leader. In contrast, the strength of the CCP had greatly increased. It had an army of nearly a million people supported by an additional force of about 900,000 **militia** men, while party membership was over a million.

Mao Zedong

1883	Born into a peasant family in Hunan
1943	Chairman of CCP
1949	Civil War ended with Mao's victory
1950	Sino-Soviet treaty
	PRC troops assist North Korea
1954	President of PRC
1957	Launched Great Leap Forward
1959	Sino-Soviet split
1966–76	Cultural revolution unleashed
1976	Died

Mao's impact on the Cold War was immense. Not only did he lead communism to success in China, but by doing so he created an alternative to Stalinism and the Soviet variant of Marxism–Leninism. Under his leadership in the 1930s the CCP escaped annihilation at the hands of KMT and by late 1944 was an effective fighting force, which was ultimately able to defeat the KMT in the Chinese Civil War 1946–9. Initially, Mao looked to Stalin as the leader of world communism and in February 1950 signed the Sino-Soviet Pact. He intervened in the Korean War in 1950, which enabled him to mobilise Chinese public opinion against the USA and to support his domestic reform programme. He also assisted the Việt Minh's struggle against the French 1949–54.

Fuelled by a growing distrust of Stalin's successors and a determination to mobilise the revolutionary potential of the PRC, Mao made the PRC by 1960 a major rival of the USSR in the Communist world. Mao distrusted Khrushchev and later Brezhnev as 'revisionists' who had effectively abandoned the struggle with the USA. The growing hostility between the two world Communist powers had a profound impact on the future of the Cold War. Its impact was to weaken the USSR's global position and make it almost impossible for it to win the Cold War.

At home, successive revolutionary programmes, the Great Leap Forward (1958–60) and then the Cultural Revolution (1966), were designed at immense human cost to achieve communism within China and to unite the Chinese against both class enemies within the PRC and well as those outside – the USA and USSR.

Exploiting this unpopularity at the end of 1944, the CCP decided on two new strategies:

- The CCP's best troops would penetrate into the area south of the Yangtze River (see map on page 134) to establish bases from which they would be able to confront the KMT after the war.
- In a political manoeuvre to challenge Chiang's claim to be the leader of China, Mao, like his Eastern European counterparts (see page 21), proposed replacing Chiang's one-party dictatorship with a coalition government that included the CCP, which would then attempt to take control of key ministries within the coalition.

Initially, Mao won US support for his coalition programme, as Roosevelt hoped that a coalition would stabilise China and lead to a more effective campaign against Japan. However, this strategy failed when Chiang declared that he would enter a coalition with Mao only if he were given complete control of the CCP's armed forces, a condition which Mao could hardly accept.

Soviet invasion of Manchuria, August 1945

When the USSR declared war against Japan on 8 August, Mao ordered his forces to co-operate closely with Soviet forces and occupy key cities and rail links in central and northern China, particularly the north-east. He was convinced that the Soviet entry into the war had created a new international dimension which would favour the CCP in its struggle with the KMT. He also instructed his generals and the party leaders to prepare for renewed conflict with the KMT once Japan had surrendered.

It was vital for Chiang, as the leader of China's internationally recognised government, to stop Mao from illegally occupying territory liberated from Japan by the USSR. On 12 August he ordered the CCP forces to remain where they were and not to accept the surrender of Japan's troops. As his own army was still in southern China, he was not in a position to enforce this without Soviet and US assistance.

Soviet and US policy in China 1945

Initially, both Soviet and US policies in China coincided. Both assumed that the KMT would eventually reassert control over China once Japan surrendered. Both also wanted Mao to accept this and ultimately join a coalition government with Chiang. Neither the USSR nor the USA yet grasped that the CCP would ultimately be much more successful than the KMT in gaining popular support for its cause in China.

The USSR

Mao and other CCP leaders were convinced that Stalin, as a Communist, would never tolerate a victory by the KMT as it would benefit the USA. Stalin's priority, as has been seen above, was the defence of Soviet interests in China, and he believed that only the KMT, as China's legal government, could deliver these concessions. On 14 August 1945 he therefore signed the Sino-Soviet Treaty of Friendship and Alliance in which Chiang acknowledged the independence of Outer Mongolia and the Soviet military occupation of Port Arthur and agreed to joint control with the USSR of the Changchun Railway (formerly the Chinese Eastern Railway). In return, Stalin agreed to recognise Chiang as China's leader, and not assist the CCP against the KMT. This agreement was a serious blow to Mao; it completely undermined his assumption that the USSR would prove to be a loyal ally in the struggle against the KMT. On the other hand, as events were to show, Stalin did not abandon Mao entirely.

The USA

Now that the war with Japan was over, the USA was concerned about the spread of Soviet influence in the Far East. It put pressure on both Chiang and Mao to negotiate a compromise agreement to stabilise China, to avoid a damaging civil war which might provide the USSR with further opportunities to strengthen its position in China. When Chiang asked for assistance in taking over the territory surrendered by the Japanese, the USA responded immediately by airlifting KMT troops to Nanjing, Shanghai, Beijing and later to Manchuria (see the map on page 134).

The Chongqing negotiations, August to October 1945

Under the joint pressure of the USA and USSR, the CCP's **Politburo** authorised Mao to meet Chiang in Chongqing on 26 August 1945. The negotiations turned out to be lengthy and complex. The main stumbling block continued to be whether the CCP should maintain an independent army. Chiang insisted that Mao should place all troops under the command of the government. Mao rejected this, but he was ready to reduce the number of his troops, provided the KMT did likewise. The two sides also failed to agree on a constitution for a new democratic China. By October, it was clear that the gap between the two sides was as wide as ever.

Even while the talks continued, clashes between the KMT and CCP escalated. In northern and north-eastern China, where the USA had succeeded in transporting large numbers of KMT troops, several major battles took place. At this stage, it seemed as if the better equipped KMT had the upper hand.

Soviet–US tension in Manchuria

Despite the Sino-Soviet Treaty, Mao received news in late August and early September that the Soviet forces of occupation in Manchuria were unofficially ready to help the CCP. After discussions between CCP commanders and a representative of Marshal Rodion Malinovsky, Soviet commander in the region, it was agreed on 14 September that CCP forces could occupy the countryside and the smaller towns of Manchuria as long as they did not enter the cities. Significantly, the Soviets also conceded that when the time came for Soviet troops to leave Manchuria, they would not automatically hand the region over to KMT forces, but would allow the two Chinese political factions to resolve the issue themselves. Since the CCP already controlled much of Manchuria, this was a formula for allowing the CCP to establish itself in the region.

In early October, Soviet troops began to halt the movement of KMT troops into Soviet-occupied areas of Manchuria, while advising the CCP to move another 300,000 troops into Manchuria. On 19 October Mao decided to launch a campaign to control the whole of the north-east of China. In response, Chiang informed US President Truman that the USSR's violations of the Sino-Soviet Treaty were a serious threat to peace in east Asia, and asked the USA to mediate. Meanwhile, Chiang accelerated the transfer of his troops to the north-east and seized control of the Shanhaiguan Pass, a major route into Manchuria from the rest of China. US naval ships also patrolled the sea off Port Arthur, which was under Soviet occupation. This appeared to the Soviets to be a deliberate provocation and there now seemed a danger not only of a full-scale civil war in

KEY TERM

Politburo The Political Bureau of the Central Committee of the Communist Party.

China, but also of a confrontation between the USA and the USSR. In the face of these dangers, the USSR reduced its assistance to the CCP and insisted that it withdraw from the areas bordering the Chinese–Changchun Railway. The CCP temporarily suspended its aim of seizing the whole of the north-east and instead concentrated on occupying the countryside and the smaller cities.

SOURCE B

? What information does Source B relay about the relations between the Red Army and the CCP?

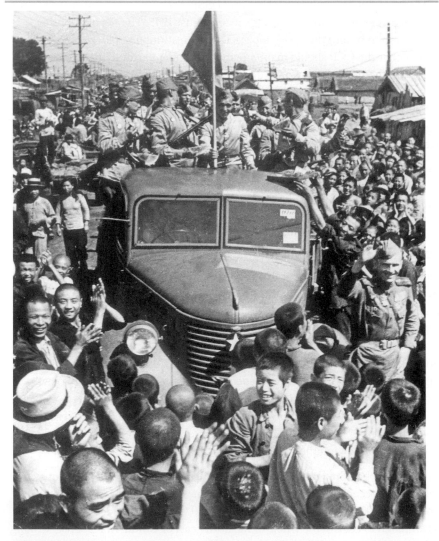

The population of Port Arthur in Manchuria celebrating Red Army soldiers marching in after the victory over the Japanese occupation troops in August 1945. The Red Army, comprising about 700,000 troops, rapidly occupied Manchuria.

The Marshall mission

The escalation of the Chinese Civil War in the autumn of 1945 confronted the USA with a major dilemma. It wanted to halt the expansion of Soviet influence in China, yet it did not want to risk military confrontation through direct intervention. President Truman announced in December 1945 that he would continue to grant assistance to the KMT, but categorically stated that he would not intervene militarily. He also sent General Marshall (see page 46) to mediate between Mao and Chiang. His aim was to establish a Nationalist-dominated government in which the CCP would be represented as a minority party. Marshall failed to negotiate a compromise, but his insistence on a truce in the spring of 1946, just at the time when the KMT were on the verge of victory in Manchuria, enabled the CCP, with the help of the Soviets, to regroup its forces. The Soviets also made available a vast amount of captured Japanese weapons to the CCP when they left Manchuria in May 1946, while also providing officer training.

Defeat of the Nationalists 1946–9

With the failure of the Marshall mission, the Civil War erupted again. In July 1946, Chiang launched a major assault, and by October had swept the CCP out of the Yangtze region. The KMT failed to capture Manchuria where the CCP had, with Soviet assistance, established a strong base, but in the spring of 1947 the Nationalists resumed the offensive and seized Yenan, the CCP's capital. By autumn, however, the war began to favour the CCP. From December 1947 to March 1948 Mao ordered a series of offensives in Manchuria and northern China, and by autumn the CCP had advanced into central China.

Soviet assistance to the CCP 1948–9

By spring 1948, Stalin had decided that the CCP had a genuine chance of success. He sent I.V. Kovalev, the Soviet commissar for transportation, to oversee the repair of bridges and railways to facilitate the advance of CCP forces and to act as his contact with Mao's headquarters. However, he still kept in contact with the KMT. He was worried that a possible victory by the Republican Party in the USA in the November 1948 elections would bring to power a president who might intervene militarily in China. Consequently, when Mao's forces moved into central and southern China, where the USA and Britain had strong economic interests, Stalin responded positively to a request from Chiang to mediate between the two sides. He informed Mao of his concern about possible US intervention, but Mao, confident of victory, firmly rejected any mediation by the USSR.

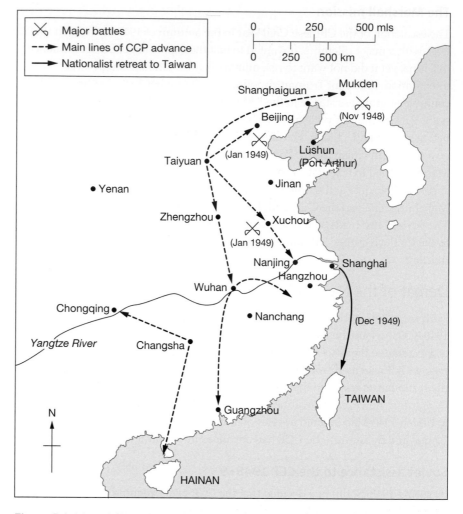

Figure 5.1 Map of China showing the major battles of the Chinese Civil War. What can be learned from this map about the strategic importance of north-east China?

US assistance to the KMT

In 1947, the USA reviewed its policy towards China. Many US diplomats, as well as the **Joint Chiefs of Staff** and the secretaries of defence and the navy, urged greater commitment and substantially more military aid to the KMT. Marshall, who was now secretary of state, and Truman rejected this on the grounds that such a policy would both prove prohibitively expensive and possibly lead to war with the USSR. The USA, therefore, limited its assistance to giving Chiang financial aid, which allowed him to purchase arms from the USA. This policy continued even when Chiang, defeated on the mainland, withdrew to Taiwan in December 1949.

SOURCE C

From 'Soviet Assessments of US Foreign Policy, 27 Sept. 1946', quoted in S.N. Goncharov, J.W. Lewis and Xue Litai, *Uncertain Partners*, Stanford University Press, 1993, pp. 229–30.

US policy in China is aimed at fully bringing that country under the control of American monopoly capital [the power of US money]. In pursuing this policy, the US Government goes so far as to interfere in China's internal affairs … how far the American government's policy towards China has already gone is seen in its current attempts to control the Chinese army. Recently the US government submitted to Congress a draft law on military aid to China under which the Chinese army would be totally reorganized, trained by American instructors, and supplied with American weaponry and ammunition …

How accurate an assessment does Source C give of US policy in China 1945–9?

Mao's triumph

CCP successes in 1949 removed any doubt about the outcome of the Chinese Civil War. In January 1949, the KMT forces north of the Yangtze River were defeated and Beijing was captured. CCP armies crossed the Yangtze in April, occupied Shanghai in late May and captured Guangzhou in October. On 1 October the People's Republic of China (PRC) was proclaimed in Beijing. Chiang Kai-shek fled to the island of Taiwan in December, with over 2 million others, where he maintained the Nationalist Government, claiming that it was still China's legal government. With US backing, his regime retained the Chinese seat on the UN Security Council until 1971, when it was taken by the PRC. The new PRC was, however, recognised by Britain, India, Pakistan and Sri Lanka in January 1950 on the grounds that it enjoyed the backing of the Chinese people. The PRC was only recognised by the US government in 1979.

SOURCE D

How does Source D seek to portray this momentous event?

Mao proclaiming the founding of the People's Republic of China from the top of Tiananmen Gate in Beijing, 1 October 1949.

The Sino-Soviet Pact

On 14 February 1950, Mao visited Moscow to celebrate Stalin's seventieth birthday and to negotiate the Sino-Soviet Pact. It was, as Mao said, 'a big political asset to deal with imperialist countries in the world'.

The pact (see Source A, page 127) committed both states to:

- co-operate in terms of defence in the case of attack by Japan or its ally (meaning the USA)
- conclude a peace treaty with Japan which would not be hostile to the interests of either state
- not conclude any hostile agreement with another power aimed at the other member of the pact
- consult closely on matters of mutual interest.

The pact was not signed without gains by Stalin. The USSR was to be supplied with valuable raw materials, tungsten, tin and antimony for ten years at very low prices. Stalin, in return, provided military support for the PRC, including the establishment of air-defence installations in coastal areas near Taiwan.

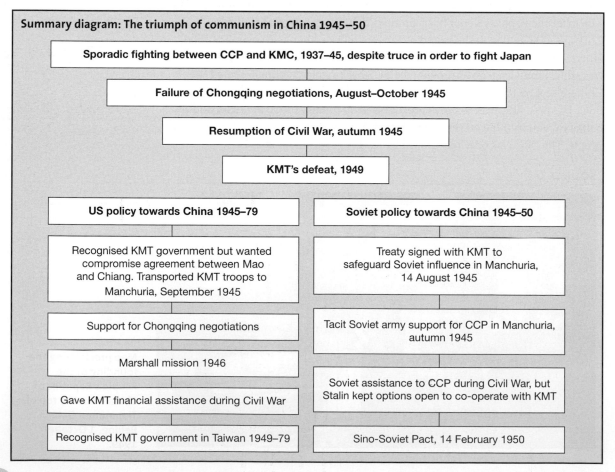

Summary diagram: The triumph of communism in China 1945–50

Sporadic fighting between CCP and KMC, 1937–45, despite truce in order to fight Japan

Failure of Chongqing negotiations, August–October 1945

Resumption of Civil War, autumn 1945

KMT's defeat, 1949

US policy towards China 1945–79

Recognised KMT government but wanted compromise agreement between Mao and Chiang. Transported KMT troops to Manchuria, September 1945

Support for Chongqing negotiations

Marshall mission 1946

Gave KMT financial assistance during Civil War

Recognised KMT government in Taiwan 1949–79

Soviet policy towards China 1945–50

Treaty signed with KMT to safeguard Soviet influence in Manchuria, 14 August 1945

Tacit Soviet army support for CCP in Manchuria, autumn 1945

Soviet assistance to CCP during Civil War, but Stalin kept options open to co-operate with KMT

Sino-Soviet Pact, 14 February 1950

The Korean War 1950–3

▶ *What caused the Korean War and how did it affect the Cold War?*

Japan had annexed Korea in 1910. During the Second World War, Koreans were conscripted into the Japanese military forces or worked as labourers. Britain, the USA and the KMT made the Cairo Declaration on 30 November 1943, stating that Korea should become free and independent. Stalin accepted this and in May 1945 agreed that once Japan was defeated there should be a **trusteeship** for Korea with supervision by the USA, the USSR, Nationalist China and Britain.

Korea 1945–9

Once the Red Army arrived in North Korea on 12 August 1945, the Soviets lost little time in installing local Communists in power in the areas under their control. Worried about Soviet intentions, the USA immediately proposed an initial division of the peninsula at the 38th parallel (see the map on page 143). In the north, Japanese troops would surrender to the Soviets and in the south to the USA. This was accepted by the USSR, but when US troops eventually arrived on 8 September, they discovered that a young Communist named **Kim Il Sung** had established a committee in the Korean capital of Seoul, announcing its intention to rule Korea as a Communist People's Republic. A rival anti-Communist group under **Syngman Rhee**, a fervent Korean nationalist who had spent most of his life in the USA, had also established a committee which claimed to be the Provisional Government for the whole nation. Kim and Rhee were each determined to unify Korea and exclude the other in the process.

The creation of North and South Korea: ROK and DPRK

Initially the USA rejected the claims of both groups, and in December 1945, at the Moscow Conference of Foreign Ministers, the USA and USSR went ahead with their plans for creating a trusteeship for Korea. A joint commission of Soviet and US officials was to advise the Koreans on creating a democratic government, but disagreements with the Soviets about which political parties should be allowed to participate led the USA, in November 1947, to refer the problem to the United Nations (UN).

Despite Soviet opposition, the UN General Assembly agreed in January 1948 to send a commission to supervise elections in both north and south Korea. When it arrived to start its work, its members were not allowed by the Soviets to enter the north. In the south, Syngman Rhee's Nationalist Party won an overwhelming majority and created the independent Republic of Korea (ROK), more commonly known as South Korea. In the north, under Soviet protection, Kim Il Sung created the Communist Democratic People's Republic of Korea (DPRK) in September 1948. Each state claimed to represent the entire nation and was hostile to the other. Each worked to unite Korea on its own terms.

> **KEY TERM**
>
> **Trusteeship** Responsibility on behalf of the UN for the government and welfare of a state handed over temporarily to other powers.

> **KEY FIGURES**
>
> **Kim Il Sung (1912–94)**
> Prime minister of North Korea 1948–72 and president 1972–94.
>
> **Syngman Rhee (1875–1960)**
> President of South Korea 1948–60.

Soviet withdrawal

Soviet troops were withdrawn from northern Korea by the end of 1948, but they left behind them much military hardware, which included not only their own equipment but also armaments seized from the defeated Japanese. These were regularly supplemented by further arms deliveries from the USSR. Indeed, according to one Soviet official, these were on a far more generous scale than those given to the CCP in China. In the winter of 1948–9, Stalin was still not entirely confident that the CCP would win the civil war in China. In the event of their defeat, North Korea would be a useful base for protecting Soviet interests in Manchuria.

US withdrawal

With the creation of the ROK, US policy makers were divided about whether the 45,000-strong US occupation army should remain or whether these troops should be withdrawn. Military planners thought that the troops could be more effectively deployed elsewhere and that Korea should not be included within the USA's **Asian defence perimeter**. Against this view was the argument that a removal of troops would weaken US prestige and result in the occupation of South Korea by a Soviet-armed North Korea. In the end, US Secretary of State Dean Acheson and President Truman were convinced that Korea was not worth the expense of a prolonged military occupation. Consequently, when the UN General Assembly passed a resolution calling on the USA and the USSR to withdraw their troops as soon as possible, the USA removed its troops by June 1949. In January 1950 Acheson, in a much publicised speech, defined the USA's Asian defence perimeter, which pointedly did not include Korea.

KEY TERM

Asian defence perimeter
A line through East and South-East Asia that the USA was willing to defend against any other nation.

? What is the importance of Source E in understanding why Mao and Stalin agreed to allow Kim's forces to invade South Korea?

SOURCE E

From US Secretary of State Dean Acheson's speech to the National Press Club in Washington, 12 January 1950, quoted in *Department of State Bulletin, XXII*, 23 January 1950, p. 116.

What is the situation in regard to the military security of the Pacific area, and what is our policy in regard to it?

In the first place, the defeat and the disarmament of Japan has placed upon the United States the necessity of assuming the military defense of Japan so long as that is required, both in the interest of our security and in the interests of the security of the entire Pacific area …

So far as the military security of other areas in the Pacific is concerned, it must be clear that no person can guarantee these areas against military attack. But it must also be clear that such a guarantee is hardly sensible or necessary within the realm of practical relationship. Should such an attack occur … the initial reliance must be on the people attacked to resist it and then upon the commitments of the entire civilized world under the Charter of the United Nations …

In April, however, the **US National Security Council** finished its assessment (NSC68) of the Communist threat after the loss of China and the distinction between the USA's vital and peripheral interests. It urged a massive increase in rearmament and containment of global communism.

Kim Il Sung seeks support from Stalin and Mao

Kim visited Moscow for talks with Stalin in April 1949. When he complained about southern violations of the frontier, Stalin urged him to 'strike the southerners in the teeth'. It is probable that Stalin envisaged that Kim would wage a guerrilla war rather than a full-scale invasion. In the summer of 1949, after US troops had left, Kim sent several well-equipped guerrilla groups across the frontier in an unsuccessful attempt to establish bases in the mountains in the south-east of the country. Kim decided that since the guerrilla operations had failed, the only way to unite Korea under his leadership was through a major invasion. To do this he needed the support of Stalin, whom he visited again in May 1950.

Stalin saw the potential of a Communist Korea as a useful economic and military ally, which would go some way to compensate the USSR's lack of influence in Japan, and after Acheson's speech was convinced that the USA would not assist South Korea. Nevertheless, he remained cautious and told Kim that the Soviets would not send troops to Korea, and that he should instead ask the PRC for assistance.

When Kim visited Beijing in April 1950, Mao also gave his consent again based on his assessment that the USA would not intervene. He was persuaded by Kim that Stalin was more enthusiastic than he was in reality.

The outbreak of the Korean War

Thanks to Soviet arms deliveries, North Korea possessed a decisive superiority over the South in terms of military strength. It launched its attack on South Korea on 25 June 1950, surprising both the South Koreans and the USA.

US/UN intervention

Initially, Kim's forces swept all before them, but the speed of the US reaction surprised the Soviets and their allies. Whereas guerrilla attacks might not have provoked a US response, a major military invasion was another matter. The US government reasoned that major aggression had to be countered or the lack of a US response would invite further invasions by Soviet puppet states elsewhere in the world, particularly in Europe (see page 72).

The USA immediately appealed to the UN Security Council to authorise a military force to intervene and end the fighting. As the USSR was boycotting the UN in protest at the exclusion of the PRC by the USA, the Soviet representative was unable to veto Resolution 83, which called on member nations to assist

KEY TERM

US National Security Council The main committee advising the US president on security issues. Created in 1947.

South Korea. The USA therefore was able to dominate the Security Council and act as the 'world policeman'. In response to this resolution, the USA, and its allies Britain and France, ordered immediate military intervention. This decision was made less risky by the fact that Stalin had secretly informed Truman that he would not see the intervention of US troops in Korea as a cause of war between the two superpowers. At the same time, Truman sent the US Navy's 7th Fleet to patrol the Taiwan Strait to prevent either the Nationalists in Taiwan or the PRC from conducting military operations against each other. The USA was determined to prevent the PRC from capturing Taiwan since aircraft based there could threaten Japan and the Philippines, both of which were in the USA's sphere of interest.

The UN counter-attack

By early August, Kim's forces had conquered 90 per cent of South Korea (see the map on page 143) and the US-led UN military task force was confined to a small area around Pusan. Supplied with equipment and reserves based in Japan, US troops were able to break out of Pusan at the end of the month. A dramatic counter-attack was launched when General Douglas MacArthur, supreme commander of allied powers, who had been appointed commander of the UN task force, landed troops at Inchon on 9 September, far behind North Korean lines. On 1 October, UN forces crossed the 38th parallel, and nearly three weeks later Pyongyang, the North Korean capital, was captured as US-led UN forces advanced to Korea's border with the PRC's province of Manchuria.

The PRC's entry into the war

In response to this military crisis, Kim sent an urgent request to Stalin on 29 September 1950 for Soviet military assistance. Stalin was not ready to risk war with the USA, but he urged Mao to intervene, warning him that failure to do so would have grave consequences not just for the PRC's north-east provinces, but for all Communist nations. The presence of the 7th Fleet in the Straits of Taiwan, the granting of military aid to the Philippines and French Indo-China, as well as the US-led advance on the Manchuria border were seen by Mao to be a direct military threat to China. Even so, he was not ready to intervene until Stalin agreed to provide further military support and air defences for both the main PRC cities and its troops in Korea.

On 18 October military intervention began. Within two weeks, PRC troops had crossed the Yalu River border and attacked UN forces, whose supply lines were over-extended. By the end of the year, UN troops had been driven back across the 38th parallel. Soviet fighter planes, which were painted in PRC colours and flown by Soviet pilots in PRC uniform, defended the Yalu crossings and gave some limited support to the Chinese army.

SOURCE F

Chinese volunteer troops near the River Yalu, October 1950. Chinese intervention marked a major escalation of the war.

The threat of nuclear war

At a press conference on 30 November, Truman hinted that the USA might use atomic bombs against PRC troops and cities, but was dissuaded from doing so by his allies, particularly British Prime Minister Clement Attlee, who feared that this might lead to the activation of the Sino-Soviet Pact and a much larger conflict, as the Soviets now possessed atomic weapons as well. Mao was undeterred by the threat and argued that atomic bombs would have relatively little impact on the PRC as it had practically unlimited manpower and could continue to field large armies!

India's ceasefire proposal

On 5 December 1950, thirteen non-Western states, headed by India, handed a peace proposal to the PRC and the UN. The proposal recommended that the PRC halt its advance at the 38th parallel, that a ceasefire should be declared and that a conference should be called to find a solution for the problem of Korea. Nine days later, the UN General Assembly approved the proposal and created a group to seek a basis on which a viable ceasefire could be arranged.

> What is the implication of Source F for the war in Korea?

India's proposal presented the USA with a dilemma. On the one hand, supporting it would lose South Korean support as well as risk the fury of the Republican-dominated Congress and much of the US press, both of which urged a tough line towards Communist states (see page 74). On the other hand, rejecting it would lead to the loss of support for the USA in the UN. In the end, the USA backed the proposal largely in the hope that the PRC would reject it. In this they were proved right, as Mao was determined to continue the war, aiming for a crushing victory over what he termed 'American imperialism'. Consequently, after PRC military successes in December 1950, he rejected the ceasefire proposal and ordered another offensive, which resulted in the capture of Seoul on 4 January 1951.

Armistice negotiations

By July 1951, fighting had stabilised along the 38th parallel. During the next two years, tortuous negotiations were conducted between the two sides, each of which constantly sought to achieve an advantage over the other. The PRC leadership understood that it lacked the resources to defeat the US-led UN force. The PRC, however, could claim that the dramatic rout of the USA in North Korea in December 1950 represented a major victory and that its armies commanded a strong position on the battlefield. Mao agreed to negotiations for a truce in the hope that this might eventually lead to the withdrawal of UN troops from Korea. He explained this strategy as 'preparing for a long war while striving to end the war through peace negotiations'. By the end of May 1951 the USA also believed that its position on the battlefield was secure enough to negotiate an end to the war, but, like Mao, the USA hoped to make further military gains which would strengthen its position at the negotiating table.

On 27 July 1953, both sides finally agreed an armistice after the newly elected US President Eisenhower (see page 84) threatened the use of nuclear weapons. This recognised the 38th parallel as a temporary dividing line between North Korea and South Korea. This division has remained the frontier ever since.

The consequences of the Korean War

The Korean War was a turning point in the Cold War and it had important consequences for the PRC, the USA, the USSR and Western Europe.

Consequences for the PRC

Mao used the Korean War to foment enthusiasm for revolutionary change within the PRC and to mobilise public opinion by stirring up hatred for what he termed 'American arrogance'. A national campaign aimed at suppressing 'reactionaries and reactionary activities' was unleashed across the PRC to remove any opponents of the government. By the time the Korean War ended, society and politics had been radically changed in the PRC. Agricultural land,

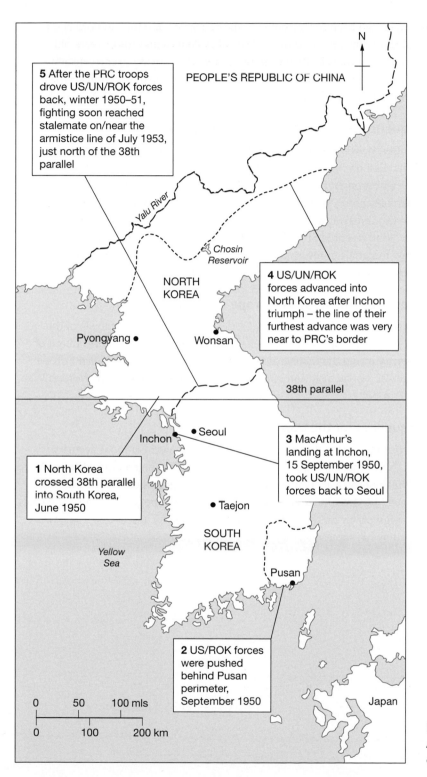

5 After the PRC troops drove US/UN/ROK forces back, winter 1950–51, fighting soon reached stalemate on/near the armistice line of July 1953, just north of the 38th parallel

PEOPLE'S REPUBLIC OF CHINA

N

Yalu River

Chosin Reservoir

NORTH KOREA

4 US/UN/ROK forces advanced into North Korea after Inchon triumph – the line of their furthest advance was very near to PRC's border

Pyongyang ●

Wonsan ●

38th parallel

● Seoul

Inchon

3 MacArthur's landing at Inchon, 15 September 1950, took US/UN/ROK forces back to Seoul

1 North Korea crossed 38th parallel into South Korea, June 1950

● Taejon

SOUTH KOREA

Yellow Sea

Pusan

2 US/ROK forces were pushed behind Pusan perimeter, September 1950

Japan

0   50   100 mls

0   100   200 km

Figure 5.2 Map of the Korean War. According to this map, what was the outcome of the Korean War?

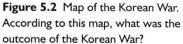

143

for example, had been redistributed to the peasantry and the landlord class eliminated, ending an economic and social system thousands of years old. PRC victories in Korea in 1950 were promoted as removing over a century of humiliating defeats at the hands of European and Japanese armies, which inevitably strengthened Mao's government.

Consequences for the USSR: Sino-Soviet relations

Throughout the war, Mao consulted with Stalin on all the key decisions and was dependent on the USSR for much of the PRC's military supplies. On one level, the war brought the USSR and China closer together, but, as the historian Chen Jian observes: 'on another level, the Chinese experience during the Korean War also ground away at some of the cement that kept the Sino-Soviet alliance together'. Mao resented Stalin's opportunism, particularly when he demanded cheap raw materials in return for signing the Sino-Soviet Pact, and made China pay excessive sums for military supplies.

Consequences for Western Europe

In the long term, the Korean War did serious damage to the interests of the Soviet Union in Europe. It strengthened NATO and led to the rearmament of West Germany and the first steps towards the integration of Western Europe (see page 72). As the historian Norman Stone concisely stated, 'the Korean War created Europe'.

Consequences for the USA

The Korean War strengthened the arguments of the US National Security Council (NSC) that communism represented a co-ordinated global threat. After the outbreak of the war, Truman accepted the NSC's proposals for a massive rearmament programme and tripled the US military budget. It became the basis of US foreign policy for the rest of Truman's presidency and in essentials was continued by his successors for the next twenty years.

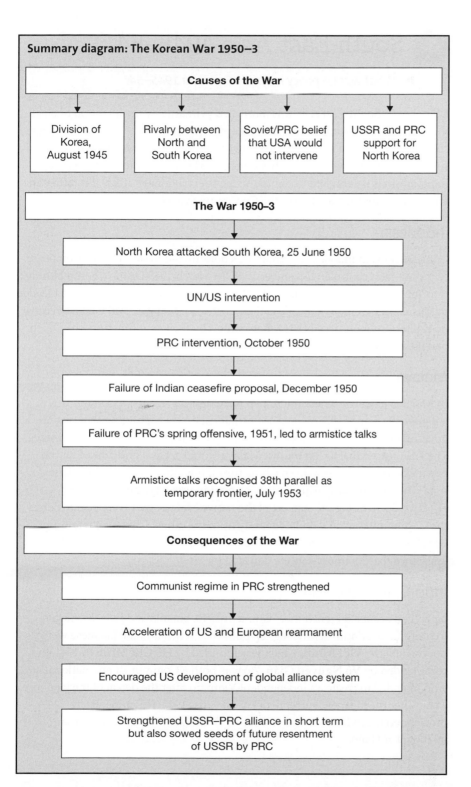

Summary diagram: The Korean War 1950–3

Causes of the War

- Division of Korea, August 1945
- Rivalry between North and South Korea
- Soviet/PRC belief that USA would not intervene
- USSR and PRC support for North Korea

The War 1950–3

North Korea attacked South Korea, 25 June 1950

↓

UN/US intervention

↓

PRC intervention, October 1950

↓

Failure of Indian ceasefire proposal, December 1950

↓

Failure of PRC's spring offensive, 1951, led to armistice talks

↓

Armistice talks recognised 38th parallel as temporary frontier, July 1953

Consequences of the War

↓

Communist regime in PRC strengthened

↓

Acceleration of US and European rearmament

↓

Encouraged US development of global alliance system

↓

Strengthened USSR–PRC alliance in short term but also sowed seeds of future resentment of USSR by PRC

4 South-East Asia 1945–54

▶ *What was US policy in South-East Asia 1945–54?*

US policy in South-East Asia was motivated primarily by the intention to block the spread of communism. Initially, it feared that attempts by the old European colonial powers to re-establish their power would merely encourage this spread. As a statement by the US Security Council in March 1949 put it: '19th century imperialism is no antidote to communism in revolutionary areas. It is rather an ideal culture for the breeding of the Communist virus.'

Indonesia

Consequently, in Indonesia, Truman was determined to stop Dutch attempts to reimpose their control in December 1948. In March 1949 Dean Acheson bluntly informed the Dutch that if they did not hand over power to the nationalist leader Sukarno, they would not only lose their portion of Marshall Aid but also receive no military support from NATO. Confronted by such an ultimatum, the Dutch had little alternative but to recognise Indonesian independence.

Malaya

In Malaya, however, where the British were fighting against a Communist-led guerrilla war, the USA could see no alternative to supporting the colonial government provided that it eventually prepared the country for independence. The USA feared that a Communist Malaya would act as a bridgehead for the expansion of communism from China throughout the whole of South-East Asia. The British counter-insurgency campaign proved to be remarkably effective. By winning the support of the native Malays, they were able to defeat the Communists, who recruited mainly from the ethnic Chinese community in Malaya. In 1957 Malaya became independent, and with continued British assistance the Communists were defeated by 1960.

Indo-China 1945–54

Japan had occupied French Indo-China in 1940, but allowed French officials to continue to administer the region. Both the French and the Japanese were opposed by the **Việt Minh**, which was founded by **Hồ Chí Minh** in 1941 and commanded by **Võ Nguyên Giáp**. Hồ was both a Communist and nationalist who intended to create an independent Vietnam after the defeat of the Japanese. Thus, after the Japanese surrender on 29 August 1945, Hồ immediately proclaimed the independent, Communist Democratic Republic of Vietnam, with its capital at Hanoi.

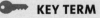

KEY FIGURES

Hồ Chí Minh (1890–1969)

Worked in the USA, Britain and France and studied Marxism in the USSR. He created the Việt Minh in 1941 and led the independence movement in Vietnam 1945–54. He was president of North Vietnam 1954–65.

Võ Nguyên Giáp (1911–2013)

Former professor of history. Military leader of the Việt Minh. He eventually unified Vietnam as a Communist state in 1975.

KEY TERM

Việt Minh 'League for the Independence of Vietnam', created in 1941.

The new republic met with opposition from both Britain and Nationalist China. In August 1945, British troops occupied southern Vietnam while the Chinese Nationalists took control of the north. Britain immediately released and rearmed French troops who had been interned by Japan, and these, reinforced by the arrival of further French military units, clashed with the Việt Minh. Hồ Chí Minh eventually compromised with the French government, agreeing that Vietnam should become a self-governing state within French Indo-China and therefore only semi-independent.

The Indo-Chinese war of 1946–54

This agreement did not last, as the French government was still determined to control Vietnam while Hồ wanted only the loosest of associations with France. Open conflict erupted in November 1946 when France bombarded Việt Minh forces in the port of Haiphong. Until 1949 France had little difficulty in confining the revolt to mountainous areas. CCP guerrillas from China occasionally assisted the Việt Minh, but it was only after his victory in 1949 that Mao was in a position to offer significant military assistance. Mao saw Hồ's war against France as part of the overall anti-imperialist struggle which he was waging against the USA, Britain and France.

France on the defensive 1950–4

In April 1950, Mao sent one of his most experienced generals, Chen Geng, to Vietnam. He organised a military campaign along the Vietnamese–PRC border where direct assistance to the Việt Minh could be provided. By November, France had lost control of the border territories, and equipment and supplies from China were able to flow unchecked into Vietnam. In December 1952, Việt Minh troops were strong enough to seize parts of north-western Vietnam. To counter this threat to Laos, France sent more reinforcements to Indo-China and appointed a new commander, General Henri Navarre. The French also received an increasing amount of US military and financial assistance.

Điện Biên Phủ

Navarre planned to eliminate the Việt Minh guerrillas in southern Vietnam and then launch a campaign to drive the Việt Minh from their stronghold in the Red River Delta in the north. The Việt Minh responded by advancing across north-western Vietnam into Laos. From there, with support of the **Pathet Lao**, they planned to move southwards into Cambodia and onwards to Saigon. To block this advance, France decided to fortify the strategically important village of Điện Biên Phủ. A large force of French paratroopers was dropped and airstrips were constructed in November 1953. The Việt Minh, however, managed to surround French positions and, with anti-aircraft guns supplied by the PRC, prevented any further supplies from reaching Điện Biên Phủ. By late April, French troops were confined to a small area of less than two square kilometres, and surrendered on 7 May 1954.

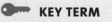 **KEY TERM**

Pathet Lao Independence movement in Laos, supported by the Việt Minh.

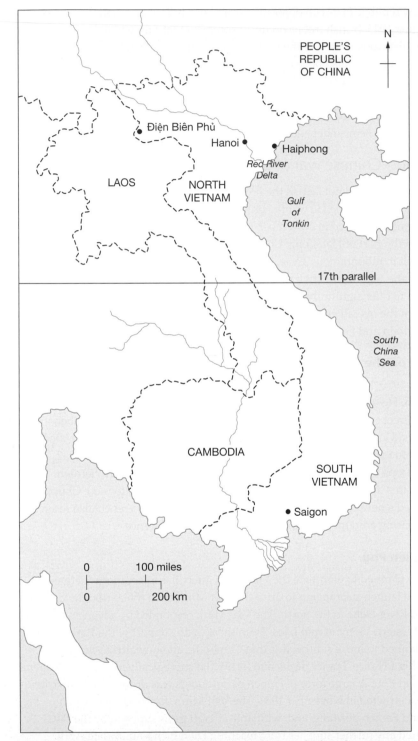

Figure 5.3 Map of Indo-China. What light does this map shed on the strategic problems facing the French in the Indo-Chinese war?

The USA and the Indo-Chinese War

The USA faced a quandary in Vietnam: should it support anti-colonialism or anti-communism? One way out of this dilemma was to find a non-Communist rival to Hồ who would be able to appeal to the people's nationalism and thus unite them against communism by setting up a strong, patriotic and capitalist government. For this to work, France would have to be pressured into granting a greater degree of independence to Vietnam while still continuing the war against the Việt Minh. In June 1949, the USA and France persuaded Bảo Đại, who from 1925 to 1945 had been the Emperor of Vietnam – controlled first by France and then ultimately by Japan – to become head of state of a semi-independent Vietnam which would still be part of France's empire.

Bảo Đại rapidly proved to be a failure. He had no programme, no ideology and little local support from the Vietnamese people; France gave him no real power. The USA found that as a consequence of its efforts to stop communism from spreading across South-East Asia, it was now supporting France in a colonial war that effectively prevented an oppressed nationality from gaining independence.

SOURCE G

What information about the war in Vietnam is conveyed by Source G?

Defeated French troops at Điện Biên Phủ. A few managed to escape to Laos. Some 11,721 French and South Vietnamese troops were captured. Of these, only about 3300 were repatriated back to France in September 1954.

In April 1954, faced with the imminent fall of Điện Biên Phủ, US Secretary of State John Foster Dulles recommended air strikes on Việt Minh positions from US aircraft flown from carriers in the South China Sea. If that failed to halt the Việt Minh, he contemplated the use of tactical nuclear weapons and the landing of ground forces. These ideas were strongly opposed by Britain and the US military chiefs of staff and therefore abandoned. The US chiefs of staff advised that this should only be considered if Vietnam was invaded by the PRC. The British government feared that US intervention would provoke full-scale PRC military intervention in Vietnam.

The Geneva Conference 1954

As early as September 1953, the Soviets suggested calling an international conference to solve the Korean and Indo-Chinese problems. Both the PRC and the USSR were ready to compromise to end the Indo-Chinese War. Both wished to avoid an escalation of the conflict which US military involvement would bring. Both too wanted to focus on domestic policies. The USSR also hoped, by being conciliatory to France, that it could weaken its support for German rearmament and the EDC (see page 89).

In the autumn of 1953, however, France agreed in principle to the conference but still optimistically hoped that an eventual victory at Điện Biên Phủ would strengthen its negotiating position. US Secretary of State John Dulles only reluctantly gave his assent as he feared that any compromise over Indo-China would result in Communist gains in South-East Asia. He was also quick to stress that the attendance of the PRC at the conference did not imply its recognition by the USA. At a press conference in early April, President Eisenhower used the term **domino principle** to illustrate his fears that if one country (in this case Indo-China) went Communist, its neighbours would follow.

Compromise reached

The Geneva Conference started on 26 April 1954. The decisive defeat at Điện Biên Phủ on 6 May finally persuaded France to reject outright US advice to continue fighting. The Việt Minh was also ready to compromise, having suffered heavy casualties at the battle for Điện Biên Phủ from which it needed time to recover. The way to a compromise was now open.

At the end of June, Britain, France, the USSR and the PRC agreed that an independent Laos and Cambodia should be established and Vietnam partitioned at the 17th parallel. The US government did not oppose this, but refused

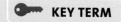
KEY TERM

Domino principle
The belief that the fall of one state to communism would result in a chain reaction, leading to the fall of other neighbouring states.

formally to sign the final Geneva Accords. It instead issued a declaration taking note of what had been decided and an undertaking not to undermine the settlement. The PRC and the USSR persuaded Hồ to agree and to aim to unify Vietnam peacefully through future elections. Zhou Enlai, the premier of the PRC, stressed emphatically that 'It is possible to unite Vietnam through elections when [the] time is ripe' and warned Hồ that force would only drive them to the US side.

The Geneva Accords

On 21 July, the agreements were signed:

- Laos and Cambodia were made independent.
- Vietnam was divided along the 17th parallel.
- French forces would withdraw from the north of this line and Việt Minh forces from the south.
- In two years' time there would be democratic elections for a united Vietnam.
- Neither North nor South Vietnam were to conclude military alliances with foreign powers, nor to allow foreign military bases on their territory.

SOURCE H

From the reminiscences of General Giap (military commander of the Việt Minh) in 1964, quoted in R.J. McMahon, editor, *Major Problems in the History of Vietnam*, D.C. Heath, 1990, pp. 122–3.

The historic Điện Biên Phủ campaign and in general the Winter 1953–Spring 1954 campaign were the greatest victories ever won by our army and people up to the present time. These great victories marked a giant progress, a momentous change in the education of the Resistance War for National Salvation put up by our people against the aggressive French imperialists propped up by U.S. interventionists. The great Điện Biên Phủ victory and the Winter–Spring victories as a whole had a far reaching influence in the world.

While the bellicose [warlike] imperialists were confused and discouraged, the news of the victories won by our army and people on the battlefronts throughout the country, especially the Điện Biên Phủ victory, have greatly inspired the progressive people the world over ... Điện Biên Phủ was also a great victory of the forces of peace in the world. Without this victory, certainly the Geneva Conference would not be successful and peace would not be reestablished in Indochina.

How reliable is the assessment in Source H of the significance of Điện Biên Phủ? **?**

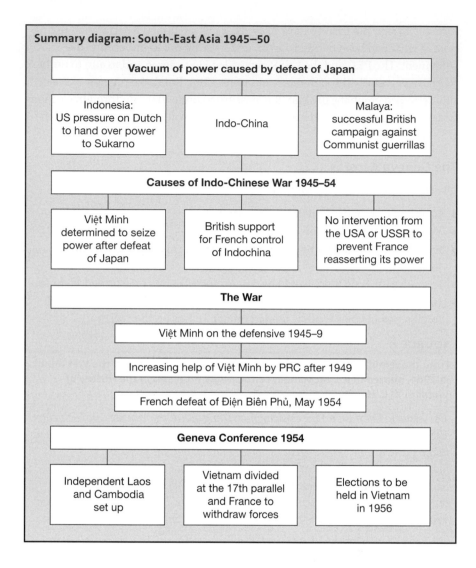

Summary diagram: South-East Asia 1945–50

Vacuum of power caused by defeat of Japan

| Indonesia: US pressure on Dutch to hand over power to Sukarno | Indo-China | Malaya: successful British campaign against Communist guerrillas |

Causes of Indo-Chinese War 1945–54

| Việt Minh determined to seize power after defeat of Japan | British support for French control of Indochina | No intervention from the USA or USSR to prevent France reasserting its power |

The War

Việt Minh on the defensive 1945–9

Increasing help of Việt Minh by PRC after 1949

French defeat of Điện Biên Phủ, May 1954

Geneva Conference 1954

| Independent Laos and Cambodia set up | Vietnam divided at the 17th parallel and France to withdraw forces | Elections to be held in Vietnam in 1956 |

Chapter summary

In August 1945, the Soviets invaded Manchuria and northern Korea while US troops occupied Japan. The USA was unwilling to share the occupation of Japan with any other power, and over the next five years ensured that Japan recovered economically to become an important part of US global defence against communism.

The CCP's victory in 1949 altered the balance of power in Asia and led to PRC support for Communist movements in Korea and Indo-China. Despite the withdrawal of both Soviet and US troops in 1949, Korea remained partitioned between the Communist North and the anti-Communist nationalist South. In June 1950 North Korean troops, encouraged by Stalin, invaded the South. Their repulse led to the intervention of the PRC and continuation of the war until 1953. The war had a profound impact on Western Europe, paving the way for West German rearmament and eventual economic integration. The PRC sent equipment and advisors to Indo-China, which helped to defeat France in 1954. At the Geneva Conference in 1954, Vietnam was partitioned into two states, while Cambodia and Laos gained independence. Elections for a united Vietnam were to be held in 1956. The USA did not sign the accords.

Refresher questions

Use these questions to remind yourself of the key material covered in this chapter.

1. What was US policy in Japan 1945–51?

2. What was the US attitude to the attempts by the European colonial powers to re-establish their power in South-East Asia?

3. Why were the USA and USSR unable to achieve a peaceful settlement in China 1945–6?

4. To what extent did Stalin support Mao?

5. Why was the Chinese Communist Party able to win the Civil War?

6. What was the significance of the Sino-Soviet Pact, 14 February 1950?

7. Why were there two Korean states by 1949?

8. To what extent did both Mao and Stalin support Kim's plans to invade South Korea?

9. Why could the Korean War not be ended until July 1953?

10. What was the impact of the Korean War on Europe?

11. To what extent did the Communist triumph in China impact on Indo-China?

12. To what extent did the Việt Minh achieve victory in the Indo-Chinese war of 1946–54?

13. Why was it possible to achieve a compromise at the Geneva Conference?

14. What was the attitude of the USA to the Geneva Conference of 1954?

15. Why was Diệm unable to consolidate his government in South Vietnam from 1960 to 1963?

Question practice

ESSAY QUESTIONS

1 'Successful US military intervention in Korea stabilised the situation in East and South-East Asia.' Explain why you agree or disagree with this view.

2 To what extent did the Communist victory in China in 1949 affect international relations from 1950 to 1955?

3 How successful were US policies in containing communism in South-East Asia in 1945–63?

SOURCE ANALYSIS QUESTIONS

1 With reference to Sources A (page 127) and E (page 138), and your understanding of the historical context, which of these two sources is more valuable in explaining the causes of the Korean War?

2 With reference to Sources A (page 127), E (page 138) and H (page 151), and your understanding of the historical context, assess the value of these sources to a historian studying the Cold War in Asia 1945–63.

CHAPTER 6

The Cold War and the era of *détente*

One of the most important consequences of the Cuban Missile Crisis was the conviction in both Moscow and Washington that there would be no winners in an all-out nuclear war. Both sides were therefore ready to pursue a policy of *détente* in Europe, especially as the USA was involved in the Vietnam War and the USSR was facing a major threat from China. These themes are studied in this chapter under the following headings:

★ The distracted superpowers 1963–72

★ The road to *détente*

★ *Ostpolitik*

★ The Helsinki Accords

Key dates

1963	Aug. 5	Test Ban Treaty	1970	Dec. 7	Warsaw Treaty
1964	Oct. 15	Fall of Khrushchev	1971	Sept. 3	Four-Power Treaty on Berlin
1965	Feb. 7	US bombing of North Vietnam began	1972	May	SALT I
1968	Aug. 21–27	Invasion of Czechoslovakia		Dec. 21	Basic Treaty between FRG and GDR
	July	Non-proliferation Treaty	1973	Jan.	Paris Peace Accords
1969	Sept. 28	Brandt became chancellor of FRG	1974	July	SALT II negotiations
1970	Aug. 12	USSR–FRG Moscow Treaty	1975	Aug. 1	Helsinki Final Act

1 The distracted superpowers 1963–72

▶ *What problems did the USSR face with China and the USA in Vietnam?*

After the Cuban Missile Crisis, the nature of the Cold War in Europe changed. A new period of stability emerged, which has sometimes been called 'the long peace'. Both the two superpowers and the Western European states sought *détente* in Europe, although they all interpreted the meaning of *détente* differently. The Americans were heavily involved in the Vietnam War, and wanted *détente* to stabilise Europe and restrain the USSR, while the USSR was also facing a growing challenge from the People's Republic of China (PRC). Consequently, it hoped that *détente* would lead Washington and its allies permanently to accept the post-war division of Europe, and to agree to something approaching nuclear parity between the USA and USSR. For the French, *détente* was a way of undermining the influence of both superpowers in Europe so that the individual European states could regain their freedom, while for the West Germans it was an essential precondition for remaining in contact with, and helping, their fellow citizens in the GDR. In London, it was welcomed by the British government, which faced mounting economic problems, as a way to terminate the arms race and save money.

Détente in Europe did not, of course, mean that the Cold War was over. Both the USSR and PRC assisted the North Vietnamese, while the USSR constructed a large navy to enable it to project its power globally. In 1976, for instance, it was able to transport some 12,000 Cuban troops along with tanks and missiles to aid the Communist Popular Movement for the liberation of Angola (see page 178).

The USSR and China

The Sino-Soviet split was caused by a mixture of both domestic and international factors, as well as by the simmering resentment in China of the long history of Russian imperialism which had encroached on its northern frontiers during the nineteenth and early twentieth centuries. Fundamentally, Mao perceived Khrushchev to be an appeaser of NATO and the USA and, above all, as a betrayer of the legacy of Stalin and Lenin. In return, the Soviet leadership was convinced that, under Mao, the PRC intended to displace the USSR as the leading Communist state.

After 1958 differences between the PRC and the USSR multiplied:

- Soviet economic advisors and technicians, who had arrived in 1956 to help the PRC industrialise, advised Mao that the economic plan, the **'Great Leap Forward'**, was both impractical and harmful to the Chinese economy. In July 1960 these experts were recalled to the USSR.
- Mao rejected plans for sharing military bases and operating joint naval units in the Pacific, which, he believed, were in reality 'imperialist' plans to subordinate the PRC's armed forces to the USSR.
- When in August 1958, the PRC began an intense bombardment of the Nationalist-controlled **Quemoy Islands** off Taiwan in order to rally the Chinese people behind the 'Great Leap Forward', Khrushchev expressed alarm that this might lead to war with the USA.
- In June 1959, Khrushchev refused to assist the PRC any further with nuclear technology on the grounds that the USA and USSR were discussing a possible ban on nuclear weapons at Geneva (see page 110).

KEY TERMS

'Great Leap Forward'
Mao's plan that aimed dramatically to increase both industrial and agricultural production. The population was to be mobilised to build dams and small-scale smelting works. By 1962 this plan had caused the deaths of at least 40 million people.

Quemoy Islands
KMT-controlled islands off Formosa.

With Khrushchev's fall from power in October 1964 (see page 166), there was initially some hope that better relations could be restored. In November a mission led by Premier Zhou Enlai was sent to the USSR to improve Sino-Soviet relations, but it was unsuccessful, and allegedly the Soviet Defence Minister Marshall Rodion Malinowski actually urged Zhou Enlai to overthrow Mao.

In August 1966 Mao launched the **Cultural Revolution**, which was meant to inspire the Chinese to recapture the revolutionary enthusiasm of 1949 and to hunt down intellectuals and Chinese Communist Party officials allegedly guilty of 'revisionist' attitudes. Mao linked the fight against the **revisionists** within China with the propaganda campaign against the 'revisionist' USSR, which was now regarded as the PRC's primary foe.

The Sino-Soviet border conflict 1969

In the nineteenth century, the Russian Empire had forced the Chinese Empire to negotiate treaties which ceded several regions to Russia. After 1917 the USSR repudiated these treaties but never returned the territory. The PRC deeply resented this and further damaged relations between the two powers.

A major territorial dispute occurred in 1969, centred on the 52,000 square kilometres of Soviet-controlled land between the Xinjiang Uighur autonomous region in western China and the Soviet-controlled region of Tajikistan. Each side massed hundreds of thousands of troops along the disputed border areas. In March 1969, two bloody conflicts erupted on Zhenbao Island, a small island on the Ussuri River, which marked the border between the PRC and the USSR. The island lay to the PRC side of the river, but was occupied by the Soviets. On the night of 1–2 March, a PRC force overwhelmed the Soviet garrison but

SOURCE A

What information does Source A convey about Sino-Soviet relations at the time?

PRC soldiers patrolling on Zhenbao Island, March 1969.

was eventually driven off the island after a massive Soviet counter-attack. On 13 August another major clash occurred in Xinjiang Province, where a PRC brigade of over 1000 men was annihilated by Soviet troops. The PRC retaliated by declaring a general mobilisation along the border with the USSR and Mongolia.

Vietnam 1954–63

The USA was determined to avoid elections for a united Vietnamese parliament, which, it was agreed on at the Geneva Conference in 1954, were to be held in 1956 (see page 151), in case they resulted in the creation of a Communist Vietnam. Instead, the USA hoped to strengthen an independent south Vietnam. In an attempt to stop the spread of communism to South-East Asia, the USA also established the Southeast Asian Treaty Organisation (SEATO), as a regional defence system, in September 1954. Its members were: the USA, Britain, France, Australia, New Zealand, Thailand, the Philippines and Pakistan. In practice, the alliance proved ineffective as its members were not legally obliged to assist each other militarily to prevent the spread of communism.

In June 1954, with US support, the head of state, Bảo Đại (see page 149), appointed **Ngô Đình Diệm** as prime minister of South Vietnam, largely on the strength of his virulent anti-communism. Diệm quickly removed Bảo Đại and temporarily managed to consolidate his own position, but then rapidly lost support. He alienated key groups, particularly the majority Buddhists, by favouring Roman Catholics, who comprised ten per cent of the population. Catholics were given preferential treatment in the allocation of posts in the army and the public service. He also did not carry out the promised programme of land reform which would have taken land away from the large landowners and redistributed it to the peasantry.

Exploiting Diệm's growing unpopularity in the spring of 1959, North Vietnam announced the resumption of the armed struggle against the South Vietnamese government and smuggled arms southwards along the newly constructed **Hồ Chí Minh Trail**. In September 1960, the Việt Cộng, the Communist movement in South Vietnam, founded the National Front for the Liberation of Vietnam (NFL), which aimed to rally all those opposed to Diệm's regime by promising reform and the creation of a united, independent Vietnam.

Diệm's fall

By the autumn of 1961, Diệm's government was in danger of collapse. The Việt Cộng had seized control of a large number of villages. In response to Diệm's demands for immediate assistance, President Kennedy sent a small force of 8000 US troops to help conduct military operations against the Việt Cộng, but this was not enough to stabilise Diệm's regime. On May 1963, Diệm's troops fired into a crowd of people celebrating the sacred occasion of Buddha's birthday because they had violated the law banning the flying of non-governmental flags.

This provoked a wave of anger across the country which resulted in protest marches and even **self-immolations** by Buddhist monks. Worried by Diệm's unpopularity and by rumours that he was considering negotiations with North Vietnam, Kennedy backed a coup mounted by the South Vietnamese army in November 1963 to remove Diệm. Both Diệm and his brother were murdered. General Nguyên Khánh was then installed as the new leader.

The war escalates

Yet Khánh, too, failed to defeat the Việt Cộng, and by 1964 the war in South Vietnam was rapidly escalating. On 2 August North Vietnamese patrol boats attacked the US destroyer, the *Maddox,* in the Gulf of Tonkin. The *Maddox* retaliated by damaging two boats and sinking a third. On 7 August, the US Congress, in an overwhelming vote, gave the president the authority 'to take all necessary measures' to defend US forces in South-East Asia (see Source B below).

In January 1965 the USA began a sustained bombing campaign against North Vietnam, Operation Rolling Thunder, and in 1966 there were over 500,000 US soldiers in South Vietnam. Despite their enormous destructive capability, US tactics were to prove ineffective against the Việt Cộng, who were supplied with weapons and provisions transported down the Hồ Chí Minh Trail. Eventually, supplies carried along this route were able to support some 170,000 Việt Cộng guerrillas. The paddy fields and dense jungles formed an ideal terrain for guerrilla fighting. The Việt Cộng were able to ambush US and South Vietnamese forces and then disappear into the safety of the jungle.

SOURCE B

From the Gulf of Tonkin Resolution, 7 August 1964, quoted in *US Department of State Bulletin* 51, 1313 (24 August 1964), p. 268.

Whereas units of the Communist regime in Vietnam, in violation of the principles of the charter of the United Nations and on international law, have deliberately and repeatedly attacked United States naval vessels lawfully present in international waters, and have thereby created a serious threat to internationals peace …

Whereas the United States is assisting the peoples of southeast Asia to protect their freedom and has no territorial, military or political ambition in that area, but desires only that these peoples should be left in peace to work out their destinies in their own way …

Now be it Resolved by the Senate and House of Representatives in Congress assembled that the Congress approves and supports the determination of the President, as Commander-in-Chief, to take all necessary measures to repel any armed attack against the forces of the United States and to prevent any further aggression.

KEY TERM

Self-immolation Burning oneself alive as a sacrifice and act of protest.

What information is conveyed in Source B about the reasons for the US involvement in the war in Vietnam?

The Sino-Soviet split and North Vietnam

North Vietnam was given substantial aid by the PRC, but it was agreed that unless US troops invaded the North, the PRC would not become directly involved in the fighting. Altogether, over 320,000 PRC troops served in North Vietnam and were engaged in the construction, maintenance and defence of transport links and important strategic targets. This freed North Vietnamese troops for deployment in the South and deterred a US invasion of the North. Between 1965 and 1967, the USSR delivered about $670 million worth of goods and aid (in the dollar values of the time), including surface-to-air missiles, mainly for the defence of North Vietnamese cities against US air attack. It also sent some 12,000 military instructors.

The PRC hoped to exploit the war not only to emphasise that it, rather than the USSR, was the true centre of communism and global revolution, but also to consolidate popular support behind the regime at a time when the 'Great Leap Forward' was obviously failing. When PRC military instructors first entered North Vietnam in August 1965, they were ordered also to work as political agents to instruct the population in the benefits of communism as practised in the PRC. The North Vietnamese authorities viewed this as interference in the internal politics of their country and rapidly stopped such activities. Their aim was first and foremost to reunite Vietnam. To them, the Sino-Soviet split was a distraction and they refused initially to take sides, while accepting help from both the USSR and the PRC.

By 1968, however, North Vietnam was increasingly siding with the USSR. When a series of fights and brawls broke out between Chinese and Soviet military experts in Vietnam, the North Vietnamese authorities supported the Soviet experts. Although the PRC reduced its assistance to North Vietnam in 1969, there was no immediate break in relations between the two countries. It was only after Vietnam joined the Soviet economic bloc in 1978 and invaded Cambodia that the PRC, as a punitive measure, briefly invaded North Vietnam, withdrawing after a month's heavy fighting.

Negotiations to end the war 1968–73

The USA lost support for the war at home when public opinion turned against the conflict. Instrumental in this was the reporting by the US media of the Tet Offensive of January to February 1968 when South Vietnamese cities and military installations were attacked by the North Vietnamese and Việt Cộng during the festival of Tết Nguyên Đán. That they managed to penetrate the US embassy compound was seized on by the USA and world media as evidence of US and South Vietnamese defeat. The fact that the offensive was halted with considerable loss of North Vietnamese and Việt Cộng life was all but ignored. Facing violent student protest and a hostile media and public opinion, **President Johnson** stated that he would not campaign for re-election in November 1968 and began negotiations with North Vietnam for a ceasefire. This was initially

🔑 **KEY FIGURE**

Lyndon Johnson (1908–73)

Democrat senator, US vice-president 1960–3, president 1963–9.

unsuccessful as North Vietnam remained adamant that the USA should withdraw its troops unconditionally.

US President Nixon 1968–72

President **Richard Nixon**'s main aim, after his election in November 1968, was to end US involvement in Vietnam 'with honour' as quickly as possible, but this was a complex task. His national security advisor, **Henry Kissinger**, hoped to link peace in Vietnam with *détente* with the USSR. He calculated that the USSR was so anxious to sign a treaty on Strategic Arms Limitation (see page 165) that it would put pressure on North Vietnam to come to the conference table, but Brezhnev rejected such a linkage and continued to supply North Vietnam with arms.

Withdrawal of US troops 1972

Nixon's military strategy was to carry out a policy of Vietnamisation, which meant transferring the burden of the land war to the South Vietnamese while withdrawing US troops. Increasingly, it was only US air power that prevented the defeat of South Vietnam. Nixon ordered the bombing of Việt Cộng military bases and supply routes in Cambodia and sent troops over the border; large stocks of Việt Cộng weapons were captured and pressure eased on South Vietnam as some 40,000 North Vietnamese troops had to be deployed in Cambodia to protect their installations and supplies.

In an attempt to reassure the US public that this was not a permanent escalation of the war, Nixon gave assurances that US troops would only advance 21 miles (34 km) into Cambodia and would withdraw by the end of June. The US Congress remained unconvinced and responded by forbidding the future deployment of US troops in either Laos or Cambodia. Shortly before the last US troops evacuated Vietnam, the North launched a massive attack against the South in June 1972, which was only halted by US air attacks. In August 1972, the last US soldier left Vietnam.

The Paris Peace Accords

In the end, the crucial factor leading to a peace agreement being signed in Paris was the realisation by North Vietnam that US air power could effectively prevent an immediate takeover of the South, despite the dominance of North Vietnamese forces on the ground. In another impressive display of US air power, Nixon sent in waves of B-52 bombers in December 1972 against the Hanoi–Haiphong area in North Vietnam (see the map on page 148), which used the new **'smart' bombs**, to target military installations with considerable effect.

On 27 January the Paris Peace Accords were at last signed:

- The USA was to withdraw its remaining forces within 60 days.
- US prisoners-of-war would be released.
- A ceasefire was declared throughout Vietnam.

KEY FIGURES

Richard Nixon (1913–94)

US president 1969–74. Resigned after the Watergate scandal (see page 162).

Henry Kissinger (1923–)

An academic and a security adviser to US presidents 1969–75.

KEY TERM

'Smart' bombs Precision-guided bombs which enable a target to be hit accurately.

? How did the picture in Source C harm the USA's image throughout the world?

- The territorial integrity of the whole of Vietnam, according to the 1954 Geneva Agreement, would be recognised by the USA.
- Elections were to be held in both North and South Vietnam.

In essence, as historian Norman Stone has observed, this peace agreement was a 'fraudulent face-saver for the Americans'. It did not halt the war. The North moved tanks and troops into the South in early 1975, and the US-trained South Vietnamese army was unable to stop them. By April 1975, Northern troops seized Saigon, the South's capital, and the USA's embassy had to be evacuated by helicopter amid scenes of panic, which were shown around the world by television. The impression given was one of American defeat and humiliation. Vietnam was now a united, Communist state.

Inevitably, the defeat in Vietnam, together with the **Watergate scandal**, did immense damage to US prestige and self-confidence, and made it reluctant to project its power in the years immediately after 1975. Nixon, Kissinger and, later, President Carter reduced direct the USA's intervention in the Developing World and instead attempted to use regional powers – Brazil, Turkey, South Africa, Iran and Indonesia – whose armed forces received aid and training, to contain communism in their regions. The humiliation of defeat disguised the fact that by 1979 the USA was in fact winning the Cold War. In the Middle East, Egypt ended its close links with the USSR, while the USA's *rapprochement* with the PRC was a serious challenge to the USSR (see below).

SOURCE C

US embassy officials being evacuated by helicopter from Saigon, South Vietnam, April 1975.

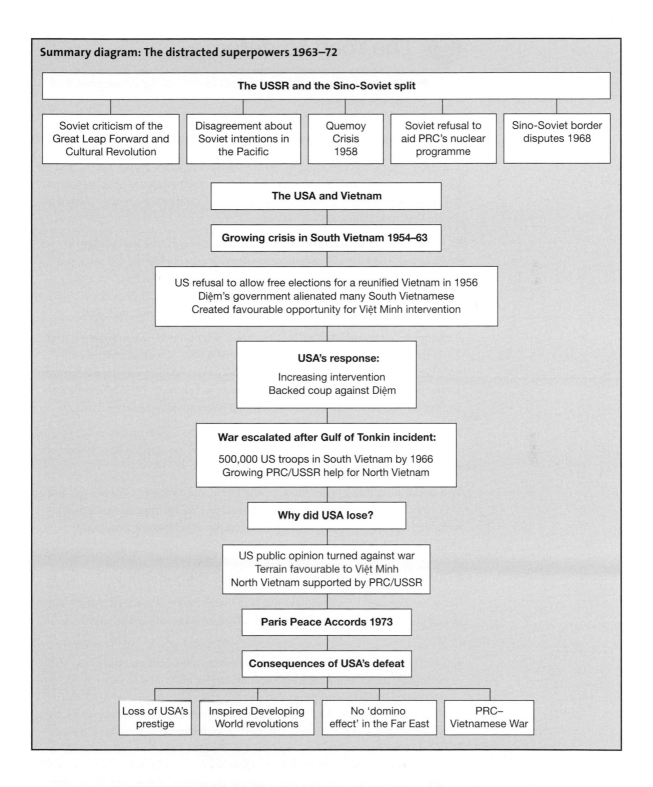

Summary diagram: The distracted superpowers 1963–72

The USSR and the Sino-Soviet split

| Soviet criticism of the Great Leap Forward and Cultural Revolution | Disagreement about Soviet intentions in the Pacific | Quemoy Crisis 1958 | Soviet refusal to aid PRC's nuclear programme | Sino-Soviet border disputes 1968 |

The USA and Vietnam

Growing crisis in South Vietnam 1954–63

US refusal to allow free elections for a reunified Vietnam in 1956
Diệm's government alienated many South Vietnamese
Created favourable opportunity for Việt Minh intervention

USA's response:

Increasing intervention
Backed coup against Diệm

War escalated after Gulf of Tonkin incident:

500,000 US troops in South Vietnam by 1966
Growing PRC/USSR help for North Vietnam

Why did USA lose?

US public opinion turned against war
Terrain favourable to Việt Minh
North Vietnam supported by PRC/USSR

Paris Peace Accords 1973

Consequences of USA's defeat

| Loss of USA's prestige | Inspired Developing World revolutions | No 'domino effect' in the Far East | PRC–Vietnamese War |

2 The road to *détente*

▶ *How successful were the attempts to control the development of nuclear weapons?*

The politics of *détente*

The Sino-Soviet split encouraged the Soviets to seek *détente* with NATO and the USA. At the same time, Sino-Soviet hostility strengthened the USA just when it was facing defeat in Vietnam, as its two great Communist enemies were now divided by mutual hostility.

In August 1969, a Soviet diplomat, almost certainly with the knowledge of Brezhnev, startled the US government when he asked what the US response would be if the USSR made a pre-emptive strike against the PRC's nuclear installations. President Nixon informed his cabinet later that the USA would not allow the PRC to be 'smashed' in a war between the PRC and the USSR.

Although tensions eased in early September, after talks between Kosygin and Zhou Enlai in Beijing where it was agreed that a PRC–Soviet conflict would only benefit the USA, diplomatic contacts between the PRC and the USA began for the first time in December. Two years later, in February 1972, Nixon flew to Beijing. After discussions with Mao the two governments declared that:

- neither would 'seek hegemony in the Asia–Pacific region and each is opposed to efforts by any other country [that is the USSR] to establish such hegemony'
- the future of Taiwan would be settled peacefully.

This declaration was a major blow for the USSR. Nevertheless, the Soviets hoped to prevent an alliance between the USA and the PRC by improving relations with the USA and agreeing to limitations on the development of nuclear weapons.

Controlling the development of nuclear weapons

Between 1963 and 1973 the following agreements were negotiated, which were aimed at stopping the spread of nuclear weapons and making the world a safer place:

- The Test Ban Treaty of 1963, signed by Britain, the USSR and the USA, banning nuclear tests in the atmosphere, under water and in outer space, was negotiated on the assumption that the only two nuclear powers who counted were the USSR and USA. It was, however, rejected by both France and China, whose leaders went on to develop their own nuclear weapons.
- In July 1968 Britain, the USA and the USSR signed the Non-proliferation Treaty, in which they pledged themselves not to transfer nuclear weapons to other countries or to assist other states to manufacture them. In November 1969 they were joined by West Germany.

- In 1970 US and Soviet experts began the Strategic Arms Limitation Talks (SALT) in Vienna.
- In May 1972 President Nixon and the Soviet leader Leonid Brezhnev signed the SALT 1 agreement at the Moscow summit. It consisted of two parts:
  - There was to be a five-year freeze on the construction of missile launchers and a freeze on intercontinental and submarine-launched ballistic missiles and long-range bombers. President Nixon accepted that the Soviets should have a greater number of missiles than the USA as the Americans had a superiority in multiple independently targetable re-entry vehicles (MIRVs), which were capable of hitting more than one target at a time.
  - The second part of the treaty concerned defence against missiles. Both sides were allowed only two **anti-ballistic screens**, one for their capital cities, Washington and Moscow, and one for their main missile sites. Both sides were left almost defenceless against attack. It was hoped that this 'mutually assured destruction', if war were to break out, would in fact guarantee peace.
- At the Moscow summit both statesmen also agreed to hold a conference on security, which the USSR hoped would result in the legal recognition of all territorial changes made in Europe since 1945.
- In July 1974 the USA and USSR agreed that negotiations should start for a SALT II treaty, which would impose permanent limitations on nuclear weapons. It was eventually concluded in June 1979 when President Carter and Brezhnev signed the SALT II Treaty in Vienna. The numbers of missile launchers and MIRV rocket warheads for both sides were further limited. However, the treaty was never ratified by the US Senate as a result of the Soviet invasion of Afghanistan (see page 182).

 **KEY TERM**

Anti-ballistic screens
Protection provided by rocket-launching pads.

Year	USA		USSR	
	Launchers	Warheads	Launchers	Warheads
1962	1653	3267	235	481
1964	2021	4180	425	771
1966	2139	4607	570	954
1968	2191	4839	1206	1605
1970	2100	4960	1835	2216
1972	2167	7601	2207	2573
1974	2106	9324	2423	2795
1976	2092	10436	2545	3477
1978	2086	10832	2557	5516
1980	2022	10608	2545	7480

Figure 6.1 Numbers of US and Soviet nuclear launchers and warheads, 1962–80, from M. Walker, *The Cold War*, Vintage, 1993, p. 214. What information do these figures convey about the US–USSR arms race? What impact did the PRC–US *rapprochement* have on USSR–US relations?

Leonid Brezhnev

1906	Born in present-day Ukraine
1941–64	Political commissar attached to the army
1963	Involved in plot to oust Khrushchev
1964	After Khrushchev's fall, became first secretary of the Russian Communist Party
1966	Appointed general secretary
1968	Ordered occupation of Czechoslovakia by Warsaw Pact forces
1972	Initiated *détente* with the USA
1975	Signed Helsinki Pact
1979	Decided to intervene in Afghanistan
1982	Died

Brezhnev was a member of the first generation to grow up in Russia without having participated as an adult in the Russian Revolution. He gained his first experiences as a Communist official during the Stalinist era. He first met Khrushchev in 1931 and became one of his favourites. After Stalin's death, he backed Khrushchev in his successful attempts to remove the Stalinist old guard from office. Up to the early 1960s he remained loyal to Khrushchev but after the Cuban Missile Crisis he helped to remove him from office in 1964. He had supported Khrushchev's more liberal policies but, once in power, he developed an increasingly conservative and repressive domestic policy. Abroad he pursued *détente* with the USA but also gave assistance to friendly regimes in Africa, Asia and the Middle East. In 1979 he committed Soviet troops to help prop up the socialist government in Afghanistan.

Developments in Western Europe 1964–8

The Test Ban Treaty of 1963 and the Nuclear Non-proliferation Treaty in 1968 were the most significant achievements in the early period of *détente*. These agreements were welcome in Western Europe, but essentially they assumed a world divided into two blocs led by their respective superpower.

By 1968 the Vietnam War was causing a rising wave of anti-Americanism. The USA was both failing to win the war and, as a result of its ruthless but ineffective military tactics, losing its position as the moral leader of the West. Its European allies rejected President Johnson's argument that the war was a vital part of the **global confrontation** with communism, and instead concentrated on easing tensions within Europe. This task was made easier by the fall of Khrushchev in October 1964 and his replacement by Brezhnev and Kosygin. Brezhnev, who rapidly emerged as the key figure in the USSR, was less erratic than Khrushchev and appeared to be more of a conciliator and **consensus** seeker, with whom the Western European leaders thought they could negotiate.

France's withdrawal from NATO

Potentially, the disagreements over the Vietnam War and the increasing assertiveness of the Western European states could have destroyed NATO and led to a US withdrawal from Western Europe. De Gaulle, the French president, took the lead in the attack on US influence in Western Europe. In 1963 he vetoed Britain's application to join the European Economic Community, on the grounds that Britain was still too pro-American, and three years later he both withdrew

French forces from NATO and expelled its headquarters from Paris. He followed this up with a visit to the USSR, where he announced that the European states should liberate themselves from the **bloc mentality** of the Cold War. He also did all he could to weaken the dollar at a time when the USA was beginning to come under financial pressure as a result of the costs of the Vietnam War.

The beginnings of *Ostpolitik*

The West Germans were meanwhile cautiously beginning to put out feelers to Eastern Europe by setting up **trade missions** in Yugoslavia and Romania. *Ostpolitik* took on a more definite shape when the Social Democrat leader, Willy Brandt, became foreign minister in December 1966. The key to his policy was that German unification was a long-term goal that could only gradually be reached within the context of a European *détente*.

The US reaction

Given the prosperity of Western Europe and its refusal to assist the USA in Vietnam, and the determination of its leading states to pursue their own ways to *détente*, it was not surprising that in 1967 a US senator, Michael Mansfield, put forward a motion in the Senate urging the withdrawal of the majority of US troops from Europe. This attracted nearly half the votes of the senate. Both to persuade Congress to continue to support the US military involvement in Europe and to prevent his allies from following the French example and leaving NATO, President Johnson committed himself to negotiate mutual and balanced force reductions with Moscow. These negotiations eventually led to the SALT I Treaty in 1972 (see above).

The Hamel Report

In December 1967 a NATO committee chaired by Belgian Foreign Minister Pierre Hamel drew up a report that committed NATO not only to defending Western Europe, but also to reaching a *détente* with the Warsaw Pact states. It stressed that:

SOURCE D

From 'The Report of the North Atlantic Council: The Future Tasks of the Alliance (Harmel Report)', 13 December 1967, available at the NATO website (www.nato. int/cps/en/natolive/topics_67927.htm).

Since the North Atlantic treaty was signed in 1949, the international situation has changed significantly and the political tasks of the Alliance have assumed a new dimension. Amongst other developments, the Alliance has played a major part in stopping Communist expansion in Europe; the USSR has become one of the two world super powers but the Communist world is no longer monolithic; the Soviet doctrine of 'peaceful co-existence' has changed the nature of the confrontation with the west but not the basic problem …

KEY TERMS

Bloc mentality A state of mind brought about by being a member of one of the two sides in the Cold War.

Trade missions Organisations to promote trade between states.

Ostpolitik West Germany's policy towards Eastern Europe, which involved recognition of the GDR and the post-war boundaries in Eastern Europe.

What information does Source D convey about the role of NATO in the period of *détente*?

The Atlantic Alliance has two main functions. Its first main function is to maintain adequate military strength and political solidarity to defend the territory of member states …

… the second function of the Alliance … [is] to pursue the search for progress towards a more stable relationship in which the underlying political issues can be solved … The way to peace and stability in Europe rests in particular on the use of the Alliance constructively in the interests of détente. The participation of the USSR and USA will be necessary to achieve a settlement of the political problems in Europe.

The Hamel Report redefined NATO's role in the age of *détente* and prevented the political fallout from the Vietnam War destroying the Western alliance.

Divisions within the Warsaw Pact

The Soviet retreat from Cuba, the growing atmosphere of *détente* and the Sino-Soviet split all combined to weaken Soviet control over Eastern Europe and provide some opportunities for the satellite states to pursue their own policies. Poland, for instance, wished to expand trade with the West, while Romania wanted to establish better relations with the Federal Republic of Germany (FRG). In an attempt to stop these independent initiatives, the Warsaw Pact issued in 1966 the Bucharest Declaration, which tried to define what the whole Soviet bloc wanted to achieve through *détente*. This called for:

- the recognition of post-war frontiers in Eastern Europe
- the creation of a new European security system
- a veto on nuclear weapons for West Germany
- a programme for economic, scientific and technical co-operation between East and West.

The Prague Spring

The Soviet government's efforts to consolidate its control over Eastern Europe and to co-ordinate the foreign and military policies of the Warsaw Pact suffered a serious setback when in January 1968 Alexander Dubček became the first secretary of the Czech Communist Party. Like Nagy in Hungary in 1956 (see page 101), he attempted to create a socialist system that would be based on the consent of the people, rather than one forced on them by the USSR, as had been the case in Eastern Europe since the late 1940s.

In April 1968 he unveiled his programme for democratic change and modernisation of the economy, which marked the start of what was called the **Prague Spring**. In April the Czech Communists announced a new programme for 'a new profoundly democratic model of Czechoslovak socialism conforming to Czechoslovak conditions'. Like Gorbachev later in the USSR (see page 187), Dubček wanted to preserve socialism, but increasingly public opinion began to press for the creation of a democracy based on the Western model. In June he abolished censorship, leading to a flood of anti-Soviet propaganda being published in Czechoslovakia.

Inevitably these developments began to worry Brezhnev and the other leaders of the Warsaw Pact, who after meeting on 15 July warned Dubček that they were 'deeply disturbed' about what was happening in Czechoslovakia. They ominously warned him that this was 'the common concern' of all the states in the Warsaw Pact.

Although Dubček reluctantly agreed to restore censorship, Brezhnev had no confidence that he would succeed and, during the night of 20–21 August 1968, twenty divisions of Warsaw Pact troops provided by the USSR, Hungary, Poland, the German Democratic Republic (GDR) and Bulgaria invaded Czechoslovakia and terminated the Prague Spring. In November Brezhnev defended the invasion by again stressing that any threat to socialism in a Warsaw Pact country was also a threat to its allies. To counter this, collective intervention, as happened in Czechoslovakia, would be justified. This became known as the Brezhnev Doctrine and was only abandoned by Gorbachev in 1989.

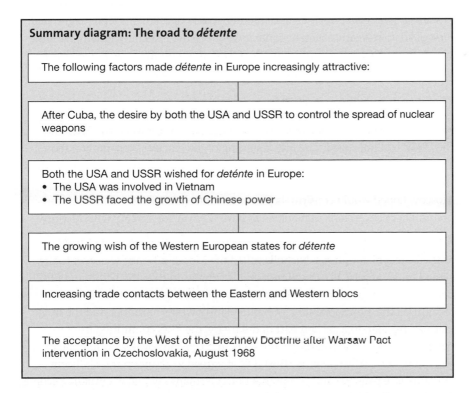

Summary diagram: The road to *détente*

The following factors made *détente* in Europe increasingly attractive:

After Cuba, the desire by both the USA and USSR to control the spread of nuclear weapons

Both the USA and USSR wished for *déténte* in Europe:
- The USA was involved in Vietnam
- The USSR faced the growth of Chinese power

The growing wish of the Western European states for *détente*

Increasing trade contacts between the Eastern and Western blocs

The acceptance by the West of the Brezhnev Doctrine after Warsaw Pact intervention in Czechoslovakia, August 1968

Ostpolitik

> ▶ What were the aims of Brandt's Ostpolitik and how did he seek to achieve them?

The invasion of Czechoslovakia was, as Michel Debré, the French prime minister, put it, 'a traffic accident on the road to *détente'*. It slowed down but did not halt progress. The elections of Richard Nixon to the US presidency in November 1968 and of Willy Brandt to the West German chancellorship in October 1969, with a mandate for his *Ostpolitik* policy, were soon to give it fresh impetus.

Brandt negotiated a complex set of interlocking treaties which marked a major turning point in the Cold War. On one level his policy was primarily a matter of coming to terms with the post-war world. This, of course, involved the recognition of the GDR regime, although his whole strategy, by defusing the tense situation between the two Germanys, was also aimed at leaving the door ajar for future unification. *Ostpolitik* was not conducted in a vacuum. Brandt had gained the support of the USA and his NATO allies by emphasising that the FRG did not intend to quit NATO or the **European Community**. In the course of 1970–2, five sets of intricate and interdependent agreements were negotiated. First of all, four treaties were negotiated between the FRG individually with the USSR, Poland, Czechoslovakia and the GDR, and then the Four-Power Treaty on Berlin between Britain, France, the USA and the USSR.

The Moscow Treaty 1970

No progress could be made in *Ostpolitik* until relations between the FRG and the USSR had improved. The FRG's signing of the Nuclear Non-proliferation Treaty in 1969, its readiness to increase technological and economic links with the USSR and willingness to agree to a European security conference, which Moscow hoped would confirm its post-war control over Eastern Europe, were all preliminary concessions that helped to pave the way for a treaty with Moscow.

After prolonged and difficult negotiations the 'foundation stone of *Ostpolitik*', as the British historian A.J. Nicholls called the Moscow Treaty, was eventually signed on 12 August 1970 by Brandt and Brezhnev. In this, the USSR and FRG declared that they had no territorial claims against any other state. The FRG recognised the 'non-violability' of both Poland's western frontier and the inner German frontier. In a second part of the treaty, the FRG committed itself to negotiating treaties with Poland, the GDR and Czechoslovakia. While the FRG still did not officially recognise the GDR, it agreed to abandon the Hallstein Doctrine (see page 91) and accept that both Germanys would eventually become members of the United Nations (UN).

The Soviets had in effect gained West German recognition of their European empire, yet this recognition was not unconditional. The West Germans also

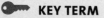 **KEY TERM**

European Community
The European Economic Community (EEC) had changed its name to the European Community (EC).

presented Brezhnev with a 'letter on German unity'. This stressed the FRG's right to work towards a state of peace in Europe in which 'the German people regains its unity in free self-determination'. Similarly, the term **inviolable** as applied to the Oder–Neisse line and the inner German frontier, rather than the preferred Soviet word **immutable**, arguably kept the door open for a later peaceful revision of the frontier. Finally, the ratification of the treaty was made dependent on a Four-Power Treaty over Berlin.

The Warsaw and Prague Treaties

Negotiations with Poland ran parallel with the Moscow talks and were completed in December 1970. Both states recognised that they had no territorial demands on each other and that the Oder–Neisse line was 'inviolable'. Trade and financial assistance from the FRG were to be increased, while the **ethnic Germans** still within Poland were to be allowed to emigrate to West Germany.

In June 1973 a similar agreement was signed with Czechoslovakia, which specifically revoked the Munich Treaty of 1938.

Four-power negotiations over Berlin

In March 1970, four-power discussions began on the thorny problem of access to West Berlin. The involvement of Britain, France and the USA in these negotiations sent signals to both NATO and the Warsaw Pact that *Ostpolitik* would not lead to a weakening of the FRG's links with the West. The Western allies wanted a settlement underwritten by the USSR that would finally confirm West Berlin's links with the FRG and guarantee its freedom of access to the West.

At first the Soviets were anxious to avoid making too many concessions, but both their desire for a general European security conference and their reluctance to annoy President Nixon at a time when he was planning to improve relations with China, made them more responsive to Western demands. The Four-Power Treaty on Berlin, signed on 3 September 1971, was, to quote the historians L. Bark and D.R. Gress, a 'milestone in the history of divided Berlin and divided Germany'. The Soviets conceded three vital principles:

- unimpeded traffic between West Berlin and the FRG
- recognition of West Berlin's ties with the FRG
- finally, the right for West Berliners to visit East Berlin.

In return, Britain, France and the USA agreed that the Western sectors of Berlin were not legally part of the FRG, even if in practice they had been so ever since West Berlin adopted the FRG's constitution in 1950.

The Basic Treaty

Once the Moscow Treaty and the agreement on Berlin had been signed, the way was open for direct negotiations between the GDR and FRG. For the

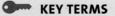

KEY TERMS

Inviolable Not to be attacked or violated.

Immutable Unchangeable.

Ethnic Germans German people who still lived in Poland. In 1945 much former German territory was given to Poland.

KEY TERMS

Magnetic social and economic forces of the FRG Brandt believed that the economy and way of life in West Germany was so strong that ultimately it would exert a magnet-like attraction on the GDR.

Social Democratisation Converting the Communist SED into a more moderate Western-style Social Democratic Party, like the SPD in the FRG.

Transit traffic Traffic crossing through another state.

GDR an agreement with the FRG was not without risk. If successful, it would undoubtedly secure the GDR international recognition, but at the continued risk of closer contact with the **magnetic social and economic forces of the FRG**. In July Leonid Brezhnev stressed to the somewhat sceptical Erich Honecker, who had just replaced Ulbricht as the GDR leader, the solid advantages of the treaty for the GDR in that '[i]ts frontiers, its existence will be confirmed for all the world to see …'. However, he also warned him that Brandt was aiming ultimately at the **Social Democratisation** of the GDR, and added: 'It … must not come to a process of *rapprochement* between the FRG and the GDR. … Concentrate everything on the all-sided strengthening of the GDR, as you call it.'

First of all, a series of technical agreements on **transit traffic**, the rights of West Berliners to visit East Berlin and postal communications were concluded. Then the two states moved on to negotiate the more crucial Basic Treaty, which was signed in December 1972. In it, the FRG recognised the GDR as an equal and sovereign state and also accepted that both states should be represented at the UN. The FRG did, however, stress that it still considered the people of the GDR to have a common German citizenship, and in a 'Letter Concerning German Unity', which it presented to East Berlin, it repeated its determination to work peacefully for German reunification.

The existence of the two Germanys now seemed to be a permanent fact confirmed by treaty. The two German states joined the UN in 1973. Within their respective blocs, both the FRG and the GDR played increasingly important economic, military and political roles. Nothing, however, had changed the essential vulnerability of the GDR, whose very existence in the last resort still depended on Soviet bayonets, as the events of 1989–90 were to show (see page 197).

Summary diagram: *Ostpolitik*

Willy Brandt needed to secure approval from the USA, USSR and NATO

Moscow Treaty, August 1970: FRG committed itself to recognising post-1945 frontiers

Berlin Treaty signed by the four occupying powers, September 1971: unimpeded transit rights to West Berlin recognised

Treaties with Poland, December 1970, and with Czechoslovakia, June 1973, confirmed 1945 borders

The Basic Treaty, December 1972: FRG gave up Hallstein Doctrine

---

The Helsinki Accords

▶ *Were the Helsinki Accords a triumph for Brezhnev?*

In July 1973 the conference on security and co-operation opened in Helsinki. A journalist, Robert Hutchings, has called it the 'centrepiece of Soviet and East European diplomacy' in the 1970s. Essentially, the USSR wanted to persuade the West to recognise as permanent the territorial and political division of Europe made at Yalta (see page 26), while stepping up economic, scientific and technological co-operation. It was anxious to exploit Western know-how and technology to modernise its economy.

The USA initially consented to holding the conference in return for a Soviet agreement on Berlin and the opening of negotiations at Vienna on mutual reductions of troops and armaments in Central Europe (see page 165). It also used the conference as a means to extract from the USSR concessions on human rights, which in time could bring about fundamental changes in the Soviet bloc and lead to a loosening of Soviet control over the satellites. The subsequent Helsinki Agreement marked the high point of *détente* and was signed on 1 August 1975 by 33 European states, Canada and the USA.

The agreement was divided into three sections, or 'baskets', as they were called:

- The first dealt with 'questions relating to security in Europe' and laid down a set of principles to guide the participating states in their relations with each other. These included peaceful settlement of disputes, non-interference in internal affairs of other states and the 'inviolability' of frontiers. Brezhnev had hoped initially that he would be able to negotiate a peace treaty permanently guaranteeing the new post-war frontiers, but under West German pressure, Henry Kissinger, the US secretary of state, managed to persuade the Soviets to accept the eventual possibility of a 'peaceful change to frontiers'.
- 'Basket two' concerned co-operation in 'the field of economics, of science and technology and the environment'.
- 'Basket three' called for 'co-operation in humanitarian and other fields'. This meant expanding trade, tourism and cultural contacts between the two blocs, as well as promoting the reunion of families split by the Iron Curtain.
- Finally, there was to be a follow-up conference two years later to work out further measures for European security and co-operation.

Who gained most from Helsinki?

At first glance, perhaps, it could be argued that Brezhnev had achieved Western recognition of the Soviet Empire and an end to all attempts to undermine it. Right-wing politicians, such as Margaret Thatcher and Ronald Reagan, saw it, to quote the latter, as a **'new Yalta'**, placing 'the American seal of approval on the Soviet Empire in Eastern Europe'. While there was some truth in this, Helsinki's stress on human rights and fundamental freedoms, as well as the increased

East–West contact it encouraged, did in the medium term contain the potential for undermining the unpopular Soviet-dominated regimes in Eastern Europe. The Helsinki treaties have been called 'a time bomb planted in the heart of the Soviet Empire'. The new US president, Jimmy Carter, for example, made human rights in Eastern Europe one of the priorities of his foreign policy. In February 1977, much to the annoyance of Brezhnev, he championed the rights of the dissident Soviet physicist, Andrei Sakharov.

? What information does Source E convey about the provisions made for safeguarding human rights by the Helsinki Accords?

SOURCE E

Excerpt from 'Declaration of Principles Guiding Relations between Participating States', 1 August 1975, US Department of State (available at www.state.gov).

The participating States will respect human rights and fundamental freedoms, including the freedom of thought, conscience, religion or belief, for all without distinction as to race, sex, language or religion … Within this framework the participating States will recognize and respect the freedom of the individual to profess and practice, alone or in community with others, religion or belief acting in accordance with the dictates of his own conscience.

The participating States on whose territory national minorities exist will respect the right of persons belonging to such minorities to equality before the law, will afford them the full opportunity for the actual enjoyment of human rights and fundamental freedoms and will, in this manner, protect their legitimate interests in this sphere.

The participating States recognize the universal significance of human rights and fundamental freedoms, respect for which is an essential factor for the peace, justice and well-being necessary to ensure the development of friendly relations and co-operation among themselves as among all States …

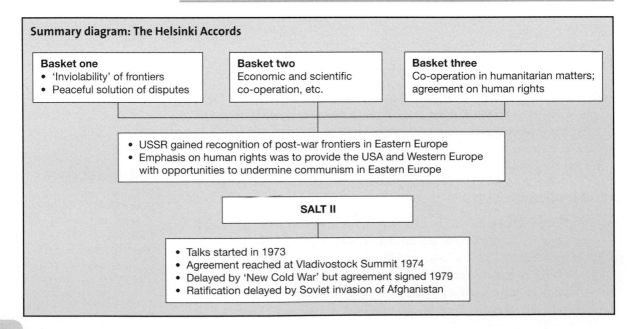

Summary diagram: The Helsinki Accords

Basket one
- 'Inviolability' of frontiers
- Peaceful solution of disputes

Basket two
Economic and scientific co-operation, etc.

Basket three
Co-operation in humanitarian matters; agreement on human rights

- USSR gained recognition of post-war frontiers in Eastern Europe
- Emphasis on human rights was to provide the USA and Western Europe with opportunities to undermine communism in Eastern Europe

SALT II

- Talks started in 1973
- Agreement reached at Vladivostock Summit 1974
- Delayed by 'New Cold War' but agreement signed 1979
- Ratification delayed by Soviet invasion of Afghanistan

Chapter summary

The years from 1963 to 1979 were a period of *détente*. The USA, distracted by the Vietnam War, wanted a stable Europe, while the USSR was facing a growing challenge from the PRC and hoped to consolidate gains made in Eastern Europe in 1945. The European allies of both the USSR and the USA increasingly exploited these superpower concerns to pursue more independent policies. In Czechoslovakia, demands for economic and political reform led to intervention by Warsaw Pact troops in August 1968, but this did not stop the development of *détente* in Europe and between the USA and USSR. Instead, it showed its limits. Within Europe, Brandt's *Ostpolitik* led to the interlocking treaties between the FRG, and the USSR, Czechoslovakia, Poland and the GDR, recognising the frontiers of 1945 and the legal existence of the GDR, 1970–2, while the Four-Power Treaty on Berlin of 3 September 1971 regulated the status of Berlin. Progress was also made in controlling the use and spread of nuclear weapons through the Test Ban Treaty of 1963, the Non-proliferation Treaty of 1968, and SALT I and SALT II. At the Helsinki Conference of 1975 the USSR again achieved the recognition of Eastern Europe's post-1945 frontiers, but at the cost of concessions on human rights.

Refresher questions

Use these questions to remind yourself of the key material covered in this chapter.

1 Why did mutual distrust between the party leadership of the PRC and USSR develop between 1958 and 1960?

2 Why did relations between the USSR and PRC continue to deteriorate between 1964 and 1969?

3 Why did the Vietnam War escalate after August 1964?

4 What difficulties did the USA encounter in its attempts to end the war in Vietnam?

5 How successful were the attempts to control the development of nuclear weapons?

6 How did the Western European states attempt to pursue a policy of *détente* with the Warsaw Pact states?

7 Why did relations deteriorate between France and the USA?

8 What was the US reaction to the assertiveness of the Western European states?

9 How divided was the Warsaw Pact during the period 1963–9?

10 To what extent was the Prague Spring a threat to Soviet control of Eastern Europe?

11 Why was the Moscow Treaty the key to Brandt's *Ostpolitik*?

12 How far did the Four-Power Treaty on Berlin solve the Berlin problem?

13 To what extent was the Basic Treaty a victory for the GDR and USSR?

14 What were the terms of the Helsinki Accord?

15 Did the East or West benefit more from the terms of the Helsinki Accord?

Question practice

ESSAY QUESTIONS

1 To what extent did the Sino-Soviet split benefit the USA?

2 Assess the reasons for improved relations between the USA and the USSR from 1963 to 1975.

3 Which of the following had the greater impact on the US failure to win the Vietnam War? i) Aid from the USSR and PRC. ii) US public opinion. Explain your answer with reference to both i) and ii).

4 How far did *Ostpolitik* benefit the USSR?

SOURCE ANALYSIS QUESTION

1 With reference to Sources B (page 159), D (pages 167–8) and E (page 174), and your understanding of the historical context, assess the value of these sources to a historian studying the development of the Cold War in 1964–75.

CHAPTER 7

The end of the Cold War

This chapter investigates the outbreak and course of what some historians refer to as the 'New Cold War' in Africa and the Caribbean as well as in Europe. It explores the cost and failure of Soviet policies and the eventual collapse of the USSR and the Warsaw Pact. It also reviews the decline of the Soviet and COMECON economies and the impact of Gorbachev's policies of *glasnost* and *perestroika* through the following themes:

★ The Cold War in Africa, the Caribbean and South America 1975–83

★ The 'Third' or 'New Cold War' 1979–85

★ Gorbachev: *glasnost* and *détente* 1985–9

★ The collapse of communism in Eastern Europe 1989–95

★ The disintegration of the USSR

Key dates

1975–6		Angolan Civil War	1989	Feb.	Soviet troops withdrawn from Afghanistan
1977	April	Soviet aid to Ethiopia began		June	Elections in Poland
1979	Dec. 27	Soviet invasion of Afghanistan		Sept.	Hungary allowed GDR citizens through frontier to Austria
1980	Dec. 13	Martial law declared in Poland		Nov. 9	Berlin Wall breached
1982	Nov.	Brezhnev succeeded by Andropov	1990	Oct. 3	Germany reunified
	March	Reagan announced development of Strategic Defence Initiative	1991	Jan.	Soviet forces intervened in Baltic republics
1985	March 12	Gorbachev became USSR party leader		July	Warsaw Pact dissolved
				Dec. 26	USSR formally dissolved
1986	Oct. 2	USSR–US summit at Reykjavík	1992–6		Croatian–Serbian war

1 The Cold War in Africa, the Caribbean and South America 1975–83

▶ *Why was the USSR able to extend its influence so successfully in Africa?*

The global Cold War

International developments during the period 1979–85 were to confirm US President Nixon's comment that '*détente* does not mean the end of danger … *détente* is not the same as lasting peace'. The USSR and its allies intensified their efforts to intervene and support sympathetic regimes in Africa, Asia, the Caribbean and South America. However, the sheer cost of these operations, taken together with the protracted Afghanistan campaign (see page 182), weakened the USSR financially and played a role in the collapse of its economy.

The USSR and Africa

Angola

By the mid-1970s the liberation movements in the former Portuguese colonies of Angola, Mozambique and Guinea-Bissau were becoming a focus for Cold War rivalry between the USA and the USSR. Having extracted itself from the Vietnam conflict, the USA was not willing to become heavily involved in Angola, but it wished to avoid a victory of the Communist **MPLA**, which would allow the Soviets influence there. It therefore allocated some $50 million for the recruiting of mercenaries and the training and equipping of troops in the rival **FNLA** and **UNITA** movements.

In the civil war that raged in Angola in 1975–6, UNITA was given powerful backing by South Africa, which was worried about the impact of a Communist victory on its own frontiers. By mid-November 1975, the UNITA army, led by South African troops, had almost reached Luanda, the capital of Angola, but the MPLA was saved by large-scale Cuban intervention approved by the USSR. Altogether, the USSR transported 12,000 Cuban troops, along with tanks and missiles, to Angola. By December 1975, the Cubans had halted the South African/UNITA advance and inflicted two defeats on their forces.

Determined to prevent a growing US military interest in Angola that might escalate into a second Vietnam, the US Senate voted to block all funding for covert operations there. Deprived of US support, the South African government had to withdraw its troops from Angola. By March 1976, the MPLA was victorious. Together with the triumph of communism in Vietnam, the victory of the MPLA seemed to confirm that the newly independent states in the Developing World were ready to embrace Soviet-style communism.

KEY TERMS

MPLA The Popular Movement for the Liberation of Angola (*Movimento Popular de Libertaçã de Angola*), headed by António Neto, was predominantly a Marxist movement influenced by the Portuguese Communist Party.

FNLA The National Front for the Liberation of Angola (*Frente Nacional de Libertação de Angola*), led by Holden Roberto, was strongly African nationalist. It was hostile both to the West and to communism but had links with the CIA and was dependent on Mobutu's Congo for bases and assistance.

UNITA The National Union for the Total Liberation of Angola (*União Nacional para a Independência Total de Angola*) was created in the mid-1960s by Jonas Savimbi to provide an alternative to what he perceived to be the military inactivity and feebleness of the two other groups (MPLA and FNLA).

Ethiopia

By early 1974, the **global oil crisis**, which saw the price of oil quadruple in many countries, caused severe economic problems and social unrest in Ethiopia. In 1974, the army seized power in Ethiopia, murdered the Emperor Haile Selassie and established a leftist regime under Colonel Mengistu, which was to give the USSR further opportunities to extend its influence in Africa.

During the 1960s, Haile Selassie had depended mainly on the USA for economic and military aid, but in 1974 the USA, enfeebled by the Watergate scandal (see page 162) and its defeat in Vietnam, did nothing to help him. In February 1977, Mengistu murdered his political rivals and established a personal dictatorship. Suspecting that the USA was covertly assisting its internal enemies, he now turned for assistance to the USSR and the Soviet bloc in Europe. In April 1978, responding to CIA reports that Mengistu was preparing to remove US advisors from Ethiopia, President Carter pre-emptively recalled all US personnel in protest at Mengistu's terror campaign against his political rivals.

Soviet intervention

Although approached by Mengistu after 1974 with requests for aid and military assistance, the USSR reacted cautiously. It was aware that the USA in 1974–6 was still supplying Ethiopia with arms, while it was itself supplying Ethiopia's enemy, Somalia, with weapons. With the coup of February 1977, the attitude of the USSR changed. Mengistu convinced the Soviet ambassador that Ethiopia would be a potentially loyal regional ally. The USSR agreed immediately to send large arms shipments to Ethiopia. By mid-April, according to Western sources, more than a hundred tanks and armoured personnel carriers had already been delivered. For the USSR, the alliance with Ethiopia became its most ambitious intervention in Africa. It gave the USSR influence in the Indian Ocean and the Red Sea area through its access to Eritrean ports such as Assab and Massawa.

Ethiopia's neighbour, Somaliland, exploited the chaos caused by Mengistu's coup to attempt to annex **Ogaden**. In 1975, the Somali government established the Western Somali Liberation Front (WSLF) to conduct guerrilla operations within Ogaden against Ethiopia. In 1977, Somali troops advanced into Eritrea and took the important town of Jijiga. After initially unsuccessful attempts to mediate, the Soviets engaged in a large-scale operation to save the Ethiopian revolution. Between September 1977 and May 1978, they flew in $1 billion worth of military equipment to Ethiopia and 1000 military personnel to organise the counter-offensive against the Somalis. Fidel Castro also sent more than 11,000 troops from Cuba. Jijiga was recaptured and the Somali army defeated.

The conventional war had been won by Ethiopia, although WSLF guerrilla groups remained active in Ogaden until 1980. The USSR had now become a major factor in African affairs. To many African leaders, the USSR was seen as a useful counter-weight to US and European influence. In Ethiopia, Mengistu attempted, largely unsuccessfully, to rebuild Ethiopian society along Soviet

🔑 **KEY TERMS**

Global oil crisis In October 1973 the Organization of Arab Petroleum Exporting Countries suspended delivery of oil to the USA and Western Europe in protest against US assistance to Israel during the October War of 1973. When deliveries recommenced in March 1974, the oil price had quadrupled.

Ogaden In the late nineteenth century, when the Somali territories were divided between Britain, France and Italy, Ethiopia acquired Ogaden. Once the British and Italian territories became independent in 1960, the two states merged and formed the new state of Somaliland and laid claim to Ogaden.

lines. He was helped by thousands of experts from the Soviet bloc, the largest assistance programme the USSR had undertaken since helping China in the 1950s.

The impact on USA–USSR relations

Large-scale Soviet intervention in Ethiopia threatened the policy of *détente* in Europe by antagonising President Carter's administration. The Republicans' argument that the USSR was exploiting the spirit of *détente* to strengthen its position in Africa helped **Ronald Reagan** to defeat Carter in the November 1980 presidential elections. It also led to increasing reluctance by the US Senate to ratify the SALT II Treaty.

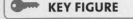

KEY FIGURE

Ronald Reagan (1911–2004)

TV and film actor, governor of California and US president 1981–9.

? According to Source A, what are Reagan's views on Soviet influence in Africa?

SOURCE A

From a speech by Ronald Reagan on 25 March 1978, quoted in *The Global Cold War: Third World Intervention and the Making of Our Times* by Odd Arne Westad, Cambridge University Press, 2005, p. 283.

If the Soviets are successful – and it looks more and more as if they will be – then the entire Horn of Africa will be under their influence, if not their control. From there, they can threaten the sea lanes carrying oil to western Europe and the United States, if and when they choose. More immediately, control of the Horn of Africa would give Moscow the ability to destabilize those governments on the Arabian Peninsula which have proven themselves strongly anti-Communist [sic] … in a few years we may be faced with the prospect of a Soviet empire of protégés and dependencies stretching from Addis Ababa to Cape Town.

US–Soviet rivalry in the Caribbean and Latin America

US influence was strengthened in South America when the socialist regime of Salvador Allende in Chile was overthrown by a military coup in 1973 and General Augusto Pinochet was installed as president. This was welcomed by President Nixon, who restarted the aid programme to Chile, which had been halted when Allende had been elected in 1970.

The Communist threat in Chile had been neutralised, but by the end of the 1970s Washington was alarmed by growing Communist influence in Nicaragua and parts of the Caribbean. In July 1979, the Marxist-leaning Sandinista political party came to power in Nicaragua after the overthrow of the country's US-backed leader Anastasio Somoza Debayle, and supported rebel activity in nearby El Salvador. In 1981, Sandinista leaders visited the USSR and succeeded in persuading the Soviets to send military equipment to Nicaragua.

US troops invaded the island state of Grenada in the Caribbean Sea in October 1983, overthrowing the Communist regime established there in 1979, and launched a covert war against the Sandinista government of Nicaragua.

President Reagan's government equipped and supplied anti-Sandinista rebels (collectively referred to as the *Contras*) despite the Senate's decision to prohibit the funding. This defiance of the Senate led to a major political scandal and subsequent investigations that weakened Reagan's government.

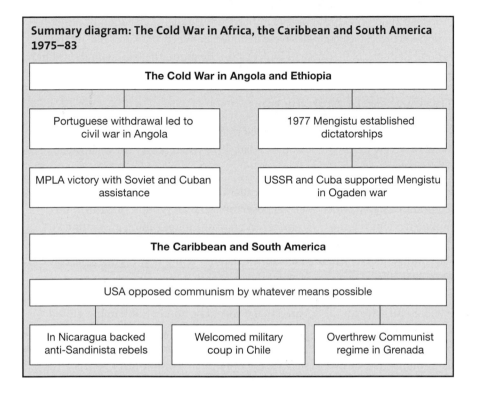

Summary diagram: The Cold War in Africa, the Caribbean and South America 1975–83

The Cold War in Angola and Ethiopia

Portuguese withdrawal led to civil war in Angola

1977 Mengistu established dictatorships

MPLA victory with Soviet and Cuban assistance

USSR and Cuba supported Mengistu in Ogaden war

The Caribbean and South America

USA opposed communism by whatever means possible

In Nicaragua backed anti-Sandinista rebels

Welcomed military coup in Chile

Overthrew Communist regime in Grenada

② The 'Third' or 'New Cold War' 1979–85

▶ *How justified are historians in calling the years 1979–85 the 'New Cold War'?*

The first blow to the Helsinki spirit occurred when the Soviet Union placed SS-20 medium-range nuclear missiles in Central Europe in 1976. These weapons could reach targets between 600 and 5000 kilometres away, threatening all NATO states in Europe. In response, NATO initiated a policy that if an arms agreement could not be reached with the Soviets, the USA would deploy Pershing and Cruise missiles in Europe by 1983.

This agreement, however, was difficult to reach as the Soviet Union had in the meantime invaded Afghanistan (see below). In November 1981, US President Ronald Reagan suggested that both sides destroy their *existing* medium-range nuclear weapons, but the Soviets immediately rejected this as a one-sided gesture that would require them to destroy their weapons, while the USA had not yet deployed its up-to-date missiles. As the Soviets calculated that growing popular opposition from the **Greens** and **left-wing protest groups** would prevent their eventual deployment in Western Europe, accepting Reagan's proposal could only undo a Soviet military advantage. Consequently, despite continued protest, the missiles were installed between 1983 and 1987 in the Federal Republic of Germany (FRG), Britain, Belgium, the Netherlands and Italy, eliminating any Soviet strategic advantage.

The invasion of Afghanistan

The historian S.R. Ashton has observed that 'if a date has to be fixed for the onset of a New Cold War, it would be late 1979 when Soviet troops invaded Afghanistan'.

In April 1978 a coup, mounted independently of the USSR by the local Afghan Communist Party, which was composed of two rival groups, overthrew the monarchy. This regime then embarked on a radical reforming programme that provoked widespread opposition from the conservative Islamic forces in the countryside, which threatened the existence of the new regime. Moscow became increasingly worried about the impact that this opposition would have on the **Islamic fundamentalism** in the Muslim republics of southern Russia. If successful, Moscow also feared that it would be another link in the **global encirclement** of the USSR at a time when China had established diplomatic relations with the USA (see page 164). It came to the conclusion that if the Communist regime was to survive, the unpopular Communist President Hafizullah Amin would have to be removed and replaced by his Communist rival Babrak Kamal.

Soviet military operations

Between 24 and 27 December 1979, 50,000 Soviet troops were flown into Kabul, the capital of Afghanistan. Within months there were 100,000 Soviet troops stationed in the country. On 27 December, Soviet soldiers attacked the presidential palace, executed President Amin and replaced him with Babrak Kamal. The Soviets hoped rapidly to crush the Muslim fundamentalist rebels and stabilise the government so that they could withdraw their troops within a few weeks. Soviet forces were able to occupy Kabul and the other major cities, but they encountered two major military problems:

- The Afghan army disintegrated, leaving Soviet forces to conduct all military actions and secure the country.
- Babrak Kamal did not have the support of the Afghan people, who felt that he was a puppet of the Soviets. This led them to support the Muslim fundamentalist guerrilla fighters, the *mujahedin*, who wished to establish an Islamic government for the country.

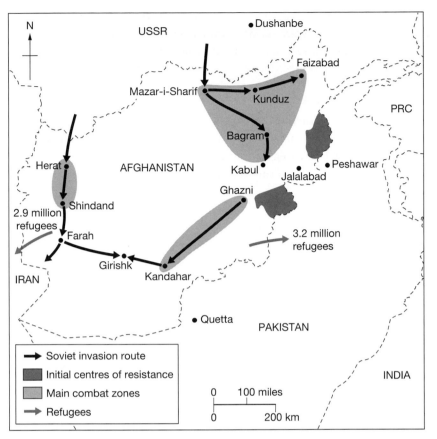

Figure 7.1 Map of the Soviet invasion of Afghanistan 1979. What information does this map convey about the Soviet invasion of Afghanistan?

Faced by up to 200,000 *mujahedin* guerrillas, the Soviet military controlled only one-fifth of the country. By 1985, it was clear that the war could not be won by the Soviets as the *mujahedin* factions had their bases in the inaccessible mountainous areas along the border with Pakistan. The unwinnable conflict demoralised Soviet forces and became a substantial financial strain on the Soviet Union.

US reaction 1979–87

The USA feared that the Soviets intended to take control of Afghanistan as a step towards further expansion towards the Indian Ocean and the Persian Gulf, which contained much of the world's oil supply. President Carter responded by banning grain exports to the USSR, while the Senate refused to ratify the SALT II Treaty (see page 165). The USA also boycotted the 1980 Olympic Games that were held in Moscow.

More importantly, the USA financed the supply of weapons to the Afghan *mujahedin* with money distributed through agencies in neighbouring Pakistan.

In 1986 President Ronald Reagan decided to send the *mujahedin* new lightweight ground-to-air missiles, which rapidly diminished Soviet air superiority, and allowed the guerrillas to share information from US satellite and communications networks.

People's Republic of China

The People's Republic of China (PRC) denounced the invasion of Afghanistan, cancelling the Sino-Soviet talks which were due to start in 1980. In May 1980, China's minister of defence, Geng Biao, visited the USA, which approved the export from the PRC of 400 items of advanced military technology to the *mujahedin*.

Western Europe

Britain, under its new prime minister, **Margaret Thatcher**, supported the line taken by the USA. The FRG and France, while condemning the invasion of Afghanistan at the United Nations (UN), were initially unwilling to let it destroy the *détente* that *Ostpolitik* had created in Europe. Many Europeans argued that the Soviet invasion of Afghanistan was no different from the invasion of Czechoslovakia in 1968 (see page 169). In both situations, the USSR acted merely to preserve Communist governments in neighbouring states.

The Solidarity crisis in Poland 1980–2

Poland was, in many ways, the key country in the Soviet bloc:

- Strategically it lay on the main route to the West.
- It provided about one-third of the combined forces of the Warsaw Pact.
- It had the largest population of the satellite states: 36 million.

Consequently, any instability in Poland inevitably threatened the whole cohesion of the Soviet bloc. By the summer of 1980, Poland was facing a major economic crisis. The rising cost of oil forced up prices and the economic recession in the West meant that Poland had no market for its exports. The government had also failed to modernise the economy and make it more competitive.

In 1980 strikes broke out in the shipyards in Gdańsk over the question of price increases. The government made far-reaching economic and political concessions, and in August recognised the **Solidarity movement** as an independent trade union. At first it tried to claim that this concession only applied to Gdańsk, but this provoked a wave of labour unrest, culminating in the threat of a national strike. Membership of Solidarity rose to nearly 8 million, and it was supported by both Polish intellectuals and the Roman Catholic Church, which had been greatly strengthened by the election of a Polish Pope in 1978.

Both Brezhnev and the other Warsaw Pact leaders urged the Polish prime minister, Stanisław Kania, to crush the 'anti-Socialist opposition forces'.

Honecker, the East German leader, wanted Brezhnev to send in troops. On 28 November 1980 he warned Brezhnev that 'any delay in acting against them would mean death – the death of socialist Poland'. Warsaw Pact forces were mobilised in early December, but at the last moment intervention was cancelled as Kania convinced Brezhnev that he could restore order himself. US warnings against the use of force were probably also a powerful deterrent.

In 1981, Solidarity began to call for further drastic political changes. At the ninth Congress of the Polish Communist Party, delegates attacked the party leaders and even began to dismantle the party organisation. Once more, the question of Soviet intervention arose. The Americans called on the USSR to allow Poland to solve the crisis itself, which arguably indicated to Wojciech Jaruzelski, Kania's successor, that Washington would tolerate a declaration of **martial law** provided Soviet troops did not cross the frontier. In December, Moscow agreed to a declaration of martial law and in October 1982 Solidarity was outlawed.

KEY TERM

Martial law Military rule involving the suspension of normal civilian government.

Ostpolitik under threat

Ostpolitik, which was a product of *détente* (see page 170), was inevitably threatened by the 'New Cold War'. Both the German Chancellor Helmut Schmidt, who had played a leading role in alerting the Western alliance to the dangers of the SS-20s, and his successor, Helmut Kohl, tried to protect it from the consequences of the sharply deteriorating East–West relations. At Tito's funeral in Belgrade in May 1980 Schmidt observed to Honecker that the European states must ensure that 'the really big brothers don't get nervous'. A month later he visited Moscow, where he managed to persuade Brezhnev in principle to negotiate with the USA on the crucial question of intermediate nuclear missiles, although little was achieved in subsequent talks in Madrid, in 1980–3.

It is arguable that by 1980 *Ostpolitik* was beginning to degenerate into an open appeasement of Moscow and the Eastern European regimes. While the West German and French governments did condemn the Soviet invasion of Afghanistan and pointedly remarked that *détente* 'could not withstand another shock' like that, they did not join London and Washington in criticising the Polish government's reaction to Solidarity. Indeed, no less a person than the former West German Chancellor Willy Brandt actually condemned Solidarity for threatening the stability of the Polish regime! When martial law was declared by the Polish government in Poland in December 1981, Schmidt went out of his way to avoid criticising it. He was unwilling to sacrifice what had already been achieved by *Ostpolitik*, in improving relations between the two Germanys, for the sake of Poland. By the time the Pershing and Cruise missiles were deployed in the FRG in November 1983, Schmidt had been replaced by Kohl, who also took great care to minimise the impact of this action on *Ostpolitik*.

Years of tension 1981–4

In January 1981, Ronald Reagan became the US president. He immediately increased expenditure on armaments, so that it amounted to 30 per cent of all government spending between 1981 and 1985.

SOURCE B

From President Reagan's speech to the British parliament, 8 June 1982 (available from www.reagan.utexas.edu/archives/speeches/1982/60882a.htm).

I have discussed on other occasions … the elements of Western policies toward the Soviet Union to safeguard our interests and protect the peace. What I am describing now is a plan and a hope for the long term – the march of freedom and democracy which will leave Marxism-Leninism on the ash-heap of history as it has left other tyrannies which stifle the freedom and muzzle the self-expression of the people. And that's why we must continue our efforts to strengthen NATO …

Our military strength is a prerequisite to peace, but let it be clear we maintain this strength in the hope it will never be used, for the ultimate determinant in the struggle that's now going on in the world will not be bombs and rockets, but a test of wills and ideas, a trial of spiritual resolve, the values we hold, the beliefs we cherish, the ideals to which we are dedicated.

'Star Wars'

In November 1982, Brezhnev died and was replaced by Yuri Andropov. In 1983, Reagan announced the Strategic Defence Initiative (SDI), also commonly called 'Star Wars', which was planned to be an anti-ballistic missile shield composed of nuclear missiles and laser-armed satellites that would protect the USA from attack. This essentially meant that, if ever fully deployed, SDI would make obsolete the Soviet Union's ability to threaten the USA, while, without this defence, the Soviet Union would remain vulnerable to attack by the USA. The ramifications of this were tremendous for international diplomacy and threatened to end the balance of power between the two superpowers in favour of the USA.

The shooting down of the South Korean airliner

On 1 September 1983, tension between the USA and USSR was further increased when a Soviet fighter aircraft destroyed a South Korean passenger aircraft, which had flown into Soviet air space, killing all 269 people on board, including 61 US citizens. The USSR refused to accept any responsibility, leading Reagan to describe the incident as 'an act of unprecedented barbarism'. Andropov responded that his government felt that it could no longer do business with the USA. In November 1983, relations were so poor that Andropov feared that an annually scheduled NATO military exercise might be a cover for a nuclear attack on the USSR.

Summary diagram: The 'Third' or 'New Cold War' 1979–85

The New Cold War 1979–85

- Solidarity crisis in Poland 1980–1
- Soviet troops occupied Afghanistan
- Deployment of SS-20 and Cruise missiles in Western Europe

③ Gorbachev: *glasnost* and *détente* 1985–9

▶ What were Gorbachev's aims, both globally and within the USSR, 1985–9?

When Andropov died in February 1984, the Soviet Politburo chose Konstantin Chernenko, a cautious and elderly man in poor health, to succeed him. He agreed to reopen negotiations with the USSR for the Strategic Arms Reduction Treaty, which had been broken off when the USA installed nuclear missiles in Europe in 1983. These opened in Geneva in March 1985, the very month that Chernenko died and was replaced by Mikhail Gorbachev.

The problems facing Mikhail Gorbachev

Gorbachev inherited a difficult situation:

- The collapse of *détente* in the late 1970s between the USA and USSR had led to a new and expensive arms race.
- The USSR, like the USA in the 1960s, was increasingly suffering from **global over-stretch**. It was fighting an unwinnable war in Afghanistan and was also giving financial and military aid to left-wing regimes that had seized power in Angola and the Horn of Africa (see pages 178–80). All of this cost a great deal of money.
- The Soviet economy was stagnating and desperately needed both technological and financial input from the West.

Gorbachev's response to these challenges was to launch an ambitious attempt to modernise the USSR within, while renewing *détente* with the West and ultimately ending the Cold War. It was a gamble that ended in the collapse of the USSR.

🔑 **KEY TERM**

Global over-stretch
The situation when great powers take on more global responsibilities than they can afford or manage easily.

Mikhail Gorbachev

1931	Born in Stavropol in southern Russia
1970	Appointed first secretary for agriculture
1979	Joined the Politburo
1985	Elected general secretary of the USSR
1986	Launched the policies of **glasnost** and **perestroika**
1987	Called for multi-candidate elections in the USSR
1988	Announced the withdrawal of Soviet forces from Afghanistan and the abandonment of the Brezhnev Doctrine
1990	Received Nobel Peace Prize for ending the Cold War
1991	Soviet hardliners launched an unsuccessful coup against him and he resigned a few weeks later

When Gorbachev became general secretary, compared to his elderly and sick predecessors, he appeared a youthful and dynamic leader. His great aim was to modernise the USSR, and the two key words *glasnost* and *perestroika* set the tone for his period in power. The ultimate survival of the USSR depended on *perestroika*. The historian S.R. Ashton, paraphrasing Henry Kissinger, observed that the USSR was in the 'unenviable position' of being threatened at the same time by two crises: 'an economic crisis if it did nothing to change its system, and a political crisis if it did anything'. Gorbachev was convinced that the USSR could no longer afford Cold War confrontation, and he renounced the idea of inevitable world conflict. Arguably, Gorbachev was therefore the single biggest force in ending the Cold War.

🔑 KEY TERMS

Glasnost Openness regarding the USSR's economic and political systems, including public discussion and debate.

Perestroika Transformation or restructuring of the Communist Party to make it more responsive to the needs of the people.

USSR's economic weakness

It was the economic weakness of the USSR and the COMECON states that was a key factor in the collapse of communism and the disintegration of the USSR by 1991. Yet until at least 1960, their economies had performed relatively well. One reason for this was that the main industrial technology of the time was based on large productive units, such as car and tractor factories, and heavy industry, particularly coal and steel, which could function effectively as large units controlled by a central planning system.

The system was poor at adapting to supplying at competitive prices the multitude of consumer goods that were available to the capitalist states. In the early 1960s, Soviet economist Yevsei Liberman and Ota Šikin from Czechoslovakia put forward ideas for decentralising the economy to allow decisions of production, design and pricing, and so on, to be taken by local factory managers. In Czechoslovakia, these ideas began to be realised between 1965 and 1968, but after the termination of the Prague Spring (see page 168), such experiments were discouraged for fear that they might lead to growing demands for political concessions.

There was, instead, a return to the Stalinist style of centralised control of the economy with its emphasis on heavy industry. For a time this did appear to work. *Détente* and *Ostpolitik* opened up the way for generous Western loans to the USSR and the satellite states, which helped to keep energy prices down and pay for massive industrial projects, but by the early 1980s the Eastern bloc economies were falling far behind the West. The total production of the USSR, for instance, was only 37 per cent of the **gross national product (GNP)** of the USA. The Western European economies had been badly hit by the escalating rises in oil prices, which started in 1973, but they had responded to this challenge by modernising their economies and developing new industries and technologies. The USSR and its satellite states had failed to do this. They were therefore very vulnerable when faced with the triple crises of inflation, rising oil prices and global economic depression in the early 1980s.

SOURCE C

From Soviet periodical *Novy Mir*, No. 6, by Nikolai Shmelevin, 1987, quoted in Martin McCauley, *Gorbachev*, Longman, 1998, p. 68.

At present our economy is characterized by shortages [and] imbalances … unmanageable, and almost unplannable … Industry now rejects up to 80 per cent of technical decisions and inventions … the working masses have reached a state of almost total lack of interest in … honest labour … Apathy, indifference, thieving … have become mass phenomena, with simultaneous aggressive envy towards those who are capable of earning. There have appeared signs of … physical degradation of a large part of the population, through drunkenness and idleness. Finally there is disbelief in the officially announced objectives and purposes, in the very possibility of a more rational economic and social organization of life. Clearly, all this cannot be quickly overcome – years, perhaps generations, will be needed.

> What information does Source C convey about the state of the Soviet economy? **?**

Gorbachev's reforms

Initially, Gorbachev aimed to reform the economy by:

- increasing investment in technology
- restructuring the economy so it was less centralised (*perestroika*)
- giving workers greater freedom and incentives to encourage them to work harder.

Glasnost

To win the support of the people for his reforms, Gorbachev realised that a policy of openness, or *glasnost*, had to be followed. In other words, economic and political issues needed to be debated openly. From the spring of 1986 onwards, state censorship of the media was progressively eased and reception of foreign broadcasts was allowed. This ensured that the disaster at the **Chernobyl** nuclear power station in 1986 received major international publicity, as did Soviet failures in the Afghanistan War. In this new climate, investigative journalism, hitherto unknown in the USSR, played a key role in exposing the corruption of the Communist Party elite with their subsidised shops, chauffeur-driven cars and other benefits. All of this did much irreparably to damage the image of the party in the eyes of many Soviet citizens.

🔑 **KEY TERMS**

Gross national product (GNP) The total production of domestic industries combined with the earnings from exports.

Chernobyl In April 1986, an explosion at Chernobyl nuclear power station released a large amount of radioactive dust into the atmosphere, which affected much of Western Russia and Eastern Europe; 31 people died.

Democratic Union
The first opposition party to the Communist Party of the USSR.

The years 1988–9 were the high points of *glasnost*. New political organisations were established, such as the **Democratic Union**, and books by former dissidents were published. Religion, too, was tolerated. Churches, mosques and synagogues were reopened and for the first time in Soviet history religious texts and books were openly on sale in the shops. There was also a sudden appearance of uncensored newspapers and journals. In May 1989, the newly constituted Congress of People's Deputies was elected in what were the first contested national elections organised by the Communists. Although the Congress was no parliament, many different strands of public opinion were represented in it, and it had complete freedom to debate and criticise the government's policies. It also had the task of selecting the members for the Supreme Soviet, which was now to become in effect a parliament in session for much of the year. In fact, in the course of 1990–1, the Congress rather than the Supreme Soviet, emerged as the most important force in Russia.

In February 1990, the cancellation of Article 6 of the old Soviet Constitution, which guaranteed the Communist Party a leading role in the USSR, destroyed the whole foundation on which the USSR's government existed. Party officials now had to have the backing of over 50 per cent of the electorate to remain in office, and in the March elections to the Congress of People's Deputies most long-term officials were rejected. Gorbachev was elected the first executive president of the USSR.

Détente renegotiated 1985–8

Gorbachev quickly showed that he was determined to negotiate major reductions in nuclear weapons. In April 1985 he stopped increasing the number of SS-20s being installed in Eastern Europe, and in October started to reduce their number. He failed at the Reykjavík Conference in 1986 to persuade Reagan to give up the SDI plan in return for the negotiation of arms control treaties. However, such was his wish to end the arms race that he accepted unconditionally the NATO plan for a total withdrawal of medium-range missiles by both sides in Europe at the Washington summit in December 1987.

For the next two years, Gorbachev showed a determination not just to restore *détente* but to end the Cold War. In December 1988 at the UN, he publicly conceded that Marxism–Leninism was not the key to ultimate truth. According to one US senator, this was 'the most astounding statement of surrender in the history of ideological struggle'.

Global *détente*

Afghanistan

Gorbachev realised that Soviet policy had failed in Afghanistan (see page 183) and in November 1986 decided that Soviet troops, regardless of the consequences within Afghanistan, would have to be withdrawn as soon as possible. The Soviets replaced Afghan President Babrak Karmal with Mohammed Najibullah, who, they believed, would be able to form a government of national unity that could negotiate a peace between the various factions fighting in Afghanistan. In April 1988, protocols were signed in Geneva, Switzerland, between Pakistan and Afghanistan, with the USSR and USA as sponsors. These consisted of the following agreements:

- neither state would interfere in the internal affairs of the other
- or allow militant groups, hostile to the other state, to train within their territory
- Afghan refugees in Pakistan would be permitted to return to Afghanistan
- the withdrawal of Soviet troops from Afghanistan would begin on 15 May 1988 and end by 15 February 1989.

These agreements did not bring peace to Afghanistan. The *mujahedin*, who were not represented at Geneva, fought on, while the USSR continued to give financial assistance and arms to Najibullah's forces. As long as this continued, the USA gave financial and military support to the *mujahedin*. Fighting continued at varying levels in Afghanistan after the collapse of the Soviet Union and into the current period.

Nicaragua

In 1988, both the USA and USSR supported a plan drawn up by the Central American states that ended foreign assistance to all fighting groups and called for free elections to resolve the Nicaraguan Civil War.

Angola

In Angola, where fighting had continued between the Cuban-backed Movement for the Liberation of Angola (MPLA) and the South African-backed UNITA (see page 178), the USA and USSR jointly persuaded Cuba, Angola and South Africa to agree to a ceasefire and the withdrawal of Cuban troops. In December 1988 South Africa, in return, agreed to implement UN Resolution 435, which called for the independence of Namibia, a huge region on Angola's southern border that was administered on behalf of the UN by South Africa.

Ethiopia

Gorbachev continued to send financial aid to assist the Mengistu regime (see page 179) in Ethiopia until 1989. In early 1990, due to the financial crisis triggered by the collapse in the prices of its coffee exports, Mengistu turned to the USA for financial aid, but in May 1991 he was ousted in a coup led by his anti-Marxist opponents. Little attention was given to Ethiopia in the final years of the Soviet Union's existence.

KEY TERM

Khmer Rouge regime
Regime established by Pol Pot, which killed over 2 million of its own people.

Cambodia

In 1979 Vietnam, supported by the USSR, invaded Cambodia and overthrew the **Khmer Rouge regime** (see page 166), establishing the pro-Vietnam People's Republic of Kampuchea (PRK). Vietnamese military units remained in Cambodia to support the new republic. The extension of Vietnamese influence into Cambodia was opposed by both the PRC and the USA, as well as many of the smaller states in South-East Asia. Gorbachev was ready to collaborate with both the USA and PRC to find a solution to the Cambodian problem. Just before his visit to Beijing in May 1989 (see below), where he hoped to end the disagreements between the PRC and the USSR, he put pressure on Vietnam to withdraw its troops from Cambodia. This did not lead to immediate peace, but a ceasefire between the PRK and the Khmer Rouge rebels was negotiated in 1991 by the UN Security Council with active US and Soviet assistance.

End of the PRC–Soviet dispute

Soviet withdrawal from Afghanistan and co-operation over Cambodia had cleared the way for improving relations between the PRC and the USSR. In May 1989, after a summit meeting in Beijing between Gorbachev and Mao's successor, Deng Xiaoping, relations were fully restored. This was helped too by Gorbachev's prior announcement that he would reduce the number of border forces on the Sino-Soviet frontier. Gorbachev was greeted by hundreds of thousands of students, who hoped their leaders would follow his example and liberalise the PRC.

Deng, who was in the process of modernising the PRC and embracing Western capitalism, sympathised with Gorbachev's desire to reform the Soviet economy, but unlike Gorbachev he was not ready to make any political concessions. He was quick to declare martial law and forcibly clear Beijing's Tiananmen Square of democratic protesters on 4 June 1989, the day after Gorbachev flew back to the USSR. The Communist Party in China managed to maintain its grip on power, while successfully modernising the economy.

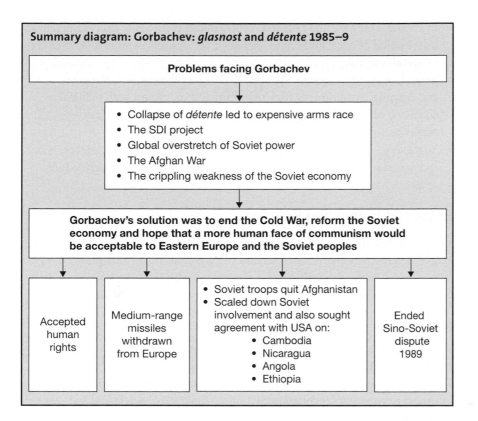

Summary diagram: Gorbachev: *glasnost* and *détente* 1985–9

Problems facing Gorbachev

- Collapse of *détente* led to expensive arms race
- The SDI project
- Global overstretch of Soviet power
- The Afghan War
- The crippling weakness of the Soviet economy

Gorbachev's solution was to end the Cold War, reform the Soviet economy and hope that a more human face of communism would be acceptable to Eastern Europe and the Soviet peoples

Accepted human rights

Medium-range missiles withdrawn from Europe

- Soviet troops quit Afghanistan
- Scaled down Soviet involvement and also sought agreement with USA on:
  - Cambodia
  - Nicaragua
  - Angola
  - Ethiopia

Ended Sino-Soviet dispute 1989

④ The collapse of communism in Eastern Europe 1989–95

▶ *Why did communism collapse in Eastern Europe?*

By withdrawing from Afghanistan and Africa, Gorbachev refocused Soviet policy on Europe. Again he hoped to safeguard Soviet security through a policy of political co-operation and negotiation. On 6 July 1989, he effectively renounced the Brezhnev Doctrine when he informed the Council of Europe in a famous speech that 'the common European home … excludes all possibility of armed confrontation, all possibility of resorting to threat or use of force … employed by one alliance against another, within an alliance, or whatever it might be.'

By 1989, Gorbachev was encouraging Communist Eastern European states to follow the USSR's example by reforming economically and liberalising politically. To understand the consequences of these radical policy changes, it is helpful to divide eastern and south-eastern Europe into three loose groups:

- In Poland, Hungary and Bulgaria, governments were ready to contemplate at least limited political and economic reform as long as Communists remained in overall control.
- In the German Democratic Republic (GDR), Czechoslovakia, Romania and Albania, governments were unwilling to experiment with political or economic reform and were compelled to reform by the dramatic events occurring in the GDR.
- Yugoslavia, even before the collapse of communism in Eastern Europe, was facing major challenges with nationalism, which would ultimately tear it apart.

Poland, Hungary and Bulgaria

The political changes in Poland, Hungary and Bulgaria have been described as 'negotiated revolutions'. What is meant by this is that the revolutionary changes that occurred in these countries were introduced with the support of the ruling Communists and decided on before the opening of the Berlin Wall.

Poland

With Poland's economy increasingly indebted to the West, General Jaruzelski was forced to introduce price rises of up to 200 per cent in 1988. This led to a series of strikes that forced the government not only to legalise Solidarity again but to enter into negotiations with both Solidarity leaders and the Catholic Church. All sides agreed at this point that relations with the USSR and the Warsaw Pact could not be discussed as they did not wish to provoke a military intervention. Neither did Solidarity challenge the dominance of the Communists in Poland. On 7 April 1989, the Round Table Agreements, as they were called, were signed between the three groups. Solidarity was recognised not just as a trade union, but also as a political party. A new constitution was also created. This allowed Solidarity to compete for 35 per cent of seats in the lower house of parliament, the Sejm, with 65 per cent reserved for Communists. The upper house of the Sejm would be elected in free elections and both houses would jointly elect the president of Poland.

Gorbachev welcomed this agreement as he felt that it safeguarded Communist power. At the same time, there were sufficient political concessions to please the West and encourage it to increase its financial assistance to Poland.

In the first round of the elections on 4 June, Solidarity won 92 out of the 100 seats in the Sejm's upper house and 160 of the 161 seats in the lower house for which they were allowed to compete. Two weeks later, Communists won all the seats reserved for them, but only 25 per cent of eligible voters voted. As there was dissent within the Communist Party regarding the inclusion of Solidarity in a possible government, it was decided that Solidarity would form the government and that the Communists would hold a minority of ministerial positions. On 18 August, Solidarity led a coalition government that contained only four Communists.

Significantly, Gorbachev made it clear on 16 August that the USSR would not intervene to reinforce an unpopular Communist regime. However, at the time it was still not obvious that a major turning point had been reached. Communists still controlled the Ministries of Defence, Interior, Transportation and Foreign Trade, while Jaruzelski remained president. Solidarity even declared that Poland would remain a member of the Warsaw Pact.

Only with the collapse of Communist rule in the GDR and Czechoslovakia (see below) did Solidarity remove Communists from control of the army and police. In January 1990 the Polish Communist Party was dissolved and then reformed as the Social Democrat Party. Jaruzelski resigned in November 1990 and **Lech Wałęsa**, the leader of Solidarity, was elected president.

Hungary

By 1987, within Hungary, criticism of both the economy and the government was growing. Living standards had declined and the country's debts to the West were the highest in Eastern Europe. As in Poland, corruption existed throughout the government.

In May 1988, responding to the atmosphere created by Gorbachev's *perestroika* and *glasnost*, the Hungarian Socialist Workers' Party (**MSZMP**) replaced Prime Minister Janos Kádár with Károly Grósz, a committed reformer. In February 1989 the party accepted that Hungary would have to become a multi-party democracy to avert revolution. When Grósz visited the USSR in March 1989, Gorbachev welcomed the developments in Hungary, but he emphasised that the dominant position of socialism in Hungary should not be threatened (see Source D on page 196).

In June, following Poland's example, 'round table' talks began between the government and the opposition groups, ending in agreement that free parliamentary elections were to be held in the spring of 1990. The party leaders accepted this because they were convinced that, having seized the initiative to reform, the Hungarian Socialist Workers' Party would emerge as the dominant force in the new parliament and safeguard socialism in Hungary. The party attempted to transform itself into a Western-style socialist party later in the year and changed its name to the Hungarian Socialist Party (HSP), but in the elections of March 1990 it won less than eleven per cent of the vote and did not take part in the next government. However, in 1994 it returned to power in alliance with the Free Democrats and in 1996 an opinion poll judged it to be the most popular party in Hungarian politics. The HSP had made a successful transformation to a left-wing social democratic party.

KEY FIGURE

Lech Wałęsa (1943–)
Co-founder of Solidarity and Polish president 1990–5.

KEY TERM

MSZMP *Magyar Szocialista Munkáspárt.* The Hungarian Socialist Workers' Party: the Communist Party in Hungary between 1956 and 1989.

What information does Source D convey about Gorbachev's views on Hungarian political reforms?

SOURCE D

From Document No. 3, Memorandum of Conversation between M.S. Gorbachev and HSWP [Hungarian Socialist Workers' Party] General Secretary Károly Grósz, 23–24 March 1989. Quoted in *Cold War International History Bulletin*, Issue 12/13, Autumn/Winter 2001, p. 78.

Comrade Grósz informed the negotiators about the Hungarian situation. He said that the events in Hungary have accelerated lately. Their direction is according to our intentions, while the pace is somewhat disconcerting. Comrade Grósz emphasized that we wish to retain political power and find a solution to our problems by political means, avoiding armed conflict.

We have a good chance for reaching our goals. People are afraid of a possible armed conflict. Workers, peasants and professionals want to work and live in peace and security …

Comrade Gorbachev emphasized that we clearly have to draw boundaries, thinking about others and ourselves at the same time. Democracy is much needed and interests have to be harmonized. The limit, however, is the safe keeping of socialism and assurance of stability.

Bulgaria

By 1989, the ruling Bulgarian Communist Party had been led by Todor Zhivkov for 35 years. Zhivkov had promoted his family into positions of authority for which they were not qualified. **Cronyism** was one of the main features of his government. Those whom Zhivkov favoured in the party were allowed to shop in special stores that stocked imported Western goods, have access to the best education for their children and receive up to 500 per cent more salary than other officials. Zhikov also launched a programme of 'Bulgarianisation', which had led to the expulsion of some 200,000 ethnic Turks from Bulgaria, and resulted in widespread international condemnation.

In July 1989, the Bulgarian foreign minister, Petar Mladenov, confidentially informed Gorbachev that he intended 'to carry out a change of direction in Bulgaria', which Gorbachev did not oppose, and on 9 November forced Zhivkov to resign. As in Poland and Hungary, talks were held with emerging opposition groups and free elections were promised for June 1990. The Bulgarian Communist Party transformed itself into the Bulgarian Socialist Party (BSP). In 1992, it entered a coalition government and narrowly won an outright majority in December 1994, only to be defeated decisively again in elections called in response to the economic crisis of the winter of 1996–7. The BSP had failed in the medium term to distance itself from the legacy of communism. In September 1996 one senior Bulgarian politician had expressed fears that the 'ghost of communism' was returning.

KEY TERM

Cronyism Favouring one's friends by granting them favours, often when they are undeserving.

The collapse of the GDR

The GDR was a product of the Cold War, and to survive into the Gorbachev era it needed to win the loyalty of its population, as it could no longer appeal to Soviet power to maintain law and order. By the summer of 1989, it seemed unlikely that it would be able to achieve this. Its economy, like the USSR's, suffered from centralised planning and a top-heavy system of bureaucratic control. Ironically, only massive West German loans in 1983–4, which were a result of *Ostpolitik* (see page 170), had saved it from bankruptcy.

The GDR faced a major challenge when the Hungarian government decided in August to open its frontiers with Austria and some 150,000 East Germans poured across the border on their way to the FRG. Under pressure from the West German Chancellor Helmut Kohl, Honecker also granted exit visas to the thousands of East Germans who had travelled to Poland and Prague, and who were quite literally besieging the West German embassies there in a desperate attempt to flee the GDR.

Honecker was now facing a crisis potentially every bit as grave as Ulbricht had in 1961 (see page 112). His belated grants of exit visas did nothing to restore confidence in the GDR. On the contrary, it merely made his handling of the crisis look unsure. In Leipzig a series of large but peaceful demonstrations took place in late September and early October 1989, which the regime reluctantly tolerated because it knew that Gorbachev would not support a hardline policy. Indeed, when Gorbachev visited Berlin on 5 October to attend the celebrations marking the fortieth anniversary of the GDR, he advised Honecker to follow the example of the Poles and Hungarians and pointedly warned him that 'life punishes latecomers'.

The Berlin Wall opens

In the absence of any effective restraints by the police or the army, crowds of demonstrators continued to grow in the cities. On 4 November, half a million congregated in East Berlin to demand further reform and the right to travel abroad. Two days later, a proposal was made by Krenz's government to issue permits for travel up to 30 days per year, but this was rejected by the *Volkskammer*, the GDR's parliament, as insufficient. On 9 November, a more sweeping concession was made that granted all GDR citizens with passports the right to an exit visa valid for any border crossing, including entry into West Berlin. Initially, this was supposed to take effect from the morning of 10 November, but it was announced prematurely in a press conference on the evening of the 9th, and that night border guards, facing a crowd of 20,000, opened up the crossing points through the Wall and into West Berlin.

Consequences of 9 November 1989

The opening of the Berlin Wall had immediate consequences not only for Germany, but also for both Czechoslovakia and Romania.

The 'Velvet Revolution': Czechoslovakia

In 1989, Czechoslovakia was still controlled by those who had called for the suppression of the Prague Spring (see page 168). Opposition was limited to small groups, such as Charter 77 led by **Václav Havel**, which attempted to monitor the government's compliance with the Helsinki Accords. As a consequence of the changes in Poland and Hungary in the summer of 1989, the opposition strengthened, and the prime minister, Ladislav Adamec, announced economic reforms which were similar to those introduced during the Prague Spring, but they were not accompanied by political reforms. It was only after the Berlin Wall was opened that the political situation changed dramatically. A demonstration officially called to honour the death of a student killed in the German occupation in the Second World War turned into a mass protest which triggered a series of events known as the Velvet Revolution.

On 19 November twelve opposition groups formed the 'Civic Forum', which demanded political change. On 7 December Adamec resigned and a new government was formed in which Communists were a minority. On 29 December, parliament elected Václav Havel as president. Havel and Civic Forum persuaded the USSR to withdraw its troops from the country while initially agreeing to remain part of the Warsaw Pact. Once it became clear that the two German states would reunite (see page 200), Czechoslovakia, together with Poland and Hungary, pressed for the pact's dissolution. In 1992, Czechoslovakia broke into two independent states: Slovakia and the Czech Republic.

Romania

The opening of the Berlin Wall and the Velvet Revolution provided the Romanians with an opportunity to oust their Communist leader, Nicolae Ceauşescu. As in the other Communist states, economic hardship and blatant corruption, symbolised by Ceauşescu's construction of a 1100-room palace, caused significant opposition to emerge against his government.

Gorbachev had been informed of plans to overthrow him as early as November 1989, and agreed, provided that the Romanian Communist Party was left as the dominant force in the country. The first revolts against the regime broke out in the largely ethnic Hungarian city of Timisoara, near the Hungarian border, and spread to Bucharest, on 21 December. Once it became clear that the army had sided with the people against the state's secret police, Ceauşescu fled the capital. He was soon arrested by the army and executed with his wife on 25 December.

On 22 December the National Salvation Front (NSF) was formed by Silviu Brucan, a former ambassador to the USA, General Militaru and Ion Iliescu, a leading Communist. After talks with opposition groups, the NSF established a Council for National Unity and held elections for a new government in May 1990. The NSF managed to win a majority and Iliescu was elected president. It was not until 1996 that the NSF was decisively defeated by a new party grouping, the Social Democratic Union.

Yugoslavia and Albania

Yugoslavia

After its expulsion from Cominform in 1948 (see page 82), Yugoslavia had followed a different pattern from the other Communist states in eastern and south-eastern Europe. It had more contact with the West and, in the 1960s and 1970s, Tito allowed greater cultural and intellectual freedom than existed in the other Communist states. However, Yugoslavia, like the other Communist states, faced growing economic and political problems that were to destroy it by 1990. It was heavily dependent on foreign investment and by 1989 inflation had reached almost 300 per cent annually.

The economic problems worsened relations between the nationalities that formed the Yugoslav state. The prestige of President Tito managed to keep ethnic rivalries in check, but after his death in 1980 leaders of the Yugoslav Federation increasingly used nationalism to strengthen their own political position. In the Soviet bloc, people's dissatisfaction with governments led to demands for democratic reform and the overthrow of communism. In Yugoslavia this was channelled into increasing ethnic rivalries.

Influenced by the events in Eastern Europe, the Communist Party's leading role in Yugoslavia was removed by the Federal Prime Minister Ante Marković from the constitution in January 1990 and multi-party federal elections were announced. These, however, only took place at state level, beginning with the northern state of Slovenia in April 1990. Each election brought to power nationalists and soon each Yugoslav state demanded independence, leading to the dismemberment of the country into independent rival states and war. Successively, Slovenia, Croatia, Bosnia and Herzegovina, Macedonia, Kosovo and Montenegro, declared their independence from Yugoslavia between 1991 and 2006. All but Macedonia and Montenegro fought wars to achieve independence, with the most brutal being the struggle in Bosnia and Herzegovina between 1992 and 1995 in which 100,000 people were killed, millions displaced and most cities destroyed.

Albania

Under Enver Hoxha, Albania had ended diplomatic and economic relations with the USSR in 1961 and had clung to a strict Stalinist interpretation of communism. On Hoxha's death in 1985, Ramiz Alia initially continued the same policies, but in February 1989 announced a very limited reform programme based on Gorbachev's *perestroika*. Ceauşescu's fall in Romania led to unrest and riots in the capital city of Tirana, which pushed the government into announcing further reforms involving the decentralisation of the economy and the legalisation of non-Communist political parties. In the election of March 1991 the former Communist Party, now renamed the Socialist Party of Albania (APL), won the majority of seats. It briefly formed a government and Alia was elected as president in May, but further unrest led to fresh elections in 1992, which the strongly anti-Communist Democratic Party won by a sizeable margin of votes. With the collapse of the old state industries, Albania experienced an acute economic crisis and in March 1997 order had to be restored by an Italian-led military task force. In the April elections, the Albanian Socialist Party (the former APL) won a large majority.

Unification of Germany

On 13 November, Prime Minister Egon Krenz was replaced by Hans Modrow, the Dresden Communist Party Secretary. Under his leadership the GDR then rapidly followed the example of Poland and agreed to free elections, which were held in March 1990. The 'Alliance for Germany' coalition, which supported reunification, won a majority of seats, and on 12 April the new government announced that it wished to join the FRG.

SOURCE E

By February 1990 GDR troops had already started to demolish the Berlin Wall. The shattered pieces of the Wall became collectors' objects. The Imperial War Museum in London has a panel on display.

? What message does Source E imply about the future of both Berlin and Germany?

Initially, neither the USSR, nor Britain nor France wanted a united Germany, and Chancellor Kohl himself was thinking only of forming a very loose confederation which would very slowly grow into a political union, or federation. Nevertheless, the strength of East German public opinion in the winter of 1989–90 convinced him that unity was the only option. The division of Germany had marked the beginning of the Cold War; its reunification marked the end.

Kohl could not reunify Germany without the agreement of the USSR, the USA and Germany's main Western European allies, Britain and France. However, only the USSR and the USA had the power to stop it. Thus, the real negotiations were between Bonn, Moscow and Washington. At first, Gorbachev was opposed to the liquidation of the GDR, and in December 1989 promised that he would 'see to it that no harm comes to the GDR'. Yet by the end of January his support for it was ebbing rapidly. On 10 February 1990 he told Kohl in Moscow that the Germans themselves should decide on the question of German unity, and at Ottowa four days later, President **Bush** also gave the green light and outlined a formula for proceeding with the negotiations, the 'two-plus-four talks', which would bring together both the two Germanys and the four former occupying powers which still had **residual rights** in Berlin.

In a series of negotiations in Bonn, Berlin, Paris and Moscow in the summer of 1990, German unity was brokered. Any lingering Soviet opposition to German unity and the membership of a united Germany in NATO was overcome by generous West German loans, which Gorbachev hoped would facilitate the modernisation of the Soviet economy. Opposition in the West, particularly in London and Paris, was stilled by Kohl's insistence on a united Germany's continued membership of NATO and on the incorporation of East Germany into the European Community.

On 12 September the Two-Plus-Four Treaty was signed in Moscow. It was in effect a peace treaty ending the partition of Germany, as it terminated the residual rights of the former occupying powers in Germany and committed the new Germany to recognising the Oder–Neisse border with Poland. At midnight on 2 October 1990 the GDR was integrated into the FRG and a reunited Germany came into existence. The West, albeit with Gorbachev's blessing, had indeed won a spectacular victory.

Concluding the Cold War in Europe

After agreement on German reunification, the Cold War was effectively ended by decisions taken in Paris in November 1990. Representatives of NATO and the Warsaw Pact, which was dissolved in July 1991, met in Paris to sign the Treaty on Conventional Armed Forces in Europe. It provided for the equal reduction of conventional weapons in both Eastern and Western Europe, agreed on a process of inspection and verification, and declared that the countries signing the pact

🔑 **KEY FIGURE**

George Bush (1924–)
US president 1989–93. (Father of George W. Bush, president 2001–9.)

🔑 **KEY TERM**

Residual rights
The remaining privileges, going right back to 1945, which the four occupying powers of Britain, France, the USA and the USSR still enjoyed.

were 'no longer adversaries'. The participants of the conference also produced the Charter of Paris for a New Europe. This established a secretariat to organise annual meetings at head-of-government level and for the creation of a Conflict Prevention Centre in Vienna to advise on conflict avoidance.

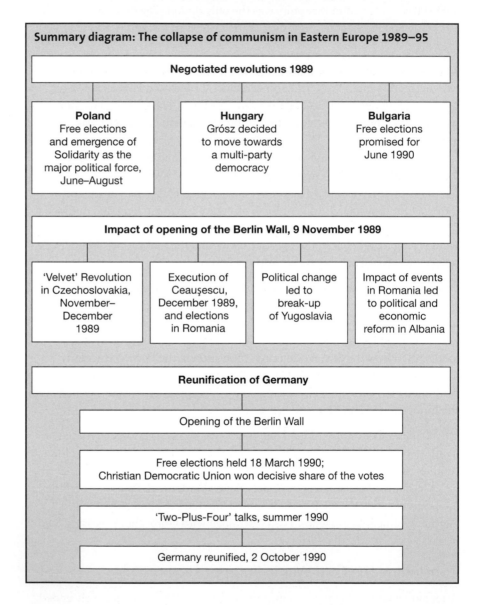

Summary diagram: The collapse of communism in Eastern Europe 1989–95

Negotiated revolutions 1989

Poland
Free elections and emergence of Solidarity as the major political force, June–August

Hungary
Grósz decided to move towards a multi-party democracy

Bulgaria
Free elections promised for June 1990

Impact of opening of the Berlin Wall, 9 November 1989

'Velvet' Revolution in Czechoslovakia, November–December 1989

Execution of Ceauşescu, December 1989, and elections in Romania

Political change led to break-up of Yugoslavia

Impact of events in Romania led to political and economic reform in Albania

Reunification of Germany

Opening of the Berlin Wall

Free elections held 18 March 1990; Christian Democratic Union won decisive share of the votes

'Two-Plus-Four' talks, summer 1990

Germany reunified, 2 October 1990

The disintegration of the USSR

▶ *Why was Gorbachev unable to prevent the disintegration of the USSR?*

▶ *To what extent was nationalism a factor in the disintegration of the USSR?*

By 1989, it was clear that *perestroika* had not managed to resolve the country's economic difficulties. The USSR's budget revenue steadily declined, while inflation rose. In 1987 the Soviet state deficit was 57.1 billion roubles; by 1989, 100 billion. The consequences of this were a growing shortage of goods and a fall in living standards.

The nationalities problem

The USSR was a federation of fifteen republics in which the Russian Soviet Federative Socialist Republic (RSFSR) was by far the largest state. *Perestroika, glasnost* and the collapse of communism in Eastern Europe led to a reawakening of nationalism in many constituent republic states that were part of the USSR and felt dominated by ethnic Russians. The collapse of the Soviet economy also removed any remaining incentive to stay within the USSR (see Source C on page 189).

The Baltic states

Estonia, Latvia and Lithuania had been parts of the Russian Empire until the collapse of Russia in the First World War, when they gained temporary independence (see page 8). They were absorbed by the Soviet Union in 1940, occupied by Germany from 1941 to 1944, and then again merged with the Soviet Union. *Glasnost* and *perestroika* encouraged reformers and nationalists to press for independence. In 1988 so-called Popular Fronts, which were coalitions of reformers, formed in all three republics. In February 1990, local elections were held throughout the USSR and pro-independence candidates won in the three Baltic republics. In March, Lithuania and Estonia declared their independence, and Latvia followed in May. They were given encouragement and support by Solidarity in Poland.

Gorbachev's reaction

Initially, Gorbachev reacted strongly against the independence movements in the Baltic. He was determined to keep the USSR together at all costs. He imposed an economic blockade on Lithuania in April 1990 and in January 1991 Soviet troops entered all three Baltic states on the pretext of searching for military deserters. In Vilnius, Lithuania, they seized the radio and television centre, killing thirteen civilians; but after encountering massive public demonstrations, they were forced to withdraw. On 11 January, President Bush contacted Gorbachev and expressed his concern. The violence only served to strengthen the determination of the nationalists to gain independence.

Transcaucasia and Central Asian Republics

Glasnost had also encouraged the emergence of historic ethnic conflicts in Georgia, Armenia and Azerbaijan, as well as in the central Asian republics of Kazakhstan and Uzbekistan.

Armenian–Azerbaijan conflict

The most serious conflict occurred in the southern Caucasus region and involved Christian Armenia and Muslim Azerbaijan. The Nagorno-Karabakh district, populated by Armenians, was claimed by Armenia but had been granted to Azerbaijan by Stalin in 1923. It was divided from Armenia by a thin strip of land. *Glasnost* enabled the Armenians to hold rallies during the winter of 1987–8 and demand its return. In February 1988, after a week of growing demonstrations in Stepanakert, the capital city, Nagorno-Karabakh voted to merge with Armenia. After this was vetoed by Gorbachev, anti-Armenian riots erupted in Azerbaijan.

Gorbachev removed the leaders in both republics, but his failure to find a solution to the intractable Nagorno-Karabakh issue led to growing nationalism in both Armenia and Azerbaijan. Early in 1988, leading Armenian intellectuals and nationalists formed the Karabakh Committee to organise a campaign for the return of Nagorno-Karabakh to Armenia. Yet in opposition to this, the Popular Front of Azerbaijan was formed in July 1988, which aimed at independence from the USSR and retention of the disputed area.

Blockade of Armenia

In July 1988, Nagorno-Karabakh was temporarily placed under direct rule of the central government in Moscow. In an attempt to find a lasting solution, Gorbachev allowed the USSR's Supreme Soviet to decide on the region's future. This, however, merely voted in November 1989 to return Nagorno-Karabakh to Azerbaijani control. In defiance of this vote, the Armenian Supreme Soviet decided to ignore the decision and integrate the territory into Armenia. In response, the Azerbaijan Popular Front organised a rail blockade of Armenia which led to shortages of petrol and food. It also held a series of demonstrations in Baku, Azerbaijan's capital, which rapidly degenerated into riots directed against the local Armenians, at least 91 of whom were killed. On 19 January, the Azerbaijan Popular Front declared a state of emergency, and the following day, its members seized government and Communist Party buildings.

Gorbachev responded by declaring martial law and sent Soviet troops to restore the government. Late at night on 19 January 1990, 26,000 Soviet troops entered Baku, smashing through barricades established by the Popular Front and attacking protesters, killing over 130. While the army gained control of Baku, it alienated the population of Azerbaijan. Most of the population of Baku attended the mass funerals of the victims and thousands of Communist Party members publicly burned their party membership cards.

Georgia

The independence movements in the Baltic and Transcaucasia inspired similar movements in Georgia. On 7–8 April 1989, troops were sent to the streets of Tbilisi, Georgia, after more than 100,000 people gathered in front of government offices and the Communist Party headquarters and called for Georgia's independence. Nineteen people were killed and more than 200 wounded. This radicalised Georgian politics, leading many to believe that independence was preferable to continued Soviet rule.

The Central Asian Republics

In Kazakhstan and Uzbekistan, Gorbachev's attempt to purge the local Communist Party organisations of corrupt officials triggered a nationalist backlash that ultimately resulted in both republics voting to leave the USSR. In 1986, Gorbachev replaced the ethnic Kazakh leader of the local branch of the Communist Party with a Russian. This was seen by the local population as humiliating and evidence of further ethnic Russian domination. On 16 December, rioting broke out in cities across the republic. The government arrested thousands in a brutal crackdown.

In neighbouring Uzbekistan, Gorbachev's attempts were equally clumsy. Over 18,000 Uzbek Communist Party members were dismissed and mostly replaced with ethnic Russian officials, who knew little of the country or the language, triggering rising nationalism which agitated for ethnic Uzbek rule and independence.

The western republics and Russia

In Belarus, Moldavia and Ukraine, demands for independence were strongest in those areas which had been annexed by the Soviet Union between 1939 and 1940.

Moldavia

The Democratic Movement of **Moldova** was created in 1988 to campaign initially for greater cultural independence from the USSR. This took the form of demands for the revival of Moldovan traditions and the recognition of Moldovan as the official language. In May 1989, inspired by events in the Baltic, the Popular Front of Moldova was founded. It successfully persuaded the Moldavian Supreme Soviet to adopt a new language law on 31 August 1989 which made Moldovan the official state language. In March 1990, it became the largest party in the elections for the Supreme Soviet.

> **KEY TERM**
>
> **Moldova** The Romanian for Moldavia, the name by which Moldova was known during its history as part of the Russian Empire.

Ukraine

The key to the future of the USSR was Ukraine, its second largest republic. If Ukraine chose independence, the USSR would be irreparably damaged. Lvov, in western Ukraine, became the centre of protests which demanded greater toleration for Ukrainian Christians and culture. Initially, local Communist authorities attempted to end demonstrations, but that became much more difficult when the republic-wide Ukrainian Popular Front Movement, *Rukh*, was created in 1989. In October 1990, it declared that its principal goal was no longer autonomy within the USSR, but complete independence.

Belarus

Again, inspired by the Baltic Popular Fronts, the Belarus Popular Front was established in 1988 as both a political party and a cultural movement demanding democracy and independence for Belarus. The discovery of mass graves in woods outside Minsk, the capital, of those executed by the NKVD during the Stalin era, added momentum to the pro-democracy and pro-independence movement in the republic. It was argued that in the future only complete independence from the USSR would protect Belarus from a recurrence of such atrocities.

Russia

Elections had taken place for the Congress of People's Deputies in March and April 1990 (see page 190) and gave a majority to reformers and outright opponents of the Communist regime. It was clear that the old USSR in the form that it had existed since the early 1920s was now doomed. Gorbachev's rival, **Boris Yeltsin**, emerged as the leading politician in Russia and was elected chairman of the Congress. On 12 June, the Congress declared that Russia was a sovereign state and that its laws took precedence over those made by the Supreme Soviet of the USSR. The term 'sovereign' asserted the moral right of the republic to self-determination. It did not necessarily rule out the possibility of voluntarily negotiating a new federation.

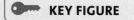

KEY FIGURE

Boris Yeltsin (1931–2007)

Head of the Communist Party in Moscow 1985–7, president of the Russian Federation 1991–9.

'The summer of sovereignty'

Elections also took place in the other republics during March and April 1990 for all the republics' Supreme Soviets. All followed Russia's example in declaring their sovereignty. The exception was Latvia, which already claimed to be independent.

The end of the USSR

The declarations of independence prompted Gorbachev to create a draft of the new Union Treaty in November 1990. In March 1991, a referendum was held on the question of creating a new union formed by the former members of the USSR. Soviet citizens were asked whether they supported the creation of a 'renewed federation of equal sovereign republics'. The referendum was boycotted by the Baltic republics, Moldavia, Georgia and Armenia, but in the other republics it was supported by 74 per cent of voters.

Gorbachev under threat

Gorbachev was in an increasingly vulnerable position. Unlike Yeltsin, he had not been democratically elected, nor did he have a secure power base. He was still president of the nearly defunct USSR and faced opposition from two quarters:

- Communists in the army, party and the KGB, who were bitterly critical of his policies, which in their eyes had led to the break-up of the USSR
- reformers led by Yeltsin, who in June 1991 became the first directly elected president of Russia.

The coup of 18–19 August 1991

On 18 August, just two days before the Union Treaty was to come into effect, leading Communists, who were opposed to change, made one last attempt to save the old USSR. They launched an abortive coup in Moscow while Gorbachev was on holiday in the Crimea. There was no public backing for the rebels and the coup collapsed. Yeltsin played a key role in rallying the crowds in Moscow against the coup and was able to emerge as the saviour of the new Russia. Gorbachev was sidelined as he was on holiday and Yeltsin was seen as the hero who saved Russia from a military coup. The once all-powerful Communist Party was made illegal in Russia in August.

The consequences: the end of the USSR

The nine republics that had agreed to the Union Treaty now refused to implement it. Gorbachev attempted to draft a new treaty, but this too was rejected by all the republics. The final blow to the USSR came when Ukraine decided on complete independence from the USSR after holding a referendum in December 1991.

In December, Ukraine, Russia and Belarus established the **Commonwealth of Independent States (CIS)**, which was then joined on 21 December 1991 by eight additional former Soviet republics: Armenia, Azerbaijan, Kazakhstan, Kyrgyzstan, Moldova, Turkmenistan, Tajikistan and Uzbekistan. Georgia joined two years later, in December 1993. On 25 December 1991, Gorbachev resigned and on 31 December, the USSR ceased to exist. The CIS was a 'ghost' of the former USSR. It was an entirely voluntary organisation whose members were sovereign states.

KEY TERM

Commonwealth of Independent States (CIS)
A voluntary organisation eventually of twelve of the successor states of the USSR. Any decision made by it was not binding on its members.

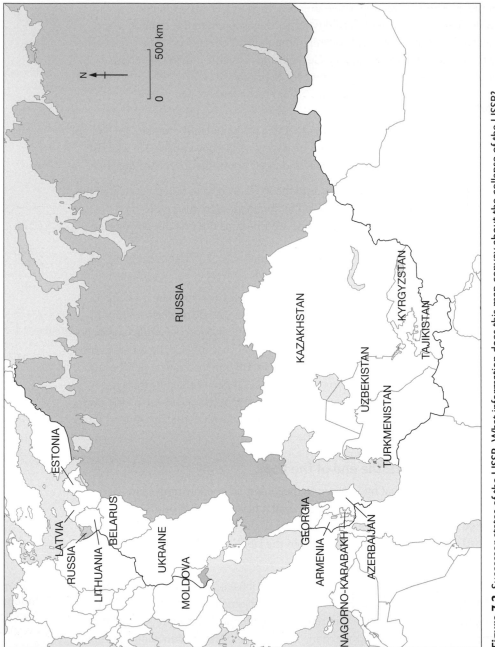

Figure 7.2 Successor states of the USSR. What information does this map convey about the collapse of the USSR?

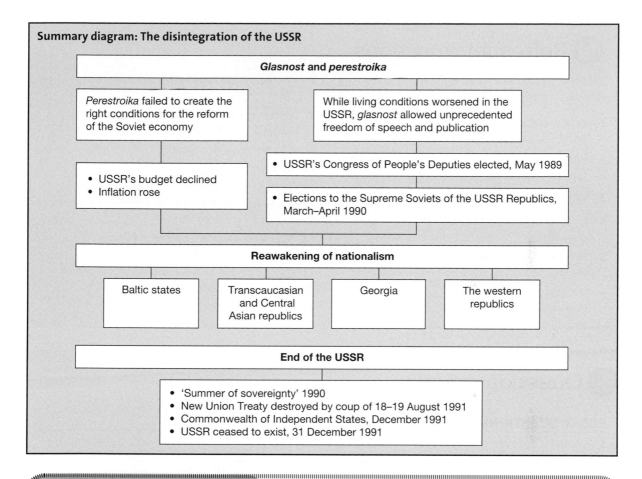

Summary diagram: The disintegration of the USSR

Glasnost and perestroika

Perestroika failed to create the right conditions for the reform of the Soviet economy

While living conditions worsened in the USSR, *glasnost* allowed unprecedented freedom of speech and publication

- USSR's budget declined
- Inflation rose

- USSR's Congress of People's Deputies elected, May 1989

- Elections to the Supreme Soviets of the USSR Republics, March–April 1990

Reawakening of nationalism

| Baltic states | Transcaucasian and Central Asian republics | Georgia | The western republics |

End of the USSR

- 'Summer of sovereignty' 1990
- New Union Treaty destroyed by coup of 18–19 August 1991
- Commonwealth of Independent States, December 1991
- USSR ceased to exist, 31 December 1991

Chapter summary

By 1980 the Soviet centralised command economy was in rapid decline. It had squandered enormous sums on armaments and failed to restructure itself to face the economic challenges of the modern world. It was weakened by the renewed arms race and the Afghan War, and could no longer afford to enforce the Brezhnev Doctrine.

Gorbachev attempted to modernise the Soviet economy by the partial introduction of free-market principles. He hoped that a reformed and economically strengthened USSR would be able to forge new links of friendship with Eastern European states which would remain Communist.

This was a miscalculation. The GDR collapsed and German unification took place on the FRG's terms. Throughout Eastern Europe, Communist regimes collapsed. Yugoslavia dissolved into several non-Communist successor states.

The liberation of Eastern Europe from communism set precedents for the republics of the USSR. Weakened by economic crisis, the USSR had little to offer them. The Baltic republics, the Transcaucasian and central Asian republics, as well as Moldavia, Belarus, Ukraine and, finally, Russia itself, decided to abandon the USSR and communism. In December 1991 the USSR was replaced by the establishment of the Commonwealth of Independent States and Gorbachev was forced to resign. The Cold War had ended.

 Refresher questions

Use these questions to remind yourself of the key material covered in this chapter.

1 What impact did the invasion of Afghanistan have on the outbreak of the 'New Cold War'?

2 What was the significance of the Solidarity crisis for East–West relations?

3 Why did the events in Poland threaten *Ostpolitik*?

4 How bad were US–USSR relations between 1981 and 1984?

5 How serious were the economic problems facing the Soviet economy 1960–85?

6 What steps did Gorbachev take to restore the policy of *détente*?

7 Why did Gorbachev inherit a difficult situation in 1985?

8 To what extent did Gorbachev support the political changes in Poland, Bulgaria and Hungary?

9 Why did the GDR collapse?

10 How was Germany reunified?

11 To what extent was the collapse of communism in Albania and Yugoslavia a consequence of the events in Eastern Europe in 1989?

12 How did communism collapse in Bulgaria, Czechoslovakia and Romania?

13 Why did the Western republics and Russia declare themselves independent?

14 Why did the USSR collapse?

Question practice

ESSAY QUESTIONS

1 To what extent can the years 1979–85 be called the 'New Cold War'?

2 Assess the consequences for the USSR of Gorbachev's policy of *Glasnost*.

3 Which of the following was of greater importance in ending the Cold War? i) Soviet economic weakness. ii) The war in Afghanistan. Explain your answer with reference to both i) and ii).

4 How successful was the USA in checking Soviet ambitions in Europe during the years 1979–85?

INTERPRETATION QUESTION

1 Read the interpretation and then answer the question that follows. '[Gorbachev] never expected communism to collapse so abruptly, and so totally, even in East Germany, let alone Russia' (from J. Haslam, *Russia's Cold War*, Cambridge University Press, 2007). Evaluate the strengths and limitations of this interpretation, making reference to other interpretations that you have studied.

SOURCE ANALYSIS QUESTION

1 With reference to Sources B (page 186), C (page 189) and D (page 196), and your understanding of the historical context, assess the value of these sources to a historian studying the reasons for the end of the Cold War.

CHAPTER 8

Interpreting the Cold War: a debate

This chapter is a general survey of the Cold War, concentrating on the following main issues that need to be considered if the Cold War is to be understood:

★ Could the Cold War have been avoided?

★ When did the Cold War actually start?

★ The Cold War in Europe

★ Why did the Cold War in Europe last for so long?

★ The Cold War in Asia

★ The Cold War in Africa, the Caribbean and South America

★ Why did the Cold War end?

The Cold War in Europe lasted for over four decades and by the mid-1960s the divisions that had grown out of the immediate post-war years were accepted as a permanent fact of international life. Twenty years later the US historian John Lewis Gaddis was able to describe the uneasy stability that it had created as the long peace. It was, however, more a truce than a peace. Even at the height of *détente* during the 1970s, tension, hostility and competition still characterised the relations between the Warsaw Pact and NATO states.

1 Could the Cold War have been avoided?

▶ *What caused the Cold War?*

Revisionist historians such as Daniel Yergin and Willy Loth argue that it was the USA that provoked the Cold War by refusing to recognise the Soviet sphere of interest in Eastern Europe or to make concessions over reparations in Germany. Could the Cold War really have been avoided if Stalin had been treated more diplomatically and greater sympathy shown to the appalling post-war problems in the USSR? It is possible to make out a case that Stalin did in fact act with greater restraint in Eastern Europe than his later Cold War critics in the West gave him credit for. He stopped Tito from intervening in Greece and, until 1948, allowed semi-democratic regimes to function in Hungary and Czechoslovakia. Loth argues that initially he also tried to restrain his own **military government officials** in the Soviet zone of Germany from applying too rigidly the Soviet Communist model. Indeed, it is arguable that, up to the summer of 1947, Stalin

KEY TERM

Military government officials Officials who worked for Soviet military governments in Eastern Europe.

gave precedence to trying to maintain the wartime Grand Alliance and failed to exploit favourable opportunities for establishing Soviet influence in such areas as Greece.

Was it, then, British and US policy that caused the Cold War? Can Stalin really be regarded as an innocent party pushed into waging the Cold War by the manoeuvrings of the Anglo-Americans? Revisionist historians point to the determination of the Americans to deny the Soviets access to raw materials in the Western hemisphere and of British attempts to force a decision on the future of Germany, which would almost inevitably lead to its division. There is no doubt that initially Stalin's policy was 'moderate' in that he did not want a third world war, as the USSR was hardly in the position to wage it.

Yet, what in retrospection can be called moderation did not necessarily seem to be so at the time. The British and Americans were alarmed by Soviet requests for control of the Black Sea Straits and of the former Italian colony of Libya. Even though Stalin withdrew these, they were seen as evidence of expansionist tendencies. Similarly, the exclusion of Western influence from Poland and most of Eastern Europe seemed to be an aggressive act and fed suspicions in London and Washington of Soviet actions. There was an ambiguity about Soviet policy. Stalin's ruthless suppression of all opposition in Poland and the **shotgun marriage** of the SPD and SED in the Soviet zone in Germany in 1946 alienated politicians in London and Washington even when he still hoped to work closely with them. On the other hand, London and Washington also gave out conflicting signals. They resented being excluded from Eastern Europe, but in their turn excluded the USSR from Western Europe and the Mediterranean.

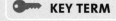 **KEY TERM**

Shotgun marriage
A forced union.

? In what ways, according to Extract 1, were the USA and USSR revolutionary powers?

EXTRACT 1

From Martin McCauley, *Russia, America and the Cold War*, Pearson, 2004, p. 3.

Both America and Russia were revolutionary powers. They possessed universal visions of how to improve the lot of humankind. From a Marxist perspective … the goal of Communism required an expansionary policy and this would continue until the goal of a Communist society world wide had been achieved. Likewise the US understood that its prosperity depended on what happened outside its borders … Truman put it succinctly: 'if Communism is allowed to absorb the free nations then we would be isolated from our sources of supply and detached from our friends'.

Great power rivalry, mutual fears about security and the rival ideologies of capitalism and Marxism–Leninism were all causes of the Cold War. Stalin's personality, too, is relevant, and it is arguable that the Cold War was an extension of the same distrust and suspicion which characterised his domestic policy. According to Gaddis, 'he functioned in much the same manner whether operating within the international system, within his alliances, within his country … or party … The Cold War we came to know was only one of many from his point of view.'

2 When did the Cold War actually start?

▶ *Why is there a debate about when the Cold War started?*

As we have seen in Chapter 1, historians disagree about when to date the beginning of the Cold War. Relations between the Allied powers, particularly the USA and the USSR, had been deteriorating ever since the defeat of Hitler, which had been the main cement holding together the Grand Alliance. The Cold War has been dated variously from the October Revolution of 1917, the dropping of the atomic bombs on Hiroshima and Nagasaki, Churchill's famous 'Iron Curtain' speech in March 1946 and the launching of the Truman Doctrine in March 1947. Although the beginnings of the Cold War are hard to pinpoint, it was certainly well under way by the end of 1947. The withdrawal of the USSR from the Paris talks on Marshall Plan aid, the creation of the Cominform and the breakdown of the London Conference were important stages in the escalation of the Cold War in that year.

3 The Cold War in Europe

▶ *Why was Europe the main theatre of the Cold War?*

Europe was the main, although not the only, theatre of the Cold War. It was there that it both began and ended. For the USSR it was essential to keep Eastern Europe under its control as a protective barrier against any possible attack from the West. It was this fact that led to Soviet intervention in Hungary in 1956 and to the formulation of the Brezhnev Doctrine 12 years later. The prize that both sides struggled for was Germany. In this the Western powers had the advantage as they controlled two-thirds of the country, which included the great industrial centre of the Ruhr. The military and economic integration of the Western two-thirds of Germany into Western Europe was what Stalin most dreaded. The Berlin Blockade was an attempt to stop this from happening, but it merely intensified Western efforts to create an independent West German state in 1949. Again, to prevent West Germany from joining NATO and/or the planned European Defence Community (EDC), Stalin orchestrated a massive peace movement, and finally, as a last desperate try, he proposed in March 1952 a plan for creating a neutral and apparently free Germany. In 1953 Lavrentii Beria, one of the key politicians in the USSR just after Stalin's death, very briefly played with the possibility of 'selling' the German Democratic Republic (GDR) to West Germany, subject to certain restrictions on its armaments, but after the East German Uprising of 1953, this idea was quickly dropped and until 1989 Soviet policy was to build up the weak and vulnerable East German state.

The division of Germany mirrored the division of Europe. The construction of the Berlin Wall confirmed the division of Germany for another 28 years, and in time brought a certain stability to Central Europe. The only problem was that in the long term the division was unstable or **asymmetrical**. As President Eisenhower's US National Security Council pointed out, the Federal Republic of Germany 'had nearly three times the population, about five times the industrial output and almost twice the size' of the GDR. Similarly, Western Europe and the USA together represented infinitely more economic power than the Soviet bloc could command.

The same lack of symmetry can be seen in the way the two superpowers influenced their respective blocs. On balance, it is true to say that the USA initially set up in Western Europe an empire by invitation. The Western Europeans in the late 1940s were desperate for US military and financial aid. On the other hand, in Eastern Europe, with the partial exceptions of Hungary and Czechoslovakia until 1947, the USSR established an empire by conquest.

In the Soviet zone of Germany the behaviour of the Red Army and the mass raping carried out by its soldiers in 1945 created an atmosphere of hate and fear, which reinforced West Germany's determination to remain within the US sphere of influence at all costs. Essentially, the Americans helped to create an independent, prosperous, economically and increasingly politically integrated Western Europe, functioning within a capitalist global system. The Soviets had little to offer Eastern Europe that could rival this. Hence, the economic strength of Western Europe exerted a magnetic attraction on the peoples of Eastern Europe.

4 Why did the Cold War in Europe last for so long?

▶ *Why did the West overestimate the power of the USSR?*

If the West had such a significant advantage over the Soviet bloc, why did the Cold War last for so long? It is possible to argue that its eventual outcome should have been predicted as early as 1968, when the crushing of the Prague Spring forced the Czech government and the other satellite states to abandon their attempts to liberalise their economies and return instead to a system of more rigid centralised control, which made them less flexible and responsive to change. Yet it still seemed inconceivable that the USSR and its Eastern European satellites would eventually collapse like a row of dominoes. The USSR seemed to be a superpower at least as strong as the USA. This overestimation of its power was caused by assessing its strength solely in terms of its nuclear weapons. This was the one area where it could effectively compete with the West. The long period of *détente* preserved the Soviet nuclear deterrent, but only slowed down its economic decline, despite massive loans from the West.

5 The Cold War in Asia

▶ *To what extent were the Cold Wars in Europe and Asia linked?*

The Cold War was a global phenomenon, even though its main theatre was in Europe. The success of communism in China in 1949 was one of the important developments in the Cold War. Together with the successful Soviet development of the atomic bomb, it strengthened the global power of communism. The outbreak of the Korean War generated fears that it would inspire a similar attack by East Germany on West Germany and accelerated Western European military and economic integration.

Initially, the USSR under Stalin remained the unchallenged capital of global communism, but the People's Republic of China (PRC) played an increasingly important role in the Far East and East Asia. Not only did the PRC intervene decisively in the Korean War, but its assistance to the Việt Minh in Indo-China played a major role in the French defeat of 1954, and indeed in the subsequent American defeat in the Vietnam War. Yet just as the global Cold War was reaching its peak with Soviet and Chinese intervention escalating in Africa, the Middle East and Far East, the two great Communist superpowers ceased to be close ideological allies and became deadly rivals. Indeed, the PRC sought protection from a possible war with the USSR by drawing closer to the USA.

EXTRACT 2

From 'China and the Cold War after Mao' by Chen Jian, in M. Leffler and O.A. Westad, editors, *The Cambridge History of the Cold War*, volume III, Cambridge University Press, 2010, p. 195.

By the mid-1980s, the Soviet Union was a superpower in decline, and China contributed in crucial ways to Moscow's problems. In a strategic sense, Beijing's partnership with Washington and its continued confrontation with Moscow completely altered the balance of power between the two superpowers. More importantly, China's market orientated reforms destroyed Moscow's claims that Communism remained a viable alternative to capitalism. ... Since the Cold War from its inception had been a global struggle between two contrasting ideological and social systems, the new course embraced by China obscured the distinctions between the two sides and favoured the capitalist world. The Soviet Union and its allies found it increasingly more difficult to sustain the course of the Cold War.

What information does Extract 2 convey about the impact on the course of the Cold War of the Sino-Soviet split?

6 The Cold War in Africa, the Caribbean and South America

▶ *How successful was communism in Africa, the Caribbean and South America?*

Decolonisation in Africa and the Caribbean and the success of Castro in Cuba turned the Cold War into a global struggle. In Africa the emergence of independent states from the wreckage of the old European empires provided opportunities for both the USSR and the PRC to exploit anti-American and anti-Western sentiment.

Cuba, with its record of successfully defying the might of the USA, became an example to Marxist parties throughout South America and the other Caribbean islands. Cuba also conducted its own foreign policy in Angola and played a crucial role in strengthening the People's Movement for the Liberation of Angola (MPLA) and other Marxist parties in Africa.

7 Why did the Cold War end?

▶ *Could the Cold War in Europe have ended before 1989?*

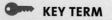 **KEY TERM**

Exoskeletons Rigid external coverings, or shells for the body.

? In what ways does Extract 3 help the historian to understand the collapse of the USSR?

Behind the nuclear façade, the whole Soviet bloc was suffering a steady economic, ideological, moral and cultural decline. This was primarily caused by its own economic inefficiencies and inability to match the West's economic growth. *Détente*, the Helsinki Agreement and *Ostpolitik* increasingly exposed the Soviet Empire to Western influences. As Gaddis has put it:

EXTRACT 3

From John Lewis Gaddis, *We Now Know*, Oxford University Press, 1997, p. 284.

*To visualize what happened, imagine a troubled triceratops [a plant-eating dinosaur]. From the outside, as rivals contemplated its sheer size, tough skin, bristling armament and aggressive posturing, the beast looked sufficiently formidable that none dared tangle with it. Appearances deceived, though, for within, its digestive, circulatory and respiratory systems were slowly clogging up, and then shutting down. There were few external signs of this until the day the creature was found with all four feet in the air, still awesome but now bloated stiff, and quite dead. The moral of the fable is that armaments make impressive **exoskeletons**, but a shell alone ensures the survival of no animal and no state.*

Until the Reagan presidency, no statesman in the West dared call the USSR's bluff. After all, even if the USA had a greater nuclear arsenal, the USSR had the capacity to land, at the very least, a few missiles on the USA, and that was still a formidable deterrent. By planning to develop the Strategic Defence Initiative, Reagan challenged the USSR in a way that had not happened since the late 1940s. The USSR simply could not keep pace with this technology. This was the context in which Gorbachev came to the conclusion that the only chance the USSR had of surviving was to modernise its economy and society along Western lines. He thus embarked on an ambitious but ultimately unsuccessful attempt to base the USSR's links with its satellite states on consent rather than coercion. This approach, however, came too late. In 1968 many Eastern Europeans could perhaps still have been won over by the prospect of 'Socialism with a human face', but twenty years later all socialist idealism had evaporated. After the grey, corrupt and repressive years of the Brezhnev era, the sudden freedom offered by Gorbachev was used by the Eastern Europeans to reject socialism and look to the US and Western European economic models.

In the PRC and Cuba, however, Gaddis's picture of a 'a troubled triceratops' is not so valid. In the former, the Chinese Communist Party under Mao's successors was successfully able to modernise its economy and embrace capitalism, thereby ending the ideological battle with the West, but unlike their colleagues in Moscow, they were able to maintain a tight grip on power. In Cuba, too, communism survived, but Castro stubbornly resisted all calls for reform. In the PRC, an economic miracle, which was denied to Gorbachev, undoubtedly enabled the Communist Party to survive. In Cuba, Castro as the great revolutionary leader – a Lenin and Mao rolled into one – could still draw on reserves of loyalty and gratitude.

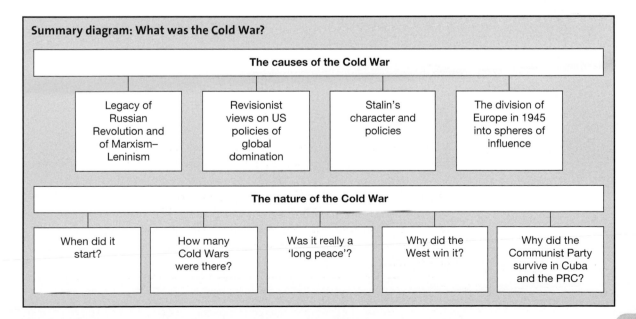

Summary diagram: What was the Cold War?

The causes of the Cold War

Legacy of Russian Revolution and of Marxism–Leninism	Revisionist views on US policies of global domination	Stalin's character and policies	The division of Europe in 1945 into spheres of influence

The nature of the Cold War

When did it start?	How many Cold Wars were there?	Was it really a 'long peace'?	Why did the West win it?	Why did the Communist Party survive in Cuba and the PRC?

Refresher questions

Use these questions to remind yourself of the key material covered in this chapter.

1 Why did the Cold War last so long?

2 Why did the USA and its allies win the Cold War in Europe?

3 Why did communism collapse in the USSR?

4 What role did Germany play in the Cold War?

5 Why was the USSR so successful in Africa in the 1970s?

AQA A level History

Essay guidance

At both AS and A level for AQA Component 2: Depth Study: The Cold War, *c.*1945–1991 you will need to answer an essay question in the exam. Each essay question is marked out of 25:

- for the AS exam, Section B: answer **one** essay from a choice of two
- for the A level exam, Section B: answer **two** essays from a choice of three

There are several question stems which all have the same basic requirement: to analyse and reach a conclusion, based on the evidence you provide.

The AS questions often give a quotation and then ask whether you agree or disagree with this view. Almost inevitably, your answer will be a mixture of both. It is the same task as for A level – just phrased differently in the question. Detailed essays are more likely to do well than vague or generalised essays, especially in the Depth Studies of Paper 2.

The AQA mark scheme is essentially the same for AS and the full A level (see the AQA website, www.aqa.org.uk). Both emphasise the need to analyse and evaluate the key features related to the periods studied. The key feature of the highest level is sustained analysis: analysis that unites the whole of the essay.

Writing an essay: general skills

- *Focus and structure.* Be sure what the question is asking and plan what the paragraphs should be about.
- *Focused introduction to the essay.* Be sure that the introductory sentence relates directly to the focus of the question and that each paragraph highlights the structure of the answer.

- *Use detail.* Make sure that you show detailed knowledge, but only as part of an explanation being made in relation to the question. No knowledge should be standalone; it should be used in context.
- *Explanatory analysis and evaluation.* Consider what words and phrases to use in an answer to strengthen the explanation.
- *Argument and counter-argument.* Think of how arguments can be balanced so as to give contrasting views.
- *Resolution.* Think how best to 'resolve' contradictory arguments.
- *Relative significance and evaluation.* Think how best to reach a judgement when trying to assess the relative importance of various factors, and their possible interrelationship.

Planning an essay

Practice question 1

'The Communist victory in China in 1949 had a huge impact on international relations, 1949–1954.' Assess the validity of this view.

This question requires you to analyse the impact of the Communist victory in China on international relations. You must discuss the following:

- The impact of the Communist victory in China on international relations (your primary focus).
- The limitations of this impact on international relations (your secondary focus).

A clear structure makes for a much more effective essay and is crucial for achieving the highest marks. You need three or four paragraphs to structure this question effectively. In each paragraph you will deal with one factor. One of these *must* be the factor in the question.

A very basic plan for this question might look like this:

- Paragraph 1: Brief background as to the potential significance of the Communist victory for international relations.
- Paragraph 2: An analysis of what changes the Communist victory in China actually brought about.
- Paragraph 3: An assessment of the limitations of the effects that the Communist victory in China had on international relations.

It is a good idea to cover the factor named in the question first, so that you don't run out of time and forget to do it. Then cover the others in what you think is their order of importance, or in the order that appears logical in terms of the sequence of paragraphs.

The introduction

Maintaining focus is vital. One way to do this from the beginning of your essay is to use the words in the question to help write your argument. The first sentence of question 1, for example, could look like this:

The Communist victory in China in 1949 had an impact on international relations in two key areas as it strengthened Communism as a global force and also affected international relations in the Far East.

This opening sentence provides a clear focus on the demands of the question, although it could, of course, be written in a more exciting style.

Focus throughout the essay

Structuring your essay well will help with keeping the focus of your essay on the question. To maintain a focus on the wording in question 1, you could begin your first main paragraph with 'Communist victory'.

The Communist victory in China was an event of considerable international significance as the largest and potentially most powerful country

in the Far East was now Communist and this would inevitably have an impact on international relations in the Far East.

- This sentence begins with a clear point that refers to the primary focus of the question (Communist victory) while linking it to a factor (communism in the Far East).
- You could then have a paragraph for each of your other factors.
- It will be important to make sure that each paragraph focuses on analysis and includes relevant details that are used as part of the argument.
- You may wish to number your factors. This helps to make your structure clear and helps you to maintain focus.

Deploying detail

As well as focus and structure, your essay will be judged on the extent to which it includes accurate detail. There are several different kinds of evidence you could use that might be described as detailed. These include correct dates, names of relevant people, statistics and events. For example, for question 1 you could use terms such as 'anti-colonialism', 'Sino-Soviet Pact' and 'Viet Minh'. You can also make your essays more detailed by using the correct technical vocabulary.

Analysis and explanation

'Analysis' covers a variety of high-level skills including explanation and evaluation; in essence, it means breaking down something complex into smaller parts. A clear structure which breaks down a complex question into a series of paragraphs is the first step towards writing an analytical essay. The purpose of explanation is to provide evidence for why something happened, or why something is true or false. An explanatory statement requires two parts: a *claim* and a *justification*. For example, for question 1, you might want to argue that the Communist victory in China affected the war in Indo-China between the Viet Minh and the French. Once you have made your point, and supported it with relevant detail, you can then explain how this answers the question. For example, you could conclude your paragraph like this:

So the Communist victory in China did have an impact on international relations in the Far East[1] because it strengthened the Viet Minh in Indo-China[2] and enabled their troops to defeat the French by 1954 and so strengthen Communism in the Far East[3].

1 The first part of this sentence is the claim while the second part justifies the claim.
2 'Because' is a very important word to use when writing an explanation, as it shows the relationship between the claim and the justification.
3 The justification.

Evaluation

Evaluation means considering the importance of two or more different factors, weighing them against each other, and reaching a judgement. This is a good skill to use at the end of an essay because the conclusion should reach a judgement which answers the question. For example, your conclusion to question 1 might read:

Clearly[1], the Communist victory in China had a major impact on international relations. The Sino-Soviet Pact of February 1950 created an alliance between the two great Communist powers, the USSR and PRC, which strengthened them both in the period 1950-4. It also enabled communism to play a more important part in international affairs in the Far East. The PRC was able directly to help the Viet Minh in Indochina. Mao, with Soviet support, also encouraged the North Koreans to invade South Korea, and when the USA threatened Manchuria in October 1950, Chinese troops actually intervened. However[2], this did not lead to a Communist victory there, as the North Korean and Chinese troops were ultimately brought to a standstill on the borders of South Korea along the 38th parallel. Therefore[3], the Communist

victory in China obviously affected international relations by strengthening the relationship between the USSR and the PRC, and encouraging Communist action in the Far East.

1–3 Words like 'clearly', 'however' and 'therefore' are helpful to contrast the importance of the different factors.

Complex essay writing: argument and counter-argument

Essays that develop a good argument are more likely to reach the highest levels. This is because argumentative essays are much more likely to develop sustained analysis. As you know, your essays are judged on the extent to which they analyse.

After setting up an argument in your introduction, you should develop it throughout the essay. One way of doing this is to adopt an argument–counter-argument structure. A counter-argument is one that disagrees with the main argument of the essay. This is a good way of evaluating the importance of the different factors that you discuss. Essays of this type will develop an argument in one paragraph and then set out an opposing argument in another paragraph. Sometimes this will include juxtaposing the differing views of historians on a topic.

Good essays will analyse the key issues. They will probably have a clear piece of analysis at the end of each paragraph. While this analysis might be good, it will generally relate only to the issue discussed in that paragraph.

Excellent essays will be analytical throughout. As well as the analysis of each factor discussed above, there will be an overall analysis. This will run throughout the essay and can be achieved through developing a clear, relevant and coherent argument.

A good way of achieving sustained analysis is to consider which factor is most important.

Page 222 has an example of an introduction that sets out an argument for question 1:

Despite its victory in China, Communism did not manage to dominate the Far East totally. Hence, Japan and Taiwan, for example, still remained under US protection[1]. However, it is undeniable that it had a major impact on international relations not only in the Far East but in Europe too, where it increased the prestige of communism and the potential military strength of the USSR through the Sino-Soviet Pact[2]. Its impact on international relations, not surprisingly, was strongest in the Far East, where the new Communist China could assist local Communist regimes and anti-colonial movements with men and equipment. The Communist victory in China played an important role in defeating the French in Indochina and checking the US advance into North Korea.[3]

1 The introduction begins with a counter-argument aimed at showing the limitations of one effect.
2 The introduction continues with another reason; this time indicating the effect it did have on international relations.
3 Concludes with an outline of detailed arguments of the most important reason for its effect on international relations.

- This introduction focuses on the question and sets out the key factors that the essay will develop.
- It introduces an argument about which factor was most significant.
- However, it also sets out an argument that can then be developed throughout each paragraph, and is rounded off with an overall judgement in the conclusion.

Complex essay writing: resolution and relative significance

Having written an essay that explains argument and counter-argument, you should then resolve the tension between the argument and the counter-argument in your conclusion. It is important that the writing is precise and summarises the arguments made in the main body of the essay. You need to reach a supported overall judgement.

One very appropriate way to do this is by evaluating the relative significance of different factors, in the light of valid criteria. Relative significance means how important one factor is compared to another.

The best essays will always make a judgement about which was most important based on valid criteria. These can be very simple, and will depend on the topic and the exact question.

The following criteria are often useful:

- Duration: which factor was important for the longest amount of time?
- Scope: which factor affected the most people?
- Effectiveness: which factor achieved most?
- Impact: which factor led to the most fundamental change?

As an example, you could compare the factors in terms of their duration and their impact. A conclusion that follows this advice should be capable of reaching a high level (if written, in full, with appropriate details) because it reaches an overall judgement that is supported through evaluating the relative significance of different factors in the light of valid criteria.

Having written an introduction and the main body of an essay for question 1, a concluding paragraph that aims to meet the exacting criteria for reaching a complex judgement could look like this:

Thus, the impact of the Communist victory in China in 1949 on international relations was complex. The Sino-Soviet Pact did much to counter the West's financial and technical superiority. In the Far East, the PRC was also able to provide decisive military help to North Korea and the Viet Minh. Indeed, it enabled the latter to defeat the French in 1953–4. In Korea, Chinese troops were engaged in open warfare with the US-led UN forces. So the Chinese revolution certainly intensified the Cold War – in Korea it became a 'hot war' between the US-led UN forces and the PRC – but between 1949 and 1954 the balance was not decisively tilted against the USA and the Western powers, as the outbreak of the Korean War accelerated Western rearmament and attempts to integrate a West German army into the EDC and NATO. Only in Indochina did communism win a clear victory, but even there, at the Geneva Conference in 1954, the USA was able to insist on the division of Vietnam along the 17th parallel. It was to take another twenty years for communism to triumph there. In Korea the PRC certainly prevented the occupation of the North by UN forces, but it was unable to drive them out of the Korean peninsula and create a united Korean Communist regime. Therefore, while the Communist victory in China saw long-reaching effects with the Sino-Soviet Pact and a more powerful PRC, the Western powers, mainly the USA, sought to limit its impact in Korea and Indo-China.

Sources guidance

Whether you are taking the AS exam or the full A level exam for AQA Component 2: Depth Study: The Cold War in Europe, 1945–1991, Section A presents you with sources and a question which involves evaluation of their utility or value.

AS exam	A level exam
Section A: answer question 1, based on two primary sources. (25 marks)	Section A: answer question 1, based on three primary sources. (30 marks)
Question focus: with reference to these sources and your understanding of the historical context, which of these two sources is more valuable in explaining … ?	Question focus: With reference to these sources and your understanding of the historical context, assess the value of these three sources to a historian studying …

Sources and sample questions

Study the sources. They are all concerned with the creation of the 'Iron Curtain'.

SOURCE 1

From Winston Churchill's speech at Fulton, Missouri, USA on the 'Iron Curtain', 5 March 1946, quoted in R. Morgan, *The Unsettled Peace*, BBC Books, 1974, pp. 67–8.

From Stettin in the Baltic, to Trieste, in the Adriatic, an iron curtain has descended across the continent. Behind that line lie all the capitals of the ancient states of Central and Eastern Europe – Warsaw, Berlin, Prague, Vienna, Belgrade, Bucharest and Sofia. All these famous cities, and the populations around them, lie in the Soviet sphere, and all are subject in one form or another, not only to Soviet influence, but to a very high and increasing measure of control from Moscow. Athens alone … is free to decide its future … The Russian dominated Polish government has been encouraged to make enormous and wrongful inroads upon Germany … The Communist parties, which were very small in all these eastern states of Europe, have been raised to pre-eminence and power far beyond their numbers, are seeking everywhere to obtain totalitarian control. Police governments are prevailing in nearly every sense, and so far, except in Czechoslovakia, there is no true democracy … An attempt is being made by the Russians in Berlin to build up a quasi-Communist party in their zone of occupied Germany by showing special favours to groups of left-wing leaders.

SOURCE 2

From Stalin's interview with the Soviet newspaper, *Pravda*, 13 March 1946, quoted in M. McCauley, *Origins of Cold War*, 1941–1949, Longman, 2003, pp. 142–3.

... The following circumstances should not be forgotten. The Germans made their invasion of the USSR through Finland, Poland, Romania and Hungary. The Germans were able to make their invasion through these countries because at the time governments hostile to the Soviet Union existed in these countries. As a result of the German invasion the Soviet Union has lost irretrievably in the fighting against the Germans, and also through the German occupation and the deportation of Soviet citizens to German servitude, a total of about seven million people. In other words, the Soviet Union's loss of life has been several times greater than that of Britain and the United States of America put together. Possibly in some quarters an inclination is felt to forget about these colossal sacrifices of the Soviet people which secured the liberation of Europe from the Hitlerite [Nazi] yoke. But the Soviet Union cannot forget about them ... And so what can there be surprising about the fact that the Soviet Union, anxious for its future safety, is trying to see to it that governments loyal in their attitude to the Soviet Union should exist in these countries? How can anyone, who has not taken leave of his senses, describe these peaceful aspirations of the Soviet Union as expansionist tendencies on the part of our state?

SOURCE 3

From Truman's speech to Congress, 12 March 1947, quoted in G. Roberts, *The Soviet Union in World Politics*, Routledge, 1999, p. 22.

One way of life is based upon the will of the majority, and is distinguished by free institutions, representative government, free elections, guarantees of individual liberty, freedom of speech and religion, and freedom from political oppression. The second way of life is based upon the will of a minority forcibly imposed upon the majority. It relies upon terror and oppression, a controlled press and radio, fixed elections and the suppression of personal freedoms. I believe that it must be the policy of the United States to support free peoples who are resisting attempted subjugation by armed minorities or by outside pressures. I believe that we must assist free peoples to work out their own destinies in their own way. ... The seeds of totalitarian regimes are nurtured by misery and want. They spread and grow in the evil soil of poverty and strife. They reach their full growth when the hope of a people for a better life has died.

AS style question

With reference to Sources 1 (page 224) and 2 (above), and your understanding of the historical context, which of these two sources is more valuable in explaining why the Cold War started after 1945?

A level style question

With reference to Sources 1 (page 224), 2 and 3 (above), and your understanding of the historical context, assess the value of these sources to a historian studying the causes of the Cold War.

The mark schemes

AS mark scheme

See the AQA website (www.aqa.org.uk) for the full mark schemes. The summary of the AS mark scheme below shows how it rewards analysis and evaluation of the source material within the historical context.

Level 1	Describing the source content or offering generic phrases.
Level 2	Some relevant but limited comments on the value of one source or some limited comment on both sources.
Level 3	Some relevant comments on the value of the sources and some explicit reference to the issue identified in the question.
Level 4	Relevant well-supported comments on the value and a supported conclusion, but with limited judgement.
Level 5	Very good understanding of the value in relation to the issue identified. Sources evaluated thoroughly and with a well-substantiated conclusion related to which is more valuable.

A level mark scheme

This summary of the A level mark scheme shows how it is similar to the AS, but covers three sources. The wording of the question means that there is no explicit requirement to decide which of the three sources is the most valuable. Concentrate instead on a very thorough analysis of the content and evaluation of the provenance of each source, using contextual knowledge.

Level 1	Some limited comment on the value of at least one source.
Level 2	Some limited comments on the value of the sources or on content or provenance, or comments on all three sources but no reference to the value of the sources.
Level 3	Some understanding of all three sources in relation to both content and provenance, with some historical context; but analysis limited.

Level 4	Good understanding of all three sources in relation to content, provenance and historical context to give a balanced argument on their value for the purpose specified in the question.
Level 5	As Level 4, but with a substantiated judgement on each of the three sources.

Working towards an answer

It is important that knowledge is used to show an understanding of the relationship between the sources and the issue raised in the question. Answers should be concerned with:

- provenance
- arguments used (and you can agree/disagree)
- tone and emphasis of the sources.

The sources

The two or three sources used each time will be contemporary – probably of varying types (for example, diaries, newspaper accounts, government reports). The sources will all be on the same broad topic area. Each source will have value. Your task is to evaluate how much – in terms of its content and its provenance.

You will need to assess the *value of the content* by using your own knowledge. Is the information accurate? Is it giving only part of the evidence and ignoring other aspects? Is the tone of the writing significant?

You will need to evaluate the *provenance* of the source by considering who wrote it, and when, where and why. What was its purpose? Was it produced to express an opinion; to record facts; to influence the opinion of others? Even if it was intended to be accurate, the writer may have been biased – either deliberately or unconsciously. The writer, for example, might have only known part of the situation and reached a judgement solely based on that.

Here is a guide to analysing the provenance, content and tone for Sources 1, 2 and 3 (pages 224–5).

Analysing the sources

To answer the question effectively, you need to read the sources carefully and pull out the relevant points as well as add your own knowledge. You must remember to keep the focus on the question at all times.

Source 1 (page 224)

Provenance:

- Source 1 is an extract from a speech from Winston Churchill, leader of the Conservative Party in Britain, at Fulton, Missouri, 5 March 1946.
- It provides the opinion of the former British wartime prime minister, who enjoyed immense global fame and prestige as the 'saviour' of the free world from Nazi tyranny.

Content and argument:

- The source warns that an 'iron curtain' is descending across Europe from Stettin to Trieste.
- East of this line countries are subject to increasing Soviet influence. In Berlin and the Soviet zone in Germany, the USSR has created what in effect is a Communist Party.
- The source argues that local Communist parties, which only represent a small minority, are with Soviet help progressively establishing control of the Eastern European states.

Tone and emphasis:

- The tone is a powerful 'wake-up' call to the USA and the countries of Western Europe to take note of what is happening in Eastern Europe.
- Shows sympathy with the fate of the Eastern European states, which are in the process of losing their liberty to the USSR.

Own knowledge:

- Use your knowledge to agree/disagree with the source, for example: Soviet policy in Germany and towards Greece and Turkey. Also, the Soviet need for security.

Source 2 (page 225)

Provenance:

- Source 2 is an extract from Stalin's interview on 13 March 1946 with the Soviet Communist newspaper, *Pravda*. It was of great importance as Stalin was dictator of the USSR with complete powers.
- *Pravda* was the official public voice of the Soviet Communist Party, and so Stalin was anxious that his views as expressed would become known to the USA, Western Europe and indeed to Communists in Eastern and Western Europe.

Content and argument:

- The source outlines Soviet sacrifices and loss of life during the Second World War.
- It argues that the USSR, having been attacked through Eastern Europe by the Germans, must ensure its security by having friendly governments in place in those Eastern European countries.

Tone and emphasis:

The article is a measured and apparently reasonable response to Churchill's accusation made on 5 March 1946.

Own knowledge:

- Use your knowledge to agree/disagree with the source, for example: detailed knowledge about Soviet policy in Eastern Europe 1944–6.

Source 3 (page 225)

Provenance:

- Source 3 is an extract from a speech by President Truman to the US Congress on 12 March 1947. As president, he is the single most powerful figure in the US government and will have well-informed views on the Soviet threats to Greece, Turkey and elsewhere.
- The extract is taken from the president's speech to Congress. He is therefore making a public announcement about the aims of the US foreign policy and its intentions to support states that are threatened by communism.

Content and argument:

- The source stresses that there are two ways of life in the world: one where the will of the majority prevails and there is individual liberty; the other where this is suppressed and dictatorship prevails.
- The aim of the USA is to assist the former and help countries maintain their liberty.
- The source argues that communism thrives where there is misery and want; the USA must remedy this.

Tone and emphasis:

- The tone is idealistic and challenging. Truman is warning the USSR that the USA is determined to block the spread of communism where it has no majority backing.

Own knowledge:

- Use your knowledge to agree/disagree with the source, for example: details about why the USA was concerned with Russian threats to independent states. The British decision to end aid to Greece and Turkey on 21 February 1946 is relevant here as it exposed these countries to threats from communism. In Greece the threat came more from Communist Yugoslavia, Albania and Bulgaria, not directly from the USSR.

Answering AS questions

You have 45 minutes to answer the question. It is important that you spend at least one quarter of the time reading and planning your answer. Generally, when writing an answer, you need to check that you are remaining focused on the issue identified in the question and are relating this to the sources and your knowledge.

- You might decide to write a paragraph on each 'strand' (that is, provenance, content and tone), comparing the two sources, and then write a short concluding paragraph with an explained judgement on which source is more valuable.
- For writing about content, you may find it helpful to adopt a comparative approach, for example

when the evidence in one source is contradicted or questioned by the evidence in another source.

At AS level you are asked to provide a judgement on which is more valuable. Make sure that this is based on clear arguments with strong evidence, and not on general assertions.

Planning and writing your answer

- Think how you can best plan an answer.
- Plan in terms of the headings above, perhaps combining 'provenance' with 'tone and emphasis', and compare the two sources.

As an example, here is a comparison of Sources 1 and 2 in terms of provenance, and tone and emphasis:

The two sources have directly opposing viewpoints and a very different provenance. Source 1 is from Winston Churchill, a man famed throughout the world for his leadership of Britain during the Second World War, but who is no longer in power. It is a strong and detailed criticism of Stalin's policies in Eastern Europe, which have resulted in the setting up of pro-Soviet or Communist regimes and the creation of a barrier between East and West Europe – the Iron Curtain. Source 2 is a direct reply to this criticism from Josef Stalin, the supreme ruler of the USSR, who enjoyed immense power and prestige in the Communist world. He makes a powerful but measured argument in support of Soviet policies.

- Then compare the *content and argument* of each source, by using your knowledge. For example:

Source 1 is arguing that Stalin's policies have resulted in setting up pro-Soviet Communist regimes in Eastern Europe. The consequence of this is that throughout this area, with the exception of Czechoslovakia, there is no democracy. Instead, these regimes are seeking to establish Soviet dictatorships and to cut off Eastern Europe from the West through the creation of the Iron Curtain. Source 2 also focuses on Eastern Europe. Stalin points out that that the USSR has suffered millions of casualties during the war, unlike the

USA and Britain, and is, therefore, determined to ensure that only regimes which are friendly and loyal to the USSR control the Eastern European states through which came the German attack in 1941.

Which is more *valuable*? This can be judged either in terms of where the source came from; or in terms of the accuracy of its content. However, remember the focus of the question: in this case, why did the Cold War start?

With these sources, you could argue that Source 2 is the more valuable because it was written by Stalin, who held complete power in the USSR. He does not deny that the USSR is seeking to install governments 'loyal in their attitude to the Soviet', which effectively means Communist, in the Eastern European states. Only through them can the USSR be sure of the loyalty of these states and that they will not ally with some future aggressor. It has the ring of truth and shows that the USSR's desire for security was one of the factors that started the Cold War. Although Source 1 is a valuable and perceptive comment on what is happening in Eastern Europe, it is from a politician who is now out of power. Its analysis is increasingly accepted by the West, but it comes from a man who, for the time being, lacks the power to take political decisions.

Then check the following:

- Have you covered the 'provenance' and 'content' strands?
- Have you included sufficient knowledge to show understanding of the historical context?

Answering A level questions

The same general points for answering AS questions (see 'Answering AS questions') apply to A level questions, although of course here there are three sources and you need to assess the value of each of the three, rather than choose which is most valuable. Make sure that you remain focused on the question and that when you use your knowledge it is used to substantiate (add to) an argument relating to the content or provenance of the source.

If you are answering the A level question on page 225 with Sources 1, 2 and 3 (pages 224–5):

- Keep the different 'strands' explained above in your mind when working out how best to plan an answer.
- Follow the guidance about 'provenance' and 'content' (see the AS guidance).
- Here you are *not* asked to explain which is the most valuable of the three sources. You can deal with each of the three sources in turn if you wish.
- However, you can build in comparisons if it is helpful, but it is not essential. It will depend to some extent on the three sources.
- You need to include sufficient knowledge to show understanding of the historical context. This might encourage cross-referencing of the content of the three sources, mixed with your own knowledge.
- Each paragraph needs to show clarity of argument in terms of the issue identified by the question.

Essay guidance

The assessment of OCR Units Y223 and Y253: The Cold War in Europe 1941–1995 depends on whether you are studying it for AS or A level:

- for the AS exam, you will answer one essay question from a choice of two, and one interpretation question, for which there is no choice
- for the A level exam, you will answer one essay question from a choice of two, and one shorter essay question, also from a choice of two.

The guidance below is for answering both AS and A level essay questions. Guidance for the shorter essay question is at the end of this section. Guidance on answering interpretation questions is on page 235.

For both OCR AS and A level History, the types of essay questions set and the skills required to achieve a high grade for Unit Group 2 are the same. The skills are made very clear by both mark schemes, which emphasise that the answer must:

- focus on the demands of the question
- be supported by accurate and relevant factual knowledge
- be analytical and logical
- reach a supported judgement about the issue in the question.

There are a number of skills that you will need to develop to reach the higher levels in the marking bands:

- understand the wording of the question
- plan an answer to the question set
- write a focused opening paragraph
- avoid irrelevance and description
- write analytically
- write a conclusion which reaches a supported judgement based on the argument in the main body of the essay.

These skills will be developed in the section below, but are further developed in the 'Period Study' chapters of the *OCR A level History* series (British Period Studies and Enquiries).

Understanding the wording of the question

To stay focused on the question set, it is important to read the question carefully and focus on the key words and phrases. Unless you directly address the demands of the question you will not score highly. Remember that in questions where there is a named factor you must write a good analytical paragraph about the given factor, even if you argue that it was not the most important.

Types of AS and A level questions you might find in the exams	The factors and issues you would need to consider in answering them
1 Assess the consequences for both Eastern and Western Europe in the years 1949–53 of the Berlin Blockade.	Weigh up the relative importance of a range of factors as to what impact the Berlin Blockade had on the development of the Cold War and Germany.
2 To what extent did the USA cause the Cold War through its policies in Europe, 1945–7?	Weigh up the relative importance of a range of factors, including comparing the impact of US actions, 1945–7, with the impact of other factors on the situation in Europe.
3 'Gorbachev's policies ended in total failure.' How far do you agree?	Weigh up Gorbachev's policies from 1985 to 1991 and assess the policies against a range of criteria to decide if they were a 'total failure'.

4 How successful was *détente* in the period from 1965 to 1979?	This question requires you to make a judgement about *détente*. You will need to think about issues such as: • Its aims as viewed from both sides: the USSR and its allies, and the USA and its allies • Its achievements in controlling nuclear weapons • Relaxation of tension in Central Europe, looking here particularly at the Helsinki Conference • For which power was *détente* the most successful?

Planning an answer

Many plans simply list dates and events: this should be avoided as it encourages a descriptive or narrative answer, rather than an analytical answer. The plan should be an outline of your argument; this means you need to think carefully about the issues you intend to discuss and their relative importance before you start writing your answer. It should therefore be a list of the factors or issues you are going to discuss and a comment on their relative importance.

For question 1 in the table, your plan might look something like this:

- The role of the blockade in the creation of East and West Germany, major factor in the short term, leads to division of Germany, ends wartime hopes and increases tensions.
- The importance of the airlift in the development of the Cold War, link to the idea of defending Western democracy against communism.
- The need to protect West Berlin without causing a third world war.
- Its role in turning Berlin into a symbol of the divide in Europe.
- West gave message to Stalin about holding on to Berlin.

- Gave message to the West that Stalin was aggressive and threatening.
- Role played in creation of NATO.
- Impact on developments in Eastern Europe and Stalin's strengthening of control.

The opening paragraph

Many students spend time 'setting the scene'; the opening paragraph becomes little more than an introduction to the topic – this should be avoided. Instead, make it clear what your argument is going to be. Offer your view about the issue in the question – what were the key consequences of the blockade for Eastern and Western Europe? – and then introduce the other issues you intend to discuss. In the plan it is suggested that the blockade had a crucial impact on Germany. This should be made clear in the opening paragraph, with a brief comment as to why the blockade made the division of Germany almost inevitable. This will give the examiner a clear overview of your essay, rather than it being a 'mystery tour' where the argument becomes clear only at the end. You should also refer to any important issues that the question raises. For example:

There are a number of reasons why the Berlin Blockade had such important consequences for Europe[1]. Stalin hoped that the blockade would force the Western Allies to give up their plans for creating a West German state. Its failure, however, made the creation of this state a virtual certainty as well as accelerating the formation of NATO and US involvement in Western Europe's defence[2]. The consequences of these developments were to lead to Stalin to setting up an East German state as well as strengthening his grip on Eastern Europe, particularly Czechoslovakia[3].

1 The student is aware that there were a number of important reasons.
2 The student offers a clear view as to what they consider to be the most important reason – a thesis is offered.
3 There is a brief justification to support the thesis.

Avoid irrelevance and description

A well-prepared plan will stop you from simply writing all you know about the Berlin Blockade and force you to weigh up the role of a range of factors. Similarly, it should also help prevent you from simply writing about the process of setting up the two Germanys. You will not lose marks if you do that, but neither will you gain any credit, and you will waste valuable time.

Write analytically

This is perhaps the hardest, but most important skill you need to develop. An analytical approach can be helped by ensuring that the opening sentence of each paragraph introduces an idea, which directly answers the question and is not just a piece of factual information. In a very strong answer it should be possible simply to read the opening sentences of all the paragraphs and know what argument is being put forward.

If we look at question 2: To what extent did the USA cause the Cold War through its policies in Europe, 1945–7? (page 230), the following are possible sentences with which to start paragraphs:

- The USA carefully cultivated its claim to be the protector of the 'West', but in reality its actions did much to provoke the Cold War, 1945–7.
- The USA did not cause the Cold War as it merely responded to Soviet actions in Eastern Europe and Germany.
- The Cold War was made inevitable by the collapse of Germany in 1945 as it created a vacuum in which the USA and the USSR, which were countries with diametrically opposed policies and ideologies, confronted each other.
- The Truman Doctrine and the Marshall Plan in 1947 played a key role in causing the Cold War, but they were an understandable response by the USA to perceived Soviet threats.
- The USA was unable to understand that the USSR's actions were influenced by an overwhelming need for security and that the establishment of what Churchill called the 'Iron Curtain' was a defensive action.

You would then go on to discuss both sides of the argument raised by the opening sentence, using relevant knowledge about the issue to support each side of the argument. The final sentence of the paragraph would reach a judgement on the role played by the factor you are discussing. This approach would ensure that the final sentence of each paragraph links back to the actual question you are answering. If you can do this for each paragraph you will have a series of mini-essays, which discuss a factor and reach a conclusion or judgement about the importance of that factor or issue. For example:

The actions and policies of the USA were important factors in the causes of the Cold War but they alone did not cause the confrontation, as other powers such as the USSR and Britain played important roles[1]. The intractable problems in Central Europe and Germany caused by the defeat of the Third Reich, the power vacuum that this opened up and the determination by the USSR to ensure that Poland and the other Eastern European states as well as Germany were controlled by friendly (that is, Communist) governments provoked the USA into attempting to consolidate and assist Western Europe to prevent the spread of communism. The question of the future of Germany brought these factors together, as we can see in the question of German reparations, the reaction of the USA and its allies to the 'shotgun marriage' between the SPD and SED in the Soviet zone in April 1946, and the USSR's reaction to the creation of the Bizone a few months later[2].

1 The sentence puts forward a clear view that the USA, while an important factor, did not alone cause the Cold War.
2 The claim that it was an important but not the sole factor is developed and some evidence is provided to support the argument.

The conclusion

The conclusion provides the opportunity to bring together all the interim judgements to reach an overall judgement about the question. Using the interim judgements will ensure that your conclusion is based on the argument in the main body of the essay and does not offer a different view. For the essay answering question 1 (see page 230), you can decide what was the most important consequence of the Berlin Blockade, but for question 2 you will need to comment on the importance of the named factor – the USA – as well as explaining why you think a different factor is more important, if that has been your line of argument. Or, if you think the named factor is the most important, you would need to explain why that was more important than the other factors or issues you have discussed.

Consider the following conclusion to question 2: To what extent did the USA cause the Cold War through its policies in Europe, 1945–7?

By the end of 1947 the Cold War was a reality. Europe, as Churchill had so graphically said, was divided by the 'Iron Curtain' from Stettin to Trieste. US policies and actions had certainly played an important part in this division. However, the USA did not cause the division by itself[1]. There were major ideological differences between the USA and USSR, both wanting to remake the world in their image. The USSR was determined to install a Communist regime in Poland by rigged elections and force, if necessary, and it had already made the SPD amalgamate with the KPD in the Soviet zone of Germany. There was no agreement on the future of Germany between the victorious members of the former Grand Alliance. By the end of 1947 US responses to these tensions had done much to make the Cold War a reality. The creation of Bizonia, which was originally proposed by the USA, was the first step in the partition of Germany, while the Truman Doctrine and the Marshall Plan forced Stalin on the defensive and accelerated the formation of both a Soviet bloc and a US-dominated western bloc in Europe[2].

1 This is a strong conclusion because it considers the importance of the named factor – the USA – but weighs that up against a range of other factors to reach an overall judgement.
2 It is also able to show links between the other factors to reach a balanced judgement, which brings in a range of issues, showing the interplay between them.

How to write a good essay for the A level short answer questions

This question will require you to weigh up the importance of two factors or issues in relation to an event or a development. For example:

Which of the following did more to consolidate the division of Germany, 1953–61?

(i) The defeat of the East German revolt in June 1953.

(ii) The construction of the Berlin Wall.

Explain your answer with reference to both (i) and (ii).

As with the long essays, the skills required are made very clear by the mark scheme, which emphasises that the answer must:

- analyse the two issues
- evaluate the two issues
- support your analysis and evaluation with detailed and accurate knowledge
- reach a supported judgement as to which factor was more important in relation to the issue in the question.

The skills required are very similar to those for the longer essays. However, there is no need for an introduction, nor are you required to compare the two factors or issues in the main body of the essay, although either approach can still score full marks. For example, you could begin with the following on page 234:

In the spring of 1953 the GDR was facing serious economic problems and growing dissatisfaction with the Ulbricht regime, which might have led to its collapse[1]. In Moscow, following the death of Stalin, a more conciliatory leadership had emerged led by Khrushchev, Beria and Malenkov. Beria had floated the idea to his colleagues that it would be cheaper in the long run to pull out of the GDR and accept German reunification in exchange for generous subsidies from the FRG. At the same time, public opinion in Western Europe was longing for the end of the Cold War, and Churchill, now prime minister again, was proposing a summit conference to achieve this[2]. We do not know whether this would have led to German reunification, but what we do know is that the East German revolt forced the USSR to drop all thoughts of a reunified Germany. It had no option but to defeat the revolt or suffer a massive blow to its prestige in Eastern Europe. The revolt encouraged the hardliners in the USSR who were opposed to giving up the GDR. At the same time it played into the hands of those in the West such as Chancellor Adenauer and US Secretary of State John Foster Dulles, who feared that a united neutral Germany would undermine the economic and military integration of the FRG into Western Europe. The defeat of the revolt thus confirmed the division of Germany, but the open frontier in Berlin remained a threat to the GDR[3].

1 The answer explains the impact on the GDR of its economic difficulties.
2 The implications of this development are considered.
3 The wider implications are hinted at and this could be developed with reference to the construction of the Berlin Wall in 1961. The answer could go on to argue that the two problems were connected.

Most importantly, the conclusion must reach a supported judgement as to the relative importance of the factors in relation to the issue in the question. For example:

Both these events were important in consolidating the GDR. The defeat of the uprising of June 1953 effectively dissuaded the USSR from compromising over the future of the GDR. Similarly, the sight of Soviet tanks on the streets of East Berlin confirmed the West's suspicions of the USSR. The GDR therefore survived, but it still faced major economic and social problems, which created instability and threatened its collapse[1]. These problems were made worse by the existence of a powerful and booming West German state, which attracted many East Germans, who could escape the GDR by crossing the open frontier in Berlin. In 1960 nearly 200,000, many of whom were skilled workers and professionals, had fled the GDR for the FRG. If this continued both the East German economy and state would collapse. The construction of the Berlin Wall on 13 August stopped this exodus and gave the GDR a chance to keep its labour force and rebuild its economy. Both events contributed to the consolidation of the GDR. The crushing of the 1953 revolt defeated an immediate threat to the GDR's existence, while the Berlin Wall averted its economic collapse for a generation[2].

1 The response explains the relative importance of the two factors and offers a clear view.
2 The response supports the view offered in the opening sentence and therefore reaches a supported judgement.

Interpretations guidance

How to write a good essay

The guidance below is for answering the AS interpretation question for OCR Unit Y253 The Cold War in Europe. Guidance on answering essay questions is on page 230.

The OCR specification outlines the two key topics from which the interpretation question will be drawn. For this book these are:

- The origins of the Cold War to 1945.
- The end of the Cold War, 1984–95.

The specification also lists the main debates to consider.

It is also worth remembering that this is an AS unit and not an A level historiography paper. The aim of this element of the unit is to develop an awareness that the past can be interpreted in different ways.

The question will require you to assess the strengths and limitations of a historian's interpretation of an issue related to one of the specified key topics.

You should be able to place the interpretation within the context of the wider historical debate on the key topic. However, you will *not* be required to know the names of individual historians associated with the debate or to have studied the specific books of any historians. It may even be counter-productive to be aware of particular historians' views, as this may lead you to simply describe their view, rather than analyse the given interpretation.

There are a number of skills you need to develop to reach the higher levels in the mark bands:

- To be able to understand the wording of the question.
- To be able to explain the interpretation and how it fits into the debate about the issue or topic.

- To be able to consider both the strengths and weaknesses of the interpretation by using your own knowledge of the topic.

Here is an example of a type of question you will face in the exam:

> Read the interpretation and then answer the question that follows:
>
> '[Gorbachev] never expected communism to collapse so abruptly, and so totally, even in East Germany, let alone Russia.'
>
> (From J. Haslam, *Russia's Cold War*, Cambridge, 2007.)
>
> Evaluate the strengths and limitations of this interpretation, making reference to other interpretations that you have studied.

Approaching the question

There are several steps to take to answer this question:

1 Explain the interpretation and put it into the context of the debate on the topic

In the first paragraph, you should explain the interpretation and the view it is putting forward. This paragraph places the interpretation in the context of the historical debate and explains any key words or phrases relating to the given interpretation. A suggested opening might be as follows:

The interpretation puts forward the view that Gorbachev initially thought that he could strengthen communism in Eastern Europe and the USSR through reform. The author implies that he disastrously misjudged the situation[1]. In using the words 'so abruptly, and so totally', the author is referring to the rapid collapse of communism between 1989 and 1991 in Russia and throughout Eastern Europe[2]. The interpretation suggests that Gorbachev believed it was possible to modernise the Russian economy and safeguard Soviet security in Eastern Europe, especially the GDR, through a policy of political co-operation and negotiation and compromise – 'glasnost' and 'perestroika' – rather than force[3].

1 The opening two sentences are clearly focused on the given interpretation. They clearly explain what Haslam thought Gorbachev intended, but there is no detailed own knowledge added at this point.
2 The third sentence explains what is meant by 'so abruptly, and so totally'.
3 The last sentence begins to place the concept of a failure in Gorbachev's judgement in the wider historical debate about reform. It suggests that this historian's emphasis on it might challenge the view that Gorbachev was a very different Soviet leader from his predecessors, who in the final analysis was ready to risk the USSR itself to reform.

In order to place Haslam's view in the context of the debate about Gorbachev's role in the collapse of the USSR, you could go on to suggest there are a wide range of other factors to consider, such as the arguably terminal economic weakness of the USSR, its defeat in Afghanistan and Gorbachev's attempts to keep the USSR as a unified state in 1990–1.

2 Consider the strengths of the interpretation

In the second paragraph, consider the strengths of the interpretation by bringing in your own knowledge that supports the given view. A suggested response might start as follows when considering the strengths of the view:

There is certainly much merit in Haslam's argument as it acknowledges that there is a problem in explaining why Gorbachev embarked on what in retrospect seem to be a series of policies which were effectively suicidal for the future of the USSR[1]. Economically, the USSR was in desperate need of reform and was finding the defence of the satellite states a heavy financial burden, but there seemed to be no reason initially why attempts to answer these problems should lead to the collapse of the USSR and communism in the Eastern Europe[2]. Thus, Haslam is right to emphasise that Gorbachev did not deliberately set about undermining his own power base. Indeed, he thought his reforms would strengthen it[3].

1 The answer clearly focuses on the strength of the given interpretation.

2 The response provides some support for the view in the interpretation from the candidate's own knowledge. This is not particularly detailed or precise, but this could be developed in the remainder of the paragraph.
3 The final sentence links together factors which support Haslam's arguments.

In the remainder of the paragraph you could explore how Gorbachev's reforms accelerated the collapse of communism.

3 Consider the weaknesses of the interpretation

In the third paragraph, consider the weaknesses or at least the limitation of the given interpretation by bringing in knowledge that can challenge or modify the given interpretation and explain what is missing from the interpretation.

A suggested response might start as follows when considering the weaknesses of the view:

There are, however, a number of ambiguities in Haslam's argument which need explanation[1]. Of course, Gorbachev did not initially intend to dissolve the USSR and end communism in Eastern Europe, but if that was so, why did he persist with his reforms? It can be argued that after a certain point Gorbachev was ready to accept that his reforms would lead to the demise of communism at least in the GDR and Eastern Europe. For instance, in December 1989 he wanted to maintain the GDR, but then by February 1990 he was willing to let the Germans decide its fate[2]. Here, one can argue that after a certain point he did understand that his reforms would lead to the collapse of communism in the GDR and to German reunification. In the USSR the picture is more complicated. Gorbachev's first reaction was to oppose nationalist movements, but after several attempts at armed intervention in Georgia and the Baltic states, for instance, Gorbachev came to terms with them and actively sought to create a new non-Communist Russian federation, which he realised marked the end of the USSR[3].

1 The opening makes it very clear that this paragraph will deal with the limitations of the interpretation.
2 It explains clearly the limitations of the argument and provides evidence to support the claim. The evidence is not detailed and could be developed, but the answer focuses on explaining the limitations rather than providing lots of detail.
3 Although more detail could have been provided about Gorbachev's reforms, the answer goes on to explain a third ambiguity in Haslam's argument. All three factors could be developed in the remainder of the paragraph.

Answers might go on to argue that Gorbachev was pursuing an ambitious policy of reform.

Thanks to the economic situation in the USSR, Gorbachev had no option but to reform, but optimistically he thought that he would be able to create a new socialism with a human face in Eastern Europe, and at the same time, through 'glasnost' and 'perestroika', reform the USSR, while enabling the Communist Party to remain in power. Haslam is right that he had no idea that this would lead to the collapse of communism in the GDR and the USSR, but quite soon he realised the logic of his reforms in the GDR and eventually in the USSR, and despite some hesitations he did, in the end, continue to support the reforms. The paragraph might therefore suggest that the interpretation provides a partial answer which needs further explanation.

There is no requirement for you to reach a judgement as to which view you find more convincing or valid.

Assessing the interpretation

In assessing the interpretation you should consider the following:

- Identify and explain the issue being discussed in the interpretation: what did Gorbachev really intend? Explain the view being put forward in the interpretation: the interpretation is arguing that Gorbachev had no intention to destroy communism.

- The idea that Gorbachev was not aware of the consequences of his reforms is certainly the most likely argument, but nevertheless you must carefully weigh up the possibility that he knew fully what he was doing.
- Explain how the interpretation fits into the wider debate about the issue of the reasons for the collapse of communism in Eastern Europe and the USSR.

In other interpretations you might need to:

- Consider whether there is any particular emphasis within the interpretation that needs explaining or commenting on, for example, if the interpretation says something is 'the only reason' or 'the single most important reason'.
- Comment on any concepts that the interpretation raises, such as 'communism', 'collapse', 'East Germany'.
- Consider the focus of the interpretation: for example, if an interpretation focuses on Russia and East Germany, what was the situation in, say, Poland or Hungary?

In summary, this is what is most important for answering interpretation questions:

- Explaining the interpretation.
- Placing it in the context of the wider historical debate about the issue it considers.
- Explaining the strengths *and* limitations of the view in the extract.

Glossary of terms

Advisory Steering Committee   A committee that would advise on priorities and the key decisions to be taken.

Airlift   The transport of food and supplies by air to a besieged area.

Allied Control Commissions   These were set up in each occupied territory, including Germany. They initially administered a particular territory in the name of the Allies.

Allied powers   Commonly referred to as the Allies during the Second World War, this group first consisted of Poland, France, Britain and others, with the USSR and the USA joining in 1941.

Allies   Britain, France, Japan, China and others were allied against Germany. The USA was 'an associated power'.

Anglo-French Guarantee   In 1939 Britain and France guaranteed Polish independence, in the hope of preventing a German invasion of Poland.

Anti-ballistic screens   Protection provided by rocket-launching pads.

Appease   To conciliate a potential aggressor by making concessions.

Armistice   The official agreement of the suspension of fighting between two or more powers as a preliminary to a negotiated peace.

Arms race   A competition or race between nations to arm themselves with the most deadly and effective weapons available.

Arrow Cross Party   A Hungarian ultra-nationalist political party that supported Germany in the Second World War.

Asian defence perimeter   A line through East and South-East Asia that the USA was willing to defend against any other nation.

Asymmetrical   Having a lack of symmetry or balance.

Atlantic Charter   A statement of fundamental principles for the post-war world. The most important of these were: free trade, no more territorial annexation by Britain or the USA, and the right of people to choose their own governments.

Autarchic economy   An economy that is self-sufficient and protected from outside competition.

Axis   The alliance in the Second World War that eventually consisted of Germany, Italy, Japan, Slovakia, Hungary, Bulgaria and Romania, as well as several states created in conquered areas.

Balance of payments   The difference between the earnings of exports and the cost of imports.

Benelux states   Belgium (Be), the Netherlands (Ne) and Luxembourg (Lux).

Berlin's open frontier   There was no physical barrier between Communist East Berlin and capitalist and democratic West Berlin.

Bilateral   Between two states.

Bizonia   Formed in January 1947 out of an amalgamation of the British and US zones of occupation.

Bloc mentality   A state of mind brought about by being a member of one of the two sides in the Cold War.

Bolshevik Party   The Russian Communist Party, which seized power in a revolution in October 1917.

Bourgeoisie   The middle class, particularly those with business interests, who Marx believed benefited most from the existing capitalist economic system.

Brinkmanship   Appearing to approach the brink of nuclear war to persuade the opposition to concede.

C-54   Large US transport plane.

CCP   Chinese Communist Party, led by Mao.

Centralised control of the economy   Control of a country's economy from the centre, as in Stalinist Russia.

Checkpoint Charlie   One of the few official crossing points between East and West Berlin. It is now a museum.

Chernobyl   In April 1986, an explosion at Chernobyl nuclear power station released a large amount of radioactive dust into the atmosphere, which affected much of Western Russia and Eastern Europe; 31 people died.

CIA   The Central Intelligence Agency was established by the USA in 1947 to conduct counterintelligence operations abroad.

Collectivising agriculture   Abolishing private farms in favour of large units run collectively by the peasantry along the lines of Soviet agriculture.

Comintern   A Communist organisation set up in Moscow in 1919 to co-ordinate the efforts of Communists around the world to achieve a worldwide revolution.

Command economy   An economy where supply and pricing are regulated by the government rather than market forces such as demand, and in which all the larger industries and businesses are controlled centrally by the state.

Commonwealth   Organisation of states that were formerly part of the British Empire.

Commonwealth of Independent States (CIS)
A voluntary organisation eventually of twelve of the successor states of the USSR. Any decision made by it was not binding on its members.

Confederation   A grouping of states in which each state retains its sovereignty. Hence, much looser than a federation.

Congress   The US parliament.

Consensus   General agreement.

Consultative Council   A council on which the member states were represented and where they could discuss mutual problems.

Conventional forces   Military forces that do not rely on nuclear weapons.

Council of [Foreign] Ministers   Composed of the foreign ministers of Britain, France, the USA and the USSR. Its role was to sort out the German problems and prepare the peace treaties.

Cronyism   Favouring one's friends by granting them favours, often when they are undeserving.

Cultural Revolution   A mass movement begun by Mao's supporters against those opposed to Mao's version of communism.

Customs union   An area of free trade unhindered by national tariffs.

Decolonisation   Granting of independence to colonies.

Democracy   A form of government in which all eligible citizens participate either directly, or more usually through elected representatives, in the government of their country.

Democratic Party   Founded in 1828. Essentially a liberal or left-of-centre party.

Democratic Union   The first opposition party to the Communist Party of the USSR.

Denazification   The process of removing all Nazi Party ideology, propaganda, symbols and adherents from every aspect of German of life.

Destalinisation   The attempts to liberalise the USSR after the death of Stalin in 1953.

Détente   A state of lessened tension or growing relaxation between two states.

Developing World   States that had been former colonies but which were now free and independent of both the USSR and the West. Used to be called the Third World.

Dictatorship of the proletariat   Marx's term suggesting that following the overthrow of the bourgeoisie, government would be carried out by and on behalf of the working class.

Dissident   Critical of the official line taken by the state.

Doctrine of containment   A policy of halting the USSR's advance into Western Europe. It did not envisage actually 'rolling back' Soviet power from Eastern Europe.

Domino principle   The belief that the fall of one state to communism would result in a chain reaction, leading to the fall of other neighbouring states.

Dutch East Indies   A Dutch colony that became Indonesia.

Economic nationalism   A policy in which every effort is made to keep out foreign goods.

Electoral bloc   An electoral alliance by a group of parties.

Embryonic state   Organisation that has some of the powers of a proper state, and is likely to grow into a fully fledged state.

Empire by invitation   The Western Europeans were in effect asking to be put under US protection and so become a part of a US 'empire' or a US-dominated region.

Ethnic Germans   German people who still lived in Poland. In 1945 much former German territory was given to Poland.

European Community   The European Economic Community (EEC) had changed its name to the European Community (EC).

ExComm   The Executive Committee of the US National Security Council.

Exoskeletons   Rigid external coverings, or shells for the body.

Federal   A country formed of several different states that enjoy considerable autonomy in domestic affairs.

Five-Year Plans   Plans to modernise and expand the economy over a five-year period.

FNLA   The National Front for the Liberation of Angola (*Frente Nacional de Libertação de Angola*), led by Holden Roberto, was strongly African nationalist. It was hostile both to the West and to communism but had links with the CIA and was dependent on Mobutu's Congo for bases and assistance.

Four-Power Control   Under the joint control of the four occupying powers: Britain, France, the USA and the USSR.

Free city   Self-governing city not incorporated into a state.

Free French   The French who supported de Gaulle after the fall of France in June 1940, when he established his headquarters in London.

French Indo-China   A French colony consisting of today's Laos, Cambodia and Vietnam.

Glasnost   Openness regarding the USSR's economic and political systems, including public discussion and debate.

Global confrontation   The attempt to stand up to the enemy anywhere or everywhere in the world.

Global encirclement   Surrounded on a global scale.

Global oil crisis   In October 1973, the Organization of Arab Petroleum Exporting Countries suspended delivery of oil to the USA and Western Europe in protest against US assistance to Israel during the October War of 1973. When deliveries recommenced in March 1974, the oil price had quadrupled.

Global over-stretch   The situation when great powers take on more global responsibilities than they can afford or manage easily.

'Great Leap Forward'   Mao's plan that aimed dramatically to increase both industrial and agricultural production. The population was to be mobilised to build dams and small-scale smelting works. By 1962 this plan had caused the deaths of at least 61 million people.

Greens   Those supporting parties or groups whose stated aim is to protect the environment.

Gross national product (GNP)   The total production of domestic industries combined with the earnings from exports.

Guerrilla groups   Fighters who oppose an occupying force using tactics such as sabotage and assassination.

Guerrilla war   A war fought by small groups of irregular troops. The term comes from the Spanish resistance to Napoleon in the early nineteenth century.

Guns and butter   A phrase used initially in the US press in 1917 to describe the production of nitrates for both peaceful and military purposes; now usually used to describe the situation when a country's economy can finance both increased military and consumer goods production.

Hallstein Doctrine   Named after Walter Hallstein, state secretary in the FRG's Foreign Ministry.

Heavy industry   Coal, iron and steel production.

High Commission   A civilian body charged with the task of defending the interests of the Western allies in Germany.

Hồ Chí Minh Trail   An infiltration route of hundreds of kilometres that allowed the movement of troops and war material through neighbouring countries into South Vietnam.

Hotline   A direct communications link between US and Soviet leaders.

Human rights   Basic rights such as personal liberty and freedom from repression.

Hydroelectric sources   Power stations that generate electricity through water power.

Hydrogen bomb   A nuclear bomb hundreds of times more powerful than an atomic bomb.

Ideologies   The ideas, beliefs and theories that constitute a religious or political doctrine on which a political party or religion is based.

Immutable   Unchangeable.

Imperialist   Britain and France, who both still had extensive colonial empires. The Soviets also regularly called the Americans imperialists.

Intercontinental ballistic missile (ICBM)   Missile capable of carrying nuclear warheads and reaching great distances.

International Ruhr Authority   An organisation to establish how much coal and steel the Germans should produce and ensure that a percentage of its production should be made available to its western neighbours. It was replaced in 1951 by the European Coal and Steel Community.

Inviolable   Not to be attacked or violated.

Iron Curtain   A term used by Churchill to describe how Stalin had separated Eastern Europe from the West.

Islamic fundamentalism   A very literal and traditional version of Islam that is hostile to Western civilisation, be it Marxist or Christian.

Joint Chiefs of Staff   Committee of senior military officers who advise the US government on military matters.

Jupiter missile   A liquid-fuelled, surface-deployed missile, which was already out of date by 1962.

Khmer Rouge regime   Regime established by Pol Pot, which killed over 2 million of its own people.

KMT   Kuomintang. Chinese Nationalist Party.

Lackey   An uncritical follower; a servant, who cannot answer back.

Land corridors   Roads, railways and canals, which the Soviets had agreed in 1945 could be used to supply West Berlin.

Lebensraum   Literally 'living space'. Territory for the resettlement of Germans in the USSR and Eastern Europe.

Left wing   Liberal, socialist or Communist.

Left-wing protest groups   Protest groups within left-wing parties such as the Labour Party in Britain or the Social Democrats in Germany.

Legal and mutually agreed framework   A legal agreement, freely negotiated, that would allow the USSR to maintain bases in Hungary.

Lend–lease   This US programme (started in March 1941) gave over $50 billion ($650 billion in today's terms) of war supplies to Allied nations. This money was to be paid back at the end of the war.

Liberation   The freeing of a country from foreign occupation.

Long peace   A period of international stability brought about by the nuclear balance between the USA and the USSR.

Magnetic social and economic forces of the FRG   Brandt believed that the economy and way of life in West Germany was so strong that ultimately it would exert a magnet like attraction on the GDR.

Make-believe constitution   A constitution that was not genuine and merely hid a dictatorship by one party: the SED.

Malaya   A British colony that became Malaysia and Singapore.

Manchuria A region in the far north-east of China, occupied by the Japanese in 1931 until the end of the Second World War.

Martial law Military rule involving the suspension of normal civilian government.

Marxism–Leninism Doctrines of Marxism which were modified by Lenin, who adapted Karl Marx's teaching to the situation in Russia. Unlike Marx, he advocated the creation of a party dictatorship, which would have absolute powers, even over the workers.

Military government officials Officials who worked for Soviet military governments in Eastern Europe.

Military governor The head of a zone of occupation in Germany.

Militia Part-time military reservists.

Missile gap Where one side has a temporary lead over the other in nuclear weapons.

Moldova The Romanian for Moldavia, the name by which Moldova was known during its history as part of the Russian Empire.

Monroe Doctrine The doctrine formulated by US President Monroe (1817–25) that the European powers should not intervene on the American continent.

MPLA The Popular Movement for the Liberation of Angola (*Movimento Popular de Libertaçã de Angola*), headed by António Neto, was predominantly a Marxist movement influenced by the Portuguese Communist Party.

MSZMP *Magyar Szocialista Munkáspárt*. The Hungarian Socialist Workers' Party: the Communist Party in Hungary between 1956 and 1989.

Munich Agreement An agreement between Britain, France, Italy and Germany that the Sudetenland region of Czechoslovakia would become part of Germany.

National federation of trade unions A national organisation representing all the trade unions.

Nationalise To take ownership of privately owned industries, banks, and so on, by the state.

Nationalist A movement or person passionately devoted to the interests and culture of their nation, often leading to the belief that certain nationalities are superior to others.

'New Yalta' US President Reagan's argument is that Yalta had allowed Soviet domination in Eastern Europe in return for liberal promises that the Soviets had no intention of honouring.

NKVD Soviet security organisation responsible for enforcing obedience to the government and eliminating opposition.

Non-aligned movement Not allied with either the USSR or the West.

Nuclear diplomacy Negotiations and diplomacy supported by the threat of nuclear weapons.

Nuclear-free zone An area, such as Central Europe, in which nuclear weapons would be neither used nor based.

Occupation Statute A treaty defining the rights of Britain, France and the USA in West Germany.

October Revolution The second Russian Revolution in October 1917, in which the Bolsheviks seized power.

Ogaden In the late nineteenth century, when the Somali territories were divided between Britain, France and Italy, Ethiopia acquired Ogaden. Once the British and Italian territories became independent in 1960, the two states merged and formed the new state of Somaliland and laid claim to Ogaden.

Organization for European Economic Co-operation (OEEC) Set up in 1948 to administer the Marshall Plan.

Ostpolitik West Germany's policy towards Eastern Europe, which involved recognition of the GDR and the post-war boundaries in Eastern Europe.

Paramilitary police force Police force that is armed with machine guns and armoured cars.

Partisan groups Resistance fighters or guerrillas in German- and Italian-occupied Europe.

Pathet Lao Independence movement in Laos, supported by the Việt Minh.

Perestroika Transformation or restructuring of the Communist Party to make it more responsive to the needs of the people.

Poland In 1815 Poland was partitioned between Austria, Russia and Prussia. In 1918 the defeat of Russia, Germany, which included Prussia, and Austria enabled it to regain independence.

Polarised Divided into two extremes (polar opposites).

Polish Home Army The Polish nationalist resistance group that fought German occupation during the Second World War.

Politburo The Political Bureau of the Central Committee of the Communist Party.

Prague Spring The liberalisation process put into effect by Alexander Dubček, the Czech prime minister.

Presidium Soviet inner council or cabinet.

Proletariat Marx's term for industrial working-class labourers, primarily factory workers.

Provisional government A temporary government in office until an election can take place.

Proxy-conflicts Wars encouraged or supported by major powers without their direct involvement.

Puppet government One that operates at the will of and for the benefit of another government.

Quemoy Islands KMT-controlled islands off Formosa.

Rapprochement Establishing close relations between two states.

Ratify When an international treaty has been signed, it can come into effect only after the parliaments of the signatory states have ratified (that is, approved) it.

Red Army The Workers' and Peasants' Red Army was the Bolsheviks' armed force, which eventually became the Soviet Army.

Reichsmark German currency before 1948; it lost most of its value after Germany's defeat in the Second World War.

Reparations Materials, equipment or money taken from a defeated power to make good the damage of war.

Republican Party Founded in 1854. Essentially an American conservative party.

Residual rights The remaining privileges, going right back to 1945, which the four occupying powers of Britain, France, the USA and the USSR still enjoyed.

Revisionist historian A historian who revises the traditional or orthodox interpretation of events and often contradicts it.

Revisionists Those accused of revising the theory of Marxism–Leninism.

Ruhr The centre of the German coal and steel industries and at that time the greatest industrial region in Europe.

Secretary of state The US foreign minister.

Self-immolation Burning oneself alive as a sacrifice and act of protest.

Shotgun marriage A forced union.

'Smart' bombs Precision-guided bombs which enable a target to be hit accurately.

Social Democratisation Converting the Communist SED into a more moderate Western-style Social Democratic Party, like the SPD in the FRG.

Socialism in one country Policy aimed at strengthening socialism within the USSR even though elsewhere revolution had failed.

Socialist A believer in socialism: the belief that the community as a whole rather than individuals should control the economy.

Solidarity movement A movement that originated in support of the strikes in the Gdańsk shipyards.

Sovereignty Independence. A sovereign state possesses the power to make its own decisions.

Soviet bloc A group of states in Eastern Europe controlled by the USSR.

Sovietisation Reconstructing a state according to the Soviet model.

Spheres of interest Areas where one power is able to exercise a dominant influence.

Splitters The SED accused the West Germans and the Western allies of splitting or dividing Germany.

Sputnik   This satellite weighed 84 kilograms and was able to orbit the Earth. In Russian the word means 'fellow traveller', or supporter of the USSR.

Stalin cult   The propaganda campaign vaunting Stalin as the great ruler and saviour of the USSR.

Supranational   Transcending national limits.

Supreme Soviet   Set up in 1936 by Stalin. It consisted of two bodies: the Soviet of the USSR and the Soviet of Nationalities. Each Soviet republic had a Supreme Soviet or parliament, as did the overall USSR.

Tactical nuclear weapons   Small-scale nuclear weapons that can be used in the battlefield.

Tariffs   Taxes placed on imported goods to protect the home economy.

Titoism   Communism as defined by Tito in Yugoslavia.

Totalitarian regimes   Undemocratic regimes such as those in Soviet Russia or Nazi Germany, which sought to control every aspect of their people's lives.

Trade embargo   A suspension of trade.

Trade missions   Organisations to promote trade between states.

Trade surplus   A surplus of exports over imports.

Transit traffic   Traffic crossing through another state.

Trust territories   Former colonial territories put in trust to the UN until they were ready for independence.

Trusteeship   Responsibility on behalf of the UN for the government and welfare of a state handed over temporarily to other powers.

UNITA   The National Union for the Total Liberation of Angola (*União Nacional para a Independência Total de Angola*) was created in the mid-1960s by Jonas Savimbi to provide an alternative to what he perceived to be the military inactivity and feebleness of the two other groups (MPLA and FNLA).

US National Security Council   The main committee advising the US president on security issues. Created in 1947.

USSR   Union of Soviet Socialist Republics, the name given to Communist Russia and the states under its control from 1922. Also known as the Soviet Union.

Việt Minh   'League for the Independence of Vietnam', created in 1941.

Watergate scandal   On 17 June 1972, Republican Party officials broke into the headquarters of the opposition Democrat Party in the Watergate Building in Washington, DC, to find material which could be used to discredit the Democrats. The break-in was discovered and eventually led to Nixon's resignation in 1974.

Western bloc   An alliance of Western European states and the USA.

Western European integration   The process of creating a Western Europe that was united politically, economically and militarily.

Western intelligence   Information gained by Western spies in Eastern Europe.

Yugoslavia   In 1918, the kingdom of Serbs, Croats and Slovenes was formed. In 1929 it officially became Yugoslavia. The Serbs were the dominating nationality within this state.

Zionist   A supporter of the foundation of a Jewish state in the historic land of Israel.

Further reading

The whole of the Cold War 1945–91

S.R. Ashton, *In Search of Détente: The Politics of East–West Relations since 1945* (Macmillan, 1989)
Published just before the Cold War ended, but it is nevertheless a useful survey, particularly on *détente*

J.P.D. Dunbabin, *The Cold War. The Great Powers and their Allies* (Routledge, 2013)
A detailed study of the global Cold War. It is arguably the most precise and detailed one-volume history of the Cold War in English

J.L. Gaddis, *The Cold War* (Allen Lane, 2005)
A helpful and readable synthesis of the Cold War

M. Leffler and O.A. Westad, editors, *The Cambridge History of the Cold War*, volume I *Origins*; volume II *Crises and Détentes*; volume III *Endings* (Cambridge University Press, 2010)
The three volumes contain chapters on all aspects of the global Cold War written by experts. The chapters can be informative, although not easy to read

J.W. Mason, *The Cold War, 1945–91* (Routledge, 1996)
An excellent introductory survey of just 75 pages. It covers the Cold War in both Europe and Asia

N. Stone, *The Atlantic and its Enemies* (Penguin, 2011)
A witty and wide-ranging book on the global Cold War

M. Walker, *The Cold War* (Vintage, 1994)
A readable, journalistic study of the whole Cold War. It covers all aspects of this struggle and contains much useful information

Historiography and problems of the Cold War

J.L. Gaddis, *We Know Now: Rethinking Cold War History* (Oxford University Press, 1997)
This puts the Cold War into its global context and assesses the changing interpretations and explanations of the Cold War

K. Larres and A. Lane, *The Cold War: The Essential Readings* (Blackwell, 2001)
Contains some interesting articles and extracts from leading Cold War historians

O.A. Westad, *Reviewing the Cold War: Approaches, Interpretations, Theory* (Frank Cass, 2000)
Brings together the often conflicting views of historians on the Cold War

The origins of the Cold War up to 1953

J.L. Gaddis, *The United States and the Origins of the Cold War, 1941–1947* (Columbia University Press, 2000)
A study of US policy towards the USSR, 1941–7

M. McCauley, *The Origins of the Cold War, 1941–49* (Longman, 1995)
A clear and well-explained introduction to the causes and early stages of the Cold War

D. Reynolds, editor, *The Origins of the Cold War in Europe: International Perspectives* (Yale University Press, 1994)
An informative survey of the historiography and the international historical debates on the Cold War covering the period 1945–55

D. Yergin, *Shattered Peace: The Origins of the Cold War and the National Security State* (Houghton Mifflin, 1977)
A revisionist study of the USA's involvement in the Cold War in Europe

Europe during the Cold War

G. Swain and N. Swain, *Eastern Europe since 1945* (Macmillan, 1993)
A detailed study of interwar Europe

J.F. Young, *Cold War Europe, 1945–91* (Arnold, 1996)
An informative chapter on the Cold War and *détente* and then further useful chapters on European integration, Eastern Europe, the USSR and the main Western European states

Studies of Cold War Germany

M. Fulbrook, *Anatomy of a Dictatorship: Inside the GDR, 1949–1989* (Oxford University Press, 1995)
An informative study of the GDR based on primary sources

W. Loth, *Stalin's Unwanted Child. The Soviet Union, the German Question and the Founding of the GDR* (Macmillan, 1998)
An interesting study that argues Stalin did not intend the division of Germany

D.G. Williamson, *Germany from Defeat to Partition, 1945–1961* (Pearson, 2001)
Covers the occupation and division of Germany

The USSR and the Cold War

J. Haslam, *Russia's Cold War From the October Revolution to the Fall of the Wall* (Yale University Press, 2011)
A study of Soviet foreign policy and its formulation during the Cold War

M. McCauley, *The Khrushchev Era, 1953–1964* (Longman, 1995)
A concise study of this dramatic period

M. McCauley, *Gorbachev* (Longman, 1998)
A biography of Gorbachev and particularly useful for the years 1989–91.

R. Pearson, *The Rise and Fall of the Soviet Empire* (Palgrave Macmillan, 2002)
An excellent but brief study of the USSR 1945–91

G. Roberts, *The Soviet Union in World Politics: Coexistence, Revolution and Cold War, 1945–91* (Routledge, 1999)
A brief but comprehensive survey of Soviet foreign policy during this period

China

J. Fenby, *The Penguin History of Modern China: The Fall and Rise of a Great Power, 1850 to the Present* (Penguin, 2008)
Good background reading on the history of China

C. Jian, *Mao's China and the Cold War* (North Carolina Press, 2001)
Essential reading for understanding China during much of the Cold War

M. Lynch, *Mao* (Routledge, 2004)
A concise biography with useful information on the Chinese Civil War

The Vietnam War

F. Logevall, *The Origins of the Vietnam War* (Pearson, 2001)
A helpful guide to the causes of the war up to 1965

R.D. Schulzinger, *A Time for War: The United States and Vietnam, 1941–1975* (Oxford University Press, 1997)
A good general account of the USA and the Vietnam War

Détente and *Ostpolitik*

O. Bange and G. Niedhart, editors, *Helsinki, 1975 and the Transformation of Europe* (Berghahn Books, 2008)
Useful for understanding the impact of the Helsinki Final Act on the Cold War

M. Bowker and P. Williams, *Superpower* Détente: *A Reappraisal* (Sage, 1988)
Gives a full account of *détente* in the 1970s

T. Garton Ash, *In Europe's Name: Germany and the Divided Continent* (Jonathan Cape, 1993)
A very useful guide to *Ostpolitik* and the reunification of Germany

The end of the Cold War

R. Garthoff, *The Great Transition: American–Soviet Relations and the End of the Cold War* (Brookings Institution, 1994)
A difficult but important book on the end of the Cold War

T. Garton Ash, *We the People – The Revolution of 1990* (Penguin, 1990)
A journalist's account of the collapse of communism in Eastern Europe

M. Hogan, editor, *The End of the Cold War: Its Meanings and Implications* (Cambridge University Press, 1992)
Contains some excellent but difficult essays on the reasons for the end of the Cold War

C.S. Maier, *Dissolution* (Princeton University Press, 1997)
An interesting account of the collapse of the GDR